T0284657

The Wizard of College Baseball

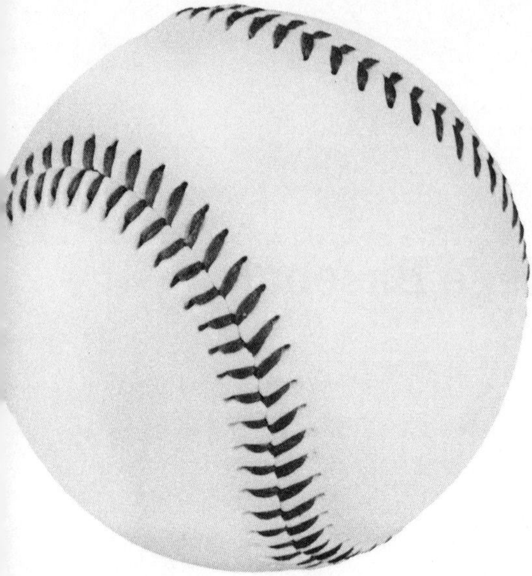

The Wizard of College Baseball

How Ron Fraser Elevated Miami and an
Entire Sport to National Prominence

DAVID BRAUER

University of Nebraska Press • Lincoln

The University of Nebraska Press is part of a land-grant institution with campuses and programs on the past, present, and future homelands of the Pawnee, Ponca, Otoe-Missouria, Omaha, Dakota, Lakota, Kaw, Cheyenne, and Arapaho Peoples, as well as those of the relocated Ho-Chunk, Sac and Fox, and Iowa Peoples.

Library of Congress Cataloging-in-Publication Data
Names: Brauer, David, author.
Title: The wizard of college baseball: how Ron Fraser elevated Miami and an entire sport to national prominence / David Brauer.
Description: Lincoln: University of Nebraska Press, [2024] | Includes bibliographical references.
Identifiers: LCCN 2023049004
ISBN 9781496220431 (hardback)
ISBN 9781496240255 (epub)
ISBN 9781496240262 (pdf)
Subjects: LCSH: Fraser, Ron. | Baseball coaches—United States—Biography. | University of Miami—Athletics. | Baseball—Florida—History. | BISAC: SPORTS & RECREATION / Coaching / Baseball | SPORTS & RECREATION / College Sports
Classification: LCC GV865.F65 B73 2024 | DDC 796.357092 [B]—dc23/eng/20240212
LC record available at https://lccn.loc.gov/2023049004

Set in Questa by A. Shahan.

To my wife, Kendra, for her support and encouragement, especially when the project seemed overwhelming. To my children, Nic and Reagan, for their enthusiasm in counting down the time to their ability to use this book for a school report.

Contents

Preface

How does someone from the Midwest end up writing a book about a South Florida legend? A love for baseball, the College World Series, and a series of serendipitous events led to this.

Growing up in the shadows of the University of Illinois, I developed a keen interest in major college athletics. The legendary Augie Garrido spent three seasons coaching the Fighting Illini and brought the team to national rankings by convincing talented players, including many from the warm California sunshine, to play in cold weather. I began following college baseball with much greater interest and learned the big-name programs through ESPN's coverage of regular season and College World Series games.

I took particular notice of the Miami Hurricanes, and something inspired me to root for them. Maybe it was the colors. Perhaps it was simply that it was one of the handful of programs that I could watch on television from afar.

In 1992 I was finally able to convince my dad to drive to Omaha to attend the College World Series. Following the scores through any coverage I could find in newspapers and the early days of the internet, I tracked Miami and hoped to see the team play. I made it to Rosenblatt Stadium, and so did the Hurricanes. One of the main storylines was the impending retirement of Head Coach Ron Fraser, a larger-than-life legend in the sport.

Wearing a Miami baseball cap and jersey to the game, I waited among the fans outside the main gate well before the stadium opened. A bus pulled up, and Miami's team poured out. As a fifteen-year-old, I was a bit shy about approaching, but I nevertheless went up to Coach Fraser and muttered some type of nervous good-luck wishes. He graciously responded with a handshake and told me to "wear that shirt with pride, son."

Fast forward twenty-five years to the genesis of this project. On a family vacation to South Florida, I spent a day in Miami and included the University of Miami (UM) Sports Hall of Fame and Alex Rodriguez Park at Mark Light Field on the itinerary list. Arriving at the Hall of Fame as visiting hours ended, I was able to view some tremendous artifacts from Canes baseball lore. The gentleman manning the front desk, who was on the phone when I walked in, sought me out, in part because I was wearing a T-shirt with the city name of my alma mater (Illinois).

After noting his connection, our conversation turned to stories of memories of Coach Fraser, who I learned was a friend of his. We carried on for an hour, leaving my wife and children to wonder what happened to my "brief" walkthrough. As if walking into a time machine, my visit rekindled my interest.

Without Earl Rubley, former UM Sports Hall of Fame president and the man at the desk that day, this book would not exist. After returning from vacation, the wheels started turning—my love for sports history, desire to write a book someday, interest in the Miami baseball, and Mr. Rubley's connections to the university, its Hall of Fame, and the Fraser family. I thought, *Why not write a book about Fraser's unique story and significant impact on college baseball?*

Throughout the process, I thoroughly enjoyed learning more about the coach and the man and connecting with those close to him. More than one hundred players, coaches, staff, friends, and family described their genuine love and adoration for Fraser. How he touched so many lives as an incredibly successful coach who won championships and developed players and head coaches is just part of the story. Fraser was a visionary who transcended the entire sport rather than simply focusing on his own program.

Within these pages, you will learn much more about Fraser's amazing accomplishments and the personal side that made him a legend. His legacy remains a significant part of today's Miami Hurricanes, and his statue outside the main entrance to Mark Light Stadium is a fitting reminder of college baseball's greatest story.

Acknowledgments

Thank you to everyone who helped me in this project by sharing their stories and insight, pointing me in the right direction, and providing additional inspiration.

A special thank you goes to the University of Miami Sports Hall of Fame, in particular Earl Rubley, who helped get this idea off the ground and aided various requests along the way, and to Ken Lee and John Routh, who provided their time and effort in aiding my research and accuracy.

My sincerest gratitude and appreciation belong to the Fraser family, Cynthia Fraser, Liz Kraut, Lynda Armitage, Liane Fraser, and Karen Fraser, for their blessing of this project, personal insight, and helpful contributions throughout the process.

Thank you to University of Nebraska Press for taking the chance on publishing this book. I am profoundly grateful to all who had touch points from proposal to finished product.

The Wizard of College Baseball

1

Early Days at Miami

Considered a second-tier option for players deemed not good enough
to sign professionally, college baseball was nearly nonexistent, even
in the Sun Belt states, as the 1960s began. The University of Miami,
despite its geography and climate, was no different. The Hurricanes
enjoyed some modest success but did not employ a full-time coach.
Fielding a successful baseball team was not a priority. The program
was once disbanded because it was without baseballs, bats, uniforms,
or interest. In the 1940s, the university's *Ibis* yearbook wrote, "Baseball, the sport in which Miami is never successful, was attempted this
year, but failed. There was no coach for the team and spring football
interfered."

Even the presence of Hall of Famer Jimmie Foxx as head coach
did not deliver success. In two seasons, Foxx sported a 20-20 record,
going one game over .500 in his first year and one game below in his
second. Whitey Campbell, considered the greatest all-around athlete in
University of Miami history with twelve combined letters in baseball,
basketball, and football, took the reins from Foxx. He posted winning
records each of his four seasons, with one season interrupted when
athletic director Jack Harding served as interim coach in 1959.

Despite compiling a 69-36-3 record, Campbell walked away from the
program without a word after the 1962 season. He switched to coaching football full-time and ascended to the NFL as special teams coach
with Hall of Fame coach Hank Stram's 1976 New Orleans Saints staff.

A popular television program and a recommendation from a rival
coach played a role in hiring the next coach. University of Miami
athletic director Jack Harding sat down one evening to watch the
popular *What's My Line?* quiz show on television. When the celebrity panelists could not unlock the subject's occupation, Harding was

intrigued. The man who stumped them? Ron Fraser, head coach of the Dutch national baseball team. Harding called Florida State coach Danny Litweiler, for whom Fraser played and served as an assistant. Litweiler recommended Fraser, and Harding hired him for a part-time salary of $2,200 per year.

A list of badly needed improvements included equipment—not upgrading equipment, but obtaining it. When Campbell left Miami, he gave the team's remaining baseball equipment to seniors who wanted mementos and returning players for use in their workouts.

"I remember when I took the job, I wanted to take a bat and ball with me to meet the team, but the program didn't own a bat or a ball," Fraser told USA Today in 1989.

To call the team's home field substandard was a compliment. The field conditions were the brunt of jokes, and the number of rocks rivaled the number of grass blades.

"I remember walking the infield foul line to foul line before practice just picking up pebbles and stones," said John Danchik, who played for Fraser in 1964. "It was part of what we did during our practices."

The diamond, lumpy and dust-blown, had a built-up ridge of dirt between the infield and outfield. Outfielders had to be wary of red ants. The dugouts were wooden shacks, and one was gutted after catching fire. A lone set of bleachers sat behind home plate, often serving as a place for football players to suntan.

The state of the program seemed a lost cause. "I remember parking my beat-up Volkswagen outside the fence and walking from the outfield all the way to home plate. I don't think I stepped on a blade of grass once. I turned around, looked back over that terrible field and thought, 'Man, we've got some work to do,'" Fraser told ESPN's Ryan McGee in 2007.

Infield conditions were bad, but the pitcher's mound was worse. Without enough quality clay to fix a reoccurring hole on the mound, assistant coach Bill McClain consulted with a maintenance worker about options to remedy the situation. The suggested "fix" included mixing mortar into the dirt to harden the mound and keep it filled. That mixture lasted barely more than an inning before an opposing pitcher called out the umpire, followed by his coach, Fraser, and McClain to discuss the conditions. Visible concrete made the clay mound look like a chewed-up driveway in need of repair.

"They asked us what the hell we were doing to come up with a mixture like that," recalled McClain. "It was like filling the hole in front of the mound with gravel instead of clay. There were a lot of really rough things we had to go through early on."

With just one set of tattered uniforms, no equipment, a facility dubbed the worst baseball field in Florida, and a mandate from his athletic director to "not spend any money," Fraser started from scratch. Bernie Rosen, the dean of sports reporting in South Florida, predicted no one in Miami would ever care about college baseball. He told Fraser, the school's sixth coach in ten years, baseball would never succeed there.

A modest salary meant Fraser needed a second job as athletic director at the Coral Gables Youth Center to bring his income to the poverty level. He typically stayed at his day job until 1:00 p.m. before heading to his campus office for practice, sometimes with borrowed equipment in tow for his team's use. His university office, much like the field itself, needed attention.

Fraser's workspace was a tiny concrete cubicle converted from a shower opening into the locker room and illuminated by one bare light bulb hanging from the ceiling. Players sometimes stole the lone bulb for use in their dorms, leaving Fraser to bring his own as a replacement. His old wooden desk had a stuck drawer due to a liquor bottle taped underneath by a predecessor. Beside the desk, the lone piece of furniture in the brick-walled dungeon was a supermarket shopping cart where players placed their dirty laundry.

The setting created a burden for recruiting visits. Recruits could only bring their fathers, and not their mothers, to Fraser's office because the only entrance was through the locker room. Fraser worked out an agreement to use football coach Andy Gustafson's office when hosting recruits and their families. Gustafson waited outside his own office if he returned while a meeting was in session.

Access to just a handful of tuition-only scholarships forced Fraser to creatively attract players and disperse financial aid among a twenty-one-man roster. He found an initial recruiting target who was already on campus. Fraser heard a mitt popping behind one of the wooden dugouts and saw All-American quarterback George Mira playing catch with a friend. New to campus and without knowing who Mira was, Fraser asked about pitching and told him he threw harder than anyone on the current roster. A news reporter overhead the conversation; an article ran about Mira joining the baseball team. Gustafson summoned Fraser to his office and handed him a list of football players he would allow to also play baseball. Mira was not on it, and Fraser got the message. He did land Mira's backup, Fred Bertrand, as a catcher.

Letting all but one senior go from the roster he inherited, Fraser opted to start his program with a young team and mold them his way. Building his program meant recruiting. And recruiting required money to travel, but no additional resources were available. Told to do the best he could with his minimal budget, Fraser resorted to writing letters instead of traveling to see prospects in person.

Fraser's first team was an experiment. The roster consisted of just two returnees. An open tryout attracted a record fifty aspiring players. He fielded the school's initial freshman team, consisting of sixteen players who played mostly against local junior colleges. Fraser quipped that he was "teaching fundamentals this year" to his young squad. He was barely familiar with his team, and the players knew very little about their young new coach.

"We had no idea who Fraser was, except that he was from Holland and brought his wooden shoes in with him," said Jerry Reisman, a freshman on Campbell's final team. "We made him bring the wooden shoes because nobody really believed they had baseball in Holland. He wasn't much older than the players, and he made it fun for us and vice versa."

Fraser quickly developed rapport and gained respect from his team. He placed an emphasis on conditioning, defense, baserunning, and pitching. With problematic field conditions, much of the first two weeks of practice moved indoors for classroom "skull sessions" that emphasized the sport's mental side. The culture Fraser put in place differed significantly from what preceded him.

"Whitey was always in shorts at practice," Reisman, the team's third baseman, said of Fraser's predecessor. "With Fraser, we had to wear our uniforms to practice and basically played a game every day. He let the players play, and we gave him respect because he gave it to us. Campbell hardly knew we were there. It was a complete difference."

As a tune-up for the regular season, Fraser scheduled the New York Yankees rookies for three games to aid his team's preparation. Even the Yankee Clipper himself, Joe DiMaggio, was complimentary of Fraser's work and praised Miami's stressing of fundamentals and a good pitching staff.

In Fraser's debut, Miami dropped a one-run, eleven-inning, decision to No. 8 Ohio State. The next game, he recorded his first victory when Elmer Harris struck out a school-record 20 Army hitters. Three weeks later, the Hurricanes split a two-game set with powerhouse Florida State University, which finished third at the College World Series the year prior. Fraser's initial squad went 18–9, including wins over No. 2 Florida and No. 3 FSU. Miami was runner-up in the Florida Intercollegiate Conference (which included Florida Southern College, Jacksonville University, Rollins College, Stetson University, and the University of Tampa) and nearly earned an NCAA District 3 tournament bid. The university's *Ibis* yearbook foretold the future in its season summary, describing Fraser as "intent on building Miami into a baseball power that someday will put his 'major league' alma mater [rival Florida State] to shame." The *Miami Hurricane* called Fraser's initial season "one of the most pleasing events of spring sports" and "the sudden emergence of Miami's dominance as a strong baseball power."

Whereas Fraser's first team showed promise, its fashion provided a visible reminder of how far things still needed to go. Miami wore hand-me-down uniforms from the U.S. Military Academy. The letters *A*, *R*, and *Y* were removed from ARMY, leaving visible outlines, while the letter *M* remained to represent Miami. Fraser compared the 100 percent wool uniforms to horse blankets.

"The players were always complaining, and you can imagine how hot those things were in the Florida heat," said McClain.

"You lost ten pounds every practice," Reisman said about donning the wool uniforms. "I had better uniforms in high school and legion, which was difficult to understand."

The dearth of equipment and shoestring budget challenged Fraser resourcefulness to fulfill the basic needs for practices and games. He found funding for new uniforms by having four players participate in a Lucky Strike cigarette advertisement at Miami Stadium. For the record, none of them used cigarettes in the ad.

Without a batting cage for his team, Fraser secured a donation to procure one approximately thirty miles away in Homestead. Bringing the fully assembled batting cage to Coral Gables, home of University of Miami, required hitching it to a truck and driving it to campus along a busy stretch of roadway. Fraser, using his Youth Center connections, arranged for help from some friends who were police officers to arrange an overnight delivery.

"The cops went down to Homestead with us," recalled Bob Sheridan, who played for Fraser in 1965. "They had the lights on and everything else. We brought that cage all the way up Highway 1, which is a pretty good ride. Everyone was so fond of Coach Fraser that they'd do anything for him, including taking a midnight ride to get a batting cage."

Even the most basic item, baseballs, were at a premium. Players in the dugout were assigned to each baseball when it was hit foul. "Get the ball or don't come back" was the player's mission. "If we lost a baseball, he'd go crazy," said Danchik.

Fraser brought a cost-containment technique learned in Holland to Miami. To appease an exceptionally tight budget, Fraser reconditioned old dark-stained baseballs by soaking them in evaporated milk. When dry, the baseballs more closely resembled their original white coloring. An unintended consequence developed when a distinct and unpleasant permeating odor emitted after exposure to the hot Florida sun.

Typically, the reconditioned baseballs were intended for practice but occasionally entered a game. When they did, opponents noticed the unfamiliar smell and sought the source.

In a 1966 game against Ohio State, one of the milk-soaked baseballs created a bigger stir. Future College Baseball Hall of Fame pitcher Steve Arlin put a ball up to his nose and called time while nearly gagging. Coach Marty Karow came out to the mound, sniffed the ball, and yelled at Fraser, "What the hell is going on?" When Fraser tried to explain that the milk had soured in the heat, Karow angrily threw the ball out of the stadium and accused Fraser of refrigerating the baseballs to deaden them.

"We're all sitting on the bench saying, 'What's wrong with him?'" recalled Sheridan of the Buckeye opponent. "We knew exactly what he was smelling. Fraser says, 'There's nothing wrong with that ball.' It was probably heavy with the PET Milk on it and stunk to the high heavens."

Harding saw evaporated milk on Fraser's expense reports and called him into the athletic director's office. He asked Fraser if his personal financial situation was so bad that he needed help feeding his family.

Supplying a college baseball team with wood bats was a significant budget strain before aluminum bats were introduced in the mid-1970s. Fraser found an ingenious way to replenish his team's lumber by taking players to Hanna Manufacturing Company in Atlanta, which produced bats at the time, during a 1965 road trip to Georgia Tech and the University of Georgia. The company graciously told his players that they each could have a dozen bats. The bats did not hold up, though, and most of them broke in batting practice before ever being used in a game. Fraser nailed some of the bats back together to keep them in use.

Fraser's purchase of forty dozen baseballs before the season, approximately twice as many as had been used before, became precious commodities. He told the *Miami News* that "every afternoon we're going to have a big Easter egg hunt." There was enough money budgeted for equipment, but not to replace any losses.

On the field, Fraser's program continued its development toward status as a major sport. He instituted a fall season of practices and exhibitions. Now a fixture on the college baseball calendar, fall practice barely existed at the time. Believing experience is the best teacher, Fraser arranged home-and-home exhibition games against Major League rookie and B-level teams from the Milwaukee Braves and New York Yankees prior to the 1964 season. Following an 11–4 win over the Yankees, he proclaimed his team could beat anyone. Miami's regular-season schedule included thirty-three games, the most in school history, and his freshmen squad took on the nation's top junior college teams. Fraser pioneered night baseball by playing the regular season opener against the University of Florida at Miami Stadium, home of the Minor League Marlins. As the season began, Fraser boldly stated, "There was no reason why we shouldn't be a major power in baseball."

In 1964 Fraser's second-year team went 20-9-1, setting a new school record for victories and qualifying for an NCAA Tournament appearance. There was one problem. University president Dr. Henry King Stanford did not allow the team to accept its invitation because the tournament coincided with final-exam week. The controversial decision nearly resulted in Fraser's departure.

Miami baseball players picketed outside the president's house through the night. Reisman represented the team and attempted to rationalize with President Stanford, but his appeal was rejected. Fraser failed to see the fairness in the decision when students from the music school were traveling overseas and had their finals rescheduled to accommodate their trip. Fraser offered his resignation, citing that he could not face his team and its disappointment, but Gustafson, then athletic director, tore his letter in two. Fraser later said that had it not been for Gustafson's reaction, he would have never come back.

Fraser needed a roster of talented players to attain his vision of consistent success. Limited to tuition waivers rather than athletic scholarships, there was heavy reliance on walk-ons. Miami had private-school tuition costs, while Florida State and University of Florida, top-level in-state options, were considerably less expensive to attend. When the number of baseball freshmen on tuition aid at Miami increased from one to seven, that still paled in comparison to other schools that had nineteen baseball scholarships.

Nearby junior colleges provided more baseball scholarships and affordable tuition rates. Coach Demie Mainieri at nearby Miami Dade–North had arguably the best college team in South Florida with future Major Leaguers Steve Carlton, Mickey Rivers, Kurt Bevacqua, Bucky Dent, and Warren Cromartie coming through his program. Dade won a junior college (juco) championship and added three national runner-up finishes and a third-place finish during a ten-year span that overlapped Fraser's first decade at Miami. The Hurricanes were left with several players no one else wanted, a group Fraser later referred to as the "tough ones" for their contributions in the program's early days.

Fraser turned to his home state of New Jersey and tapped into connections for players who could help him win. Friends coaching from the area were instrumental in helping him find and land recruits. The 1965 incoming class featured four out-of-state players, including three from New Jersey, and three Miami-area products. The prize recruit was Warren Bogle, a daunting lefthanded pitcher from Lyndhurst, New Jersey, who stood 6 feet 4 and weighed 220 pounds. His prowess drew attention from professional teams that tried to sign him before he opted for Coral Gables.

"Many of the kids who came down to play would normally have not come to Miami if it weren't for Fraser's contacts in the area," said McClain. "He did a remarkable job recruiting guys from New Jersey, New York, and the Northeast to come into the program on partial scholarships."

Fraser divided the handful of available scholarships into as many pieces as possible. He even borrowed from the tennis or football teams to supplement aid for his players. The patchwork approach meant some players might get half or a third tuition scholarships. Others received books and room or meals. While it was not much, any aid helped. Still, the limitations put players and their families in a financial crunch. Fraser told them if they came in and did well, "we'll take care of you." Sometimes the available money did not match the amount needed and resulted in additional burdens.

"We had some kids who were coming to us under a lot of pressure to perform well so they could maintain the scholarship amounts they were originally given and hopefully try to induce an increase," recalled McClain. "Dealing with that every year, when it was not the case for other schools, put a lot a pressure on Frase."

Players received meal tickets from the football program to eat. Others got housing assistance by working as residence hall advisors. Fraser lined up various jobs, including some at the Coral Gables Youth Center, so they could pay their remaining tuition bills. It meant being creative in developing work-study opportunities.

"Coach told me he had a job for me at the Coral Gables Youth Center, and at the time, I didn't realize he also worked there," recalled John Danchik. "He said, 'You're going to coach youth soccer,' and I said, 'What?' Being from western Pennsylvania, I didn't know anything about soccer. He told me to go to the library and read up on it."

The following year Danchik roomed with tennis players because there was an extra unused scholarship. To earn his meal tickets, Danchik had to maintain the school's clay tennis courts. Fraser told him it would not be that bad and simply required watering them and washing them down at 7:00 a.m. and 7:00 p.m. each day. When Danchik reported for duty, he found the water automatically came on without any effort. A few days later, the tennis coach asked Danchik if Fraser had mentioned the sprinklers were on automatic timers.

"Coach would smile, wink and ask me, 'How's that job going with the tennis courts?'" Danchik recalled. "I'd say, 'Fine, coach, I've got it under control.' He knew exactly what was going on from the beginning."

Lacking the scholarships and type of facility that would entice prospective players, Fraser resorted to his best sales pitches. Fraser sold blue sky, green grass, and the opportunity to play a lot of baseball. By 1966 the schedule had sixty games before the end of May, a ledger that included exhibitions against big league teams preparing for spring training. The facility was still lackluster, but Fraser was resourceful.

On his recruiting visit from Wisconsin, Randy Olen was likely heading to Arizona State University, one of the nation's preeminent programs and the College World Series champion two of the previous three seasons. He decided to visit Miami on a professional scout's recommendation. After meeting at the Coral Gables Youth Center, Olen hopped in Fraser's Dodge Dart. Fraser told him to roll down the window and touted his car's radio as the best ever.

"You thought about the radio instead of how hot it was," recalled Olen. "We drove and drove and got to this baseball field. It was new and one of the best I have ever seen."

Fraser told Olen that one day he would play baseball on that field. The two resumed driving and talking, and before they knew it, they were back at the student union.

"The clouds rolled in, and the rain came down, and he looked up and said, 'I know these things, it will stop raining within five minutes,'" Olen recalled. "It did. The sun came out, and I thought he was a magician."

The impressive tour, immaculate baseball field, immediate acceptance into the business school, and a partial scholarship sold Olen on Miami. A month later, he reported to campus, found the location of the baseball field, and went to visit.

"I promise you there was a hump on third base that was about eight inches tall," said Olen, who wondered if it was the same field he saw during his visit and asked Fraser about it. "He said, 'What did I tell you? I told you one day you'd play on it. And how many games have we played at Dade South?' He was right. That was the fun-loving guy he was and personality he had. He would do anything he could to convince a guy with talent to come to the university and then would figure out how to put the pieces in place."

Recruiting was more than clever sales tactics. Fraser made personal visits and charming presentations to recruits and families, including Larry Pyle in New Jersey.

"I had scholarship offers from all over the country, including Arizona State and Florida State, but he was the only one who took the time and effort to come to see me and my parents, which I thought was great," recalled Pyle, who went on to a UM Sports Hall of Fame career as the school's first first-team baseball All-American. "He showed concern for me and meeting my parents. I thought that was important. My parents loved it and loved him too."

Additional games on summer international trips became another recruiting enticement to playing at Miami. In 1965 Fraser began an annual goodwill tour to South America, stopping in multiple cities and countries, including Coral Gables's sister city of Cartagena, Colombia. The trips were part of People to People International, a program of student experiences around the world. His initial team of fourteen players were mostly Hurricanes along with a handful of others from area junior colleges and schools around the state. The team conducted clinics during the day and played exhibition games against local or national teams in the evening. As many as four hundred children attended clinics, and Fraser distributed equipment, along with the Spanish translation of a baseball manual he authored. A highly sought publication across Latin countries and one of the few baseball publications available in Spanish, Fraser's manual taught fundamentals and described basic techniques for instructing the sport. The Colombians loved sports and Fraser's squad drew ninety-four thousand fans to eight games, including a crowd of sixteen thousand and fourteen thousand on three other occasions, surpassing typical attendance of most Minor League teams. By comparison, the Class A Florida State League Miami Marlins drew just under seventy-two thousand to Miami Stadium during its entire home schedule.

Back on campus, Fraser continued to battle through his budget and sought additional ways to pay the bills. He made a revolutionary decision to charge admission to attend Miami baseball games, beginning in 1966. No one in the country charged to attend college baseball games at the time. The risk was alienating about one hundred regular fans attending games free of charge. Having a crowd made the program look good, which in turn furthered interest. Crowds were so thin that Fraser once fielded a call from a woman with twelve grandchildren asking when the night's game started and asked her, "What time can you get here?"

Fraser's initial goal was to gate $50 per game, enough to pay the umpires. His friend Harry Diehl, who came to games in a wheelchair after a fall a few years prior left him paralyzed from the waist down, volunteered to sell tickets at the gate. He told Fraser that "no one was going to get angry at a guy in a wheelchair." Diehl ended up as ticket manager, ticket collector, parking director, usher, and security, all in one. He told the *Miami News* in 1983 that "if I saw a guy who looked like he was hurting for dough, I'd let him in free. But anybody who came in a suit had to pay."

To give fans an additional experience to justify their purchase, Fraser arranged for a skydiver to land on second base and deliver the game ball. "To charge them, I had to give them something else," Fraser said.

After pushing the pregame promotion in the newspapers, a better-than-expected crowd assembled. It was game time, but there was no skydiver. Restless fans began booing while waiting for the game to start and the skydiver to appear. The game could no longer wait and moved ahead without the special appearance. As the story goes, the skydiver missed his mark, in part due to strong winds, and landed on Dixie Highway. He walked up U.S. 1 in his full regalia and reached the gate well after the game was underway. When informed of the skydiver's late arrival, Fraser told his ticket taker that the performer would have to buy his ticket to get in the gate.

To bulk up Miami's home schedule, Fraser scheduled early season tournaments against some of the top northern teams. A desired destination for early season baseball, northern schools came to Miami to prepare for their season much in the same way Major League teams spent spring training in Florida. For many of them, the trip was their first opportunity to practice, let alone play, outdoors. Fraser brought in strong Ohio State and Michigan State teams along with a number of northeast squads to face the Hurricanes and play games against each other. A round-robin format allowed teams to play several games during their visit.

Miami had a distinct edge because its season was already underway after full fall and winter schedules. Fraser used the sunshine and warm weather to his advantage and scheduled games against northern teams late in the day. That allowed the visitors an opportunity to enjoy the Florida sunshine, whether at the beach or by the hotel pool. Fraser's rationale went beyond hospitality. The northern players showed effects of the sun by the time they took the field against the Hurricanes.

"Their players were sunburned and had difficulty being comfortable and moving around real well," said McClain. "They weren't always in the best shape to be able to play baseball, and that gave us a bit of an edge. We were very successful in the tournaments. Sometimes the coaches would ask why we weren't playing earlier in the day."

In some seasons, the round-robin schedules had as many as twenty-four games. Fraser strategically created the schedule with another baseball advantage in mind. He typically did not face a northern team playing its first game. Instead, Miami played those teams after they had played one or two games against each other.

"Most of the northern teams had one or two really good pitchers and wanted to throw them as much as they could down south," recalled John Danchik. "Fraser knew they would throw their best pitcher in the first or second game, so he would always schedule them for the third game and usually faced their No. 3 pitcher. He was always looking for an advantage. That was coach."

Just as the Hurricanes were poised to break out after a school-record 27 wins in 1968, Fraser's tenure at Miami was nearly ended by his alma mater.

Florida State's head coach Fred Hatfield left the school for a position in the St. Louis Cardinals organization. Speculation centered on Fraser taking over, and FSU announced him as a candidate. His progress at Miami, where he inherited a far-less successful program, was appealing. The Seminoles, meanwhile, spent part of the previous season ranked first in the nation and were described by the *Miami Hurricane* as "the Notre Dame of baseball with better facilities, a larger budget, more scholarships, and more tradition" than Miami. By December, the student paper reported that Fraser had or would soon accept the job. A student group began a Keep Fraser campaign and lobbied the university to do everything in its power to keep him.

Fraser made it known he would stay at Miami if promised lights at UM Field to help grow the program. He chose to stay and cited a fondness for the Miami area and the university. "It's tough to leave a place where you feel you've built up the program . . . and there is still so much more to do here," Fraser said. He claimed that his challenge of "making Miami baseball a major sport . . . will be done within five years." By retaining its coach and his vision, Miami baseball was headed in the right direction.

"He put his heart and soul into it and tried everything he possibly could do," said Danchik. "He certainly paid his dues early on."

2

Progress

Success bred expectation, and the momentum of Fraser's program was palpable. As the team gained acclaim for its winning ways, Fraser added some new wrinkles to home games. Miami had batboys in previous seasons, but he decided to add batgirls in 1968. Fraser's idea employed university co-eds to retrieve bats and foul balls during games and assist with game operations and promote the team at events.

The selection process was similar to that of selecting the school's cheerleaders. The interview panel included the three baseball captains, three UM intramural staff, and one sportswriter from the *Miami News*. Selections were based on personality and appearance.

Fraser oversaw the batgirls in a very protective way, much like a big brother, uncle, or father would. His players were very respectful and treated them as an extension of the team. The batgirls became a key part of the Miami baseball family.

Officially known as the Sugarcanes, the batgirls had a voice in decisions, including input on their uniform design. The uniforms were tight-fitting tops and short shorts, far different than batboys who dressed like the players. Seated on stools near the dugouts, the Sugarcanes provided a visual distraction for visiting teams.

"Guys would come down from someplace up north and they hadn't seen anyone in anything but an overcoat all winter," chuckled Joel Green, a standout shortstop from 1969 to 1971 and a future professional baseball player and doctor of chiropractic. "The batgirls would kind of mesmerize the other team."

Fraser said the batgirls made it easier to retrieve foul balls from spectators, providing an economical advantage. Fans typically opted to keep foul balls as souvenirs rather than turning them back to be put in play again. Fraser found when an attractive young lady made a polite request, fans were more apt to return the ball, which meant purchasing fewer baseballs to replenish the team's supply.

The Sugarcanes were more than a unique feature of Miami's game-day atmosphere. Each had specific duties, ranging from keeping the manual scoreboard to staffing concessions and souvenir stands. They sold tickets and passed out promotional materials, created player scrapbooks, and handled an array of business duties. Fraser took pride in their work in supporting the baseball program.

"Coach loved having batgirls and thought it was great marketing," recalled Nicki (Dacquisto) Cluney, who joined the team in 1971. "Initially, it was more about bringing attention to the program. People who may not be as interested in baseball would come out to see what the batgirls did at the games. A few of us sat up by the manual scoreboard and changed the numbers. If we were wrong, coach would look over at us and point."

The Sugarcanes nearly doubled their squad size within the first few seasons and became program ambassadors with goodwill-building publicity roles. Fraser included them on the team's regular season road trips and international summer tours.

"We were a close organization, and some of us learned the game as we went," said Linda DiMare, a Sugarcane in the early 1970s and a cousin of future player and coach Gino DiMare. "It was fun. Coach Fraser wanted us to build the program, get money back into it, and help gain fans. The love of the game, love of the program, and love for coach kept us going. He kind of raised us and gave us those character qualities that we were seeking."

A distinct transformation to the game experience began when a young freshman searching for a job introduced himself to Fraser.

Jay Rokeach went searching for a team-manager position with the basketball team after moving to campus. While walking back after rejection, he stopped at baseball practice and introduced himself to Fraser, who was standing behind the batting cage.

"I asked if he needed a student manager," recalled Rokeach. "He told me they could certainly use some help, and about an hour later, I was in the clubhouse doing laundry and cleaning uniforms."

Rokeach's manager duties extended to bagging peanuts for the concession stands before games and serving as official scorer for in-game statistics. He asked Fraser, who was always open to ideas, if he could add the role of public-address announcer. Fraser agreed.

Using a primitive table-and-chair setup behind the backstop, Rokeach became the voice narrating games, often with a modest crowd. He took it a step further and pioneered the integration of music into college baseball games. His selections went beyond playing songs to fill the void between innings and included music corresponding to on-field situations. For example, Rokeach played "Three Blind Mice" when the umpires would come out to meet with the coaches prior to the game. It was all in the name of fun and entertainment during the game experience, core staples of Fraser's vision.

"My love of the game led me to do walk-up songs," Rokeach said of playing music when announcing batters for their at-bats. "I don't claim to have invented the walk-up song, but certainly back in the day, we really went out of our way to be entertaining and play music that applied to the game.

"I literally had one hundred cassette tapes piled up next to me and was the only one who knew to cue them where needed for a special occasion. I took a lot of pride in making sure the music at the ballpark was something people noticed and would say or think, 'That was really cool they just played that.'"

On the field, a *Miami Hurricane* newspaper headline at the start of the 1969 season read "Miami Baseball Team Best Ever." Buoyed by a trio of returning captains in All-American center fielder Larry Pyle and the senior battery of catcher Jorge Maduro and left-handed pitcher Thom Lehman, the squad lived up to its preseason hype.

The Hurricanes reeled off 11 wins in 12 games during a midseason stretch, dropping only a highly controversial, one-run decision at Saint Leo University. After objectionable calls drew Fraser out to argue on multiple occasions, the game ended after umpires deliberated for ten minutes and overturned an out that would have pushed the game into extra innings. Instead, they decided Saint Leo's runner was safe and handed the home team an 11–10 victory. Fraser was so incensed that he refused to play the two-game series finale the following day. Eight years elapsed before Saint Leo appeared on Miami's schedule, and the team never again hosted the Hurricanes.

Miami finished the season with a 31-11 record, its best under Fraser, and set school offensive records in almost every category. *Collegiate Baseball* ranked the Hurricanes fourteenth in its final poll, a first for the program. Pyle earned the school's initial All-American honor when selected to the American Baseball Coaches Association (ABCA) and Rawlings first team. Despite the records and accolades, the year ended in disappointment when Miami was denied its first NCAA postseason bid.

The NCAA operated its baseball tournament by dividing schools into eight districts, and each winner advanced to the College World Series. Miami was in District 3, a large geographic footprint encompassing the southeast part of the country from Florida north to Maryland, west to Kentucky and south along the Mississippi River to Louisiana. That season, Virginia Tech received the final District 3 bid over Miami. Mississippi advanced from the tournament to the College World Series with an 18-15-1 record after defeating North Carolina and Furman. It was a difficult pill to swallow for Fraser's most talented team to date with six players signing pro contracts after the season.

"We were one of the best teams he ever had," recalled Green. "I remember coach had to come in and tell us we didn't get the bid. We should have gone to the College World Series that year."

Pyle was Fraser's first superstar at Miami. In an era when freshmen did not play on the varsity team, he made a memorable debut after being pulled out of the stands while watching a game. Fraser called for Pyle to go to the football office and get his uniform on. When he got back to the field, Pyle entered the game as a pinch hitter with the bases loaded and the Hurricanes down three. Like a perfectly written script, he belted a grand slam.

After turning down a lucrative signing bonus from the Atlanta Braves, Pyle hit .431 during his 1969 All-America campaign. That mark came during the wood-bat era and stood atop the Miami record book for three decades. Nicknamed the "Blonde Bomber," Pyle's stock peaked, and he signed with the New York Yankees for nearly $60,000. Upon learning his decision, Fraser told Pyle in jest, "You stiff, I wanted you back here again next year. What's your problem?"

Featuring a retooled roster, Fraser's 1970 squad won its first ten games but dropped seven of its last nine to finish 28-15-1 and fall short of a postseason bid. Miami's elusive first NCAA Tournament appearance remained on hold for another year.

Despite being on the precipice of postseason berths, Fraser feared his program could be dropped altogether. The university decided to cut a program from its athletics department to trim costs. Football was struggling mightily but too high-profile. That left basketball, which had even more problems, or baseball, which did not make money. Anticipating his program could be dropped, Fraser convinced baseball legends Joe Garagiola and Stan Musial to host a fundraiser. Having former athletes on the banquet speech circuit was a new concept, and Garagiola agreed to headline the event. Fraser then turned to Musial, who owned a hotel in Miami and provided a ballroom for use. The successful fundraising event built excitement for Fraser's program through significant publicity and much-needed donations. The attention and funding were enough to get the administration's attention. Baseball dodged the bullet, and basketball was cut following the 1970–71 season, a surprising move, given the sport's status on the college landscape.

Baseball became highly respected by the students and the university. It had surpassed basketball in popularity and was nearly on par with football, especially given the lack of gridiron success. Even then, baseball remained hindered by its subpar facility.

As Fraser's program inched closer to reaching the national tournament, he established key relationships with prominent community members who helped lift baseball with financial donations. As the football program struggled to occasionally reach the .500 mark, some donors chose to support Fraser's efforts instead.

"He had all these donors giving him money and thanking coach for the opportunity to give him money. That's talent. It was unbelievable," said Al Marsicano, who was on the Hurricanes roster for two years before a postgraduate business career that included advising Fraser on finances. "He was way ahead of his time, extraordinarily creative, and the best promoter I've ever come across."

"He could sell you the swamp, and you would think you got the greatest deal in the world," said Tony Segreto, longtime Miami television anchor and host of the Fraser coach's show. "He was a true visionary who had a belief."

One benefactor was Wilburt "Burt" Chope, founder and CEO of Industrial Nucleonics, which later changed its name to AccuRay, a manufacturer of industrial process controls. He held patents for several inventions, including an aircraft midair refueling system.

Fraser lined his players up with jobs to help maintain Chope's $163 million property, one of his two Miami homes. Some watered the coconut trees and cleaned up the fallen fruit. Others gave private baseball instruction to Chope's son and coached his Little League team.

"When I was coaching his son in Little League, Burt asked what I thought he needed for equipment," recalled Green. "I told him a glove, some baseballs, and bats. He said, 'What about a batting cage?' and I said, 'Sure.'" In two days, he had two batting cages with pitching machines that were better than any I had ever seen—two cages for one kid.

"He asked me about a field, and I said, 'A field?' He had these beautiful royal palms removed behind his house and in two weeks had an artificial-turf field. Burt was a character and was right up Coach Fraser's alley. They knew how to promote."

The field featured artificial turf and clay imported from Georgia. When the local Little League reached its capacity for participants, Chope started his own league and had Fraser's players work on the field, sometimes for $20 per week. To determine which position his son should play, Chope funded a study and found that more balls are hit to shortstop and center field and had him play there. Chope's son took batting practice recorded on closed-circuit TV for the Miami players to watch and review.

As their friendship grew, Chope attended Canes games with his driver and kept score. He loaned a bus and use of his personal driver to Fraser for the team's road trips—not just any bus, but one resembling a house on wheels with modern amenities far ahead of its time: a sauna, televisions, a stereo system, beds, and sofas. It was easily the best transportation in college baseball and rivaled top Major League accommodations. Traveling in a $250,000 bus, the Hurricanes were like touring rock stars.

Fraser saw an opportunity to enhance his team's media coverage and forged a partnership with the University of Miami's student radio station, wvum-fm, in 1971. For the first time, all Miami home games aired live at a time when broadcasting college baseball games was new to most of the country. The broadcasts provided a way to follow games for those unable to attend the 3:00 p.m. start times necessitated by the lack of lights at um's field. Students and Coral Gables residents comprised the audience due to wvum's limited range, but having game broadcasts gave the program a big-time feel.

"He looked at the radio station as a vehicle in the promotion of his team," Marty Connors, who spent four years on the wvum broadcast team, said of Fraser. "He utilized that to a greater extent than I think any coach I've seen before or since. He realized that even though we had only ten watts, the reach we had and the number of people around campus and the Gables community who listened to the games was remarkable."

Determined to make the next step, the Hurricanes entered 1971 with a solid lineup and trademark speed and defense. Fraser believed the team's pitching depth, a question mark at the start of the season, would come along.

Just over two weeks into the season, Miami hosted Florida State and dropped the opener of a two-game set, 5-4, in ten innings. The following day, the Canes countered with a 5–4, ten-inning victory of their own to snap a twelve-game skid against fsu. The Seminoles were the Southeast's behemoth and coming off a runner-up finish to usc at the College World Series.

The win was just the third in nineteen tries for Fraser against his alma mater, but it was more significant than that. In his column titled "And the Jinx Finally Ended," *Miami Hurricane* sports editor Ed Lang called it the greatest baseball win he covered. Miami's series split, repeated a month later in a two-game set in Tallahassee, proved it was a legitimate challenger to fsu's reign.

Still early in the season, the victories bolstered Miami's hopes for a postseason bid. By the end of March, the Hurricanes achieved its first top-ten ranking, sitting at No. 8 in the United Press International (upi) poll. Considered the clear frontrunner in District 3, excitement grew about the team, and so did the crowds.

When NCAA bids were announced, Fraser's squad joined conference champions Maryland (Atlantic Coast) and Mississippi State (Southeastern), and at-large selection Georgia Tech for the District Tournament in Gastonia, North Carolina. "I've been waiting for this for nine long years," Fraser told the media.

"To get a bid as an independent was rewarding itself," said Bob Bartlett, a pitcher on the first NCAA Tournament team. "It was made clear to us that this was quite an accomplishment, and Ron was able to persuade the university to come up with the money for travel. Getting an invitation was a goal of ours, and once that was extended, his interest turned to whether we could go or not."

After a 4–3 win over Georgia Tech in Miami's postseason debut, losses to Mississippi State and in the rematch with Georgia Tech ended the season. The Hurricanes took another step forward while earning an all-time best twelfth final ranking from *Collegiate Baseball*.

The next season proved a great disappointment despite a 32-17 record. There was no postseason, however. Fraser saw it as a rebuilding year and experimented with different player combinations after many key performers proved irreplaceable. Falling short of expectations took a toll on Fraser. His team played uninspired baseball, and camaraderie was missing. Attendance suffered, and much of the optimism about the program faded. Fraser vowed it would never happen again.

"The season was a failure; there is no other way to put it," recalled Connors. "Fraser admitted that to me a couple of times and said, 'I did not do as a good a job in recruiting as I should.' What Fraser did to build that program with basically nothing to work with was spectacular. It really took, as a first step, getting to the tournament to catch people's attention."

Fraser needed a bounce-back season to prove the postseason appearance two seasons prior was the precursor of success rather than an anomaly. The program's future was bright beyond wins and losses.

A series of generous contributions by local businessman George Light, a plastics magnate, made Fraser's ballpark vision a reality. Light announced a $100,000 donation to fund lights and an artificial playing surface at UM Field. One year later, he nearly matched that figure with a separate $95,000 contribution to build permanent seating to hold up to 3,700 fans. The news of the initial donation came as a shock to Fraser, who learned about it during a late-season luncheon.

Fraser had long pushed for lights. Illuminating the field meant avoiding scheduling games in the hot afternoon sun. Furthermore, it allowed for increased attendance and making Hurricane baseball an evening entertainment destination. It was much easier to sell fans on coming to the ballpark after work hours than for a late-afternoon start time.

Adding a Tartan Turf surface eliminated the cost for field maintenance, a concern throughout Fraser's first decade. Becoming the first college team to play on turf made Miami unique. It provided a competitive advantage in both recruiting and games. Gone were the days of a rock-infested infield and spectators on borrowed bleachers and personal lawn chairs.

Light, the catalyst of these improvements, was president of Modern Plastics in Hialeah, a factory he opened in 1940 with a $2,000 investment. Appointed to the university's Citizens Board in 1965, he made several contributions, including purchasing motion-picture equipment for the mass communications department. Light sought to make a six-figure donation and let the university decide its allocation.

A former baseball player himself, Light nearly lost an eye in prep school after being struck in the face by a thrown ball, leaving him legally blind. Until 1970 he had never seen a Canes game or met Fraser. A year later he was hooked, hanging around the dugout, and often sitting on the bench with the team, though never offering advice. An unassuming gentleman, he preferred to stay behind the scenes and told people to call him George, rather than Mr. Light.

Light and his wife, Ethel, made their donations with a request to name the newly developed baseball facility after their late adopted son. Bound to a wheelchair at age seven, Mark Light never played baseball because of his muscular dystrophy, which ultimately claimed his life in 1957 at age sixteen. George wanted to honor his son and his love for baseball by creating a place where people could enjoy watching the sport.

Light told the *Miami News* in 1975 that he felt great satisfaction in his contributions because it triggered a lot, including Fraser's ascension from part-time to full-time coach, additional substantial financial donations, and the team's burgeoning success. "Being involved in that kind of progress in such a short time is an exciting thing," Light said.

Fraser lobbied that a synthetic-turf field could benefit the university in several ways beyond being the nation's premier baseball facility. The football team could hold night practices or freshman football games. Students could have a venue for intramurals and outdoor concerts, and the community could hold soccer and high school events. It was a win-win situation. Groundbreaking on the complex and new home for Hurricanes baseball began in the summer of 1972.

Other off-field developments accelerated the program's forward trajectory. The athletic department nearly doubled baseball scholarships to thirteen, comparable with other top-ten programs, yet well below the NCAA limit of twenty-four.

Fraser received a full-time salary comparable or better than many of the nation's top coaches. No longer having to work as part-time baseball coach and part-time Coral Gables Youth Center director, Fraser focused full energy on his program while adding a role of assisting the UM Athletic Federation during the fall. His office was upgraded with wood-paneling, air conditioning, carpeting, and even a secretary. Although not as visible as facility improvements, the changes signified progress and, in many ways, a new starting point, all of which came together quickly.

The new ballpark and an improved team created excitement as the season approached. Advanced tickets were sold. Assistant coaches McClain and Red Berry helped bring in an influx of junior college and high school talent to the roster with the added scholarships. Fraser's office began fielding an average of sixty letters per month from players nationwide expressing interest in playing for Miami.

"Entertainment, the warm climate, a 60–75 game schedule, bat girls, and colorful uniforms . . . all of them add flair to entice top athletes," McClain told the *Miami Hurricane* when asked about the team's surge in recruiting.

Collegiate Baseball ranked Miami third in the season's initial poll, its highest position in history and behind only perennial powers Arizona State and USC. The mix of key holdovers and talented newcomers gave Fraser his deepest roster yet.

One newcomer, Clarence "Gully" Poitier, a talented junior college All-American and cousin of Academy Award–winning actor Sidney Poitier, broke the color barrier as Miami's first Black baseball player that season. Fraser successfully recruited Black players in previous years, but each opted to sign professionally. Unphased by portrayal as a trailblazer, Poitier told media he was "just here to play ball and that's all." As Fraser successfully blended players from different national-ities and parts of the country, the addition of a Black player to a mix of Cubans and Caucasians was no big deal in his program. The team fully embraced Poitier, making his race a nonfactor.

"We all molded together and never thought anything of it," said Wally Pontiff, who was Poitier's roommate after transferring to Miami when Loyola University in New Orleans dropped its program. "Everybody loved him. We never thought of him as Black. You just thought of him as Gully, a good guy who loved being part of the team. I never saw one problem that he had with another player. The guys he played against on other teams loved him."

When the season began, Miami players relished the new turf, and it provided a distinct competitive advantage. True and faster hops eliminated concern that a bad hop would ruin a defensive play and leave a fielder in the wrong position. Miami's offense and speed game benefitted. Hit balls got through the infield more rapidly, and bounces sometimes careened over heads of opponents unfamiliar with the turf's springiness. Most visiting teams practiced on the turf the day before their game, while local commuting squads had only a couple of hours to prepare. Intrigued by the surface, opponents often took baseballs and bounced them when first walking onto the field.

The turf had one drawback for home and visitor alike. Heat reso-nating from the surface on sunny afternoons made it extremely hot. "With the turf, your feet would be burning up after an inning or two," McClain recalled. "For a day game in the sun, the temperature would be well over one hundred degrees."

Not only did players need shoes different from those worn on tra-ditional grass-and-dirt infields, but they also needed protection from the temperatures. Fraser prepared for the concerns by touring MLB clubs and learning about special innersoles manufactured specifically to guard against heat.

The highly anticipated season opener against rival Florida State marked the first home night game in Miami baseball history. A pre-game dedication ceremony officially opened the new facility. Always thinking big, Fraser expressed a desire to invite President Richard Nixon to throw out the first pitch. "Why not?" Fraser told the *Miami News*. Instead, he got the university president dressed in a tuxedo to lead the dedication ceremony. Despite a cool and windy night, excitement abounded through the crowd of 4,235 fans, well beyond the facility's 3,700 seating capacity and the 3,000 expected attendance.

The game started inauspiciously when Florida State's first two batters reached base. A ball hit toward the right-center-field gap appeared destined for a double and an early 2–0 lead but instead set the stage for the first instance of "Mark Light magic." Outfielder Manny Trujillo, who got a great jump, snared it, pivoted, and made an incredible throw to the infield. Jim Crosta caught the ball and, with both baserunners already past third base, stepped on second and threw to first to complete a triple play. The improbable play set the tone for the historic night.

"Manny turned his back—you could see his number—and made a basket catch," recalled first baseman Orlando González. "He turned and threw to second and then the throw came to me for the triple play. Those were the first three outs made at the new stadium. The magic started there."

"Fraser was already turning into a legend, and his program had turned the corner," recalled Gary Chrisman, who called games from WVUM that season. "At the very first game at Mark Light, there was a special feeling with the turf and lights and dedication of this beautiful state-of-art facility in memory of George Light's son. Then the Hurricanes ended the first inning threat with an improbable triple play. You thought something special is going to happen in this place for Fraser and the Hurricanes and it sure did because they didn't lose very much."

The only thing missing from the night was the new scoreboard, which debuted later in the season due to logistical matters. Fraser was very proud of his new purchase and the color it brought to the ballpark—the board was green and had permanent markings for "Miami" as the home team and "Visitors" on top—and could not wait to have it installed when it arrived on campus shortly after the season began. The installation was quintessential Fraser in getting things done but not always through the proper channels. The university's purchasing department asked Fraser why a scoreboard was delivered and informed him it required a bid process.

"They told him he couldn't just order a scoreboard, but Ron's feeling was 'What are they going to do about it?'" recalled Rokeach. "There's a scoreboard sitting in the receiving area. It's green. It has Miami on the bottom of it. What are they going to do with it? And that's how we got our scoreboard. Obviously, the people in purchasing were not very happy."

WVUM announcer Marty Connors overheard some of the conversation between the purchasing department and Fraser while passing by his office.

"When Ron called the university maintenance department to have the scoreboard installed, he was asked for a requisition number," recalled Connors. "He said, 'What the hell is a requisition?'"

The maintenance department proceeded to inform Fraser that it needed a requisition number before performing any work.

"Ron says, 'Nobody told me about a requisition,'" Connors said. "He desperately wanted his new scoreboard for the showpiece it represented. He's calling all over campus and is upset he can't order maintenance to come over and install his scoreboard. It's driving him insane."

The maintenance department dug in its heels in and played hardball with Fraser. The maintenance representative informed him that the department would not install the scoreboard because he was rude to them.

"The madder Ron gets, the madder maintenance gets," said Connors. "He says, 'I'm the baseball coach; I have people here. I need my scoreboard up.'"

The back-and-forth continued for almost six weeks before the scoreboard finally moved out of the university's physical plant and was installed midseason.

The Mark Light magic seen on opening night continued that season. The following weekend's series against Jacksonville began with a fourteen-inning Hurricane victory, the longest game in school history. The next day, Miami recorded a most improbable comeback. Trailing by 8 to start the bottom of the ninth, the Canes rallied for 9 runs and a 9–8 win. Miami won its first nine games, including a sweep of Southern Illinois University, which had finished as College World Series runner-up just two seasons prior.

The highly ranked Hurricanes were poised to put the disappointments of previous seasons behind them. Fraser felt like a weight had been lifted off him. As well as his team played, its postseason prospects took a hit after a three-game skid in Tallahassee with a loss to FSU and a doubleheader sweep at Florida A&M. With a 28-14 record, Fraser challenged his team.

"He was a motivator and would play mind games with us sometimes," said Pontiff. "He told us, 'You're not making regionals. You're not going anywhere. You're not good enough.' He was just chewing us out. I remember saying, 'Yes, coach, we're going to make it. From this point on we're going to get it done. There will be no talk about if we're going to get it done.'"

Finishing the season 11-1 earned the Hurricanes the final District 3 bid over Florida State and Georgia Tech. The team headed to Starkville, Mississippi, focused on reaching its first College World Series. A win over the University of South Alabama was followed by a 1–0 loss to Ron Polk's Georgia Southern University squad. After rolling past Appalachian State University, the Canes notched a thrilling one-run victory over Vanderbilt to set up a rematch against Georgia Southern for a berth in the College World Series. A former assistant coach at Miami Dade Community College–South, Polk knew all the Canes recruits and scouted the team during the year whenever he could. Georgia Southern shut Miami out four days earlier and again had its number, holding the offense in check in a 4–1 decision.

Despite finishing one game short of Omaha, Fraser called it a great year. Although the players did not get where they wanted to be, the program was in a position it wanted to be. Miami finished ninth in the *Collegiate Baseball* rankings, its highest finish to date. Even the Sugarcanes gained national accolades, finishing as co–national champions with Brigham Young University in the All-American Batgirl contest.

3

Omaha

By the early 1970s, college baseball's landscape revolved around its two most successful teams. Southern California and Coach Rod Dedeaux dominated the sport—the Trojans won five of six national championships from 1968 through 1973. The other preeminent power, Arizona State coached by Bobby Winkles, claimed the 1969 title and finished runner-up in both 1972 and 1973. The sport's axis of power clearly tilted to the West Coast.

Three significant rule changes took effect in 1974. The introduction of aluminum bats allowed schools a cost-effective option to replacing broken wood bats. The new bats performed similarly to their wooden counterparts but were heavier, unlike today's lightweight versions. Initially, aluminum bats did not create a clear advantage and made only a minimal impact on offense. Many players continued to use wood bats.

The NCAA implemented the American League's 1973 designated-hitter rule after the previous two College World Series combined to average just seven runs per game. Officials anticipated an offensive boost without pitchers batting.

NCAA Division I schools also saw the number of baseball scholarships capped at nineteen after being unlimited. The move provided more parity rather than a handful of teams like USC and Arizona State stockpiling talent.

Miami entered the 1974 season with seven returning starters from a club that finished one win from its first College World Series. Media called the roster the most talented ever assembled at the school. The buzz grew, and there was a sense that baseball was on the verge of something big.

With the additional scholarships, Fraser's recruiting territory expanded to California. He attracted Rich Reichle, son of UCLA's legendary baseball coach Art Reichle. He also tapped into the state's rich junior college pipeline to shore up a key position of need.

When Fraser signed Ron Scott, he told him that he was a catcher away from a special team. Scott signed and seized the opportunity to contribute. Fraser used the same pitch to Tom Holliday, another touted backstop, hoping to sign one of the two. He ended up with both.

Season preparation took on a new wrinkle. Fraser turned down an opportunity to play exhibition games against Latin and Central American teams and opted for a trip to the Kansas City Royals Academy in Sarasota. At the time, the Royals Academy was the only center preparing young athletes for future Major League and Minor League careers. Miami's visit included additional training and instruction, just as other attendees received, plus five exhibition games against academy teams on the complex's lavish fields.

A season-opening sweep of Jacksonville included Fraser's three hundredth career victory. Following a 1–0, ten-inning loss at Florida Southern that dropped the Hurricanes to 7-3, Fraser expressed displeasure with his touted team for not playing to its capability. Without uttering anything other than "get on the line," he had his team run sprints for an hour even after ballpark's lights were turned off and sprinklers went on.

Miami got hot and rolled through its tournaments with wins over Southern Illinois and Seton Hall University, which both appeared in the College World Series the previous year. From March 9 through April 12, Miami did not lose a game, reeling off a twenty-six-game winning streak and moving up to No. 2 in the national rankings, one vote behind No. 1 Arizona in the *Collegiate Baseball* poll and one spot ahead of USC. "I never expected being ranked number two. Everyone was figuring we would be ranked fifth or sixth," said Fraser of the news.

The streak drew national attention. As Miami closed in on the NCAA record of thirty-two consecutive wins, CBS planned a Coral Gables visit to produce a feature about the team for its *60 Minutes* news show. Rollins College, an in-state opponent that seemingly had the Hurricanes' number, ended the streak, and the television crew never made its visit. Florida State then swept a doubleheader and extended Miami's season-long losing streak to three.

With a talented roster led by Orlando González, whom Fraser called the most complete college baseball player he had ever seen, the Hurricanes won eleven of thirteen to close the regular season. Despite a collection of dirtbag-type players, the team dynamic gave Fraser one of his most challenging seasons. The roster featured future Major Leaguer Wayne Krenchicki, No. 1 starting pitcher Stan Jakubowski, and starting third baseman Jim Crosta, all from New Jersey. He had a group of Miami Cubans known as "the family" in González, Joe Vega, Benny Castillo, Manny Trujillo, and Hugo Rams. Competitive drive galvanized the eclectic roster.

"Coach Fraser pushed the right buttons all season," said Tom Baxter, a pitcher on the 1974 squad. "All we wanted to do was win, and we pushed one another. Guys knew this was a competition and you have to be your best every day."

Sporting a gaudy 44-8 record, Miami entered Starkville, Mississippi, as the District 3 NCAA Tournament favorite. The six-team field had plenty of competition. North Carolina State featured basketball standouts Monty Towe and Tim Stoddard, who went on to become the first player to win an NCAA Basketball Championship and MLB World Series. South Carolina was coached by New York Yankees legend Bobby Richardson, and Georgia Southern, coached by Polk, handed Miami its two postseason losses the previous season.

"In the back of our mind we thought College World Series, but we knew it was not going to be easy in Starkville," recalled Baxter. "To Coach Fraser's credit, I don't recall him ever bringing up going to the College World Series. It was 'let's win today, and we'll keep moving.'"

The Hurricanes edged Georgia Southern, 2–1, topped Vanderbilt, 7–1, and shut out South Carolina, 5–0, to reach the championship. A loss to South Carolina in the first rematch set up a winner-take-all contest between the sixth-ranked Canes and fourth-ranked Gamecocks the next day. Fraser's pitching staff, the team's lone question mark entering the season, saw its depth further tested by already playing four games.

Fraser started Jerry Brust in the deciding game, even though Brust pitched two days prior. The decision was based on his confidence in Brust after blanking the Gamecocks and because the righthander's sidewinding throwing motion caused less arm strain and allowed him to bounce back more quickly.

South Carolina led off the game with a home run before Miami countered with a pair of runs in the bottom half of the first inning. When asked what went through his mind when Brust was in an early jam, Fraser quipped, "I figured I made the biggest mistake ever."

With the Hurricanes still holding a 2–1 lead, Eddie Ford, South Carolina's fastest baserunner and son of Yankees legend Whitey Ford, reached base to lead off the ninth. With one out, Richardson gave Ford the steal sign, and Scott made a perfect throw to nail him at second, thwarting the threat and preserving a victory that sent Miami to its first College World Series.

Despite sharing the No. 1 ranking with Texas, Miami was relatively unknown entering Omaha. On his first visit, Fraser compared walking into Rosenblatt Stadium to walking into Yankee Stadium.

Miami defeated Harvard, 4–1, in its College World Series debut. When rain pushed back the next game, Jakubowski returned to the mound for his second consecutive start, a 5–1 win over Oklahoma. The two wins set up a showdown with juggernaut USC.

Despite having won four consecutive College World Series championships, USC was not considered a favorite that season. Its .703 winning percentage was considered an off year and a product of a tougher road to Omaha. Still, the Trojans were an imposing veteran squad led by NCAA RBI record-holder Rich Dauer, along with fellow future Major Leaguer Steve Kemp, and All-American running back Anthony Davis.

USC defeated Texas and rode an impressive ten-game College World Series winning streak into its matchup against the Hurricanes, playing their third-ever game in Omaha. Unphased, Miami toppled college baseball's Goliath, 7–3, and sat in the driver's seat for the title. The following day's *Omaha World-Herald* headline read "Trojans' Nose Bloodied by the New CWS Bully." The Omaha crowd embraced Miami and cheered the fresh faces wearing the wild orange and green uniforms.

"I remember being very impressed with them, especially when they beat us," recalled Justin Dedeaux, an assistant coach for his legendary father. "We said, 'Boy, these guys are really good.' They were a really strong team and were definitely on the map after that game."

Next up for Miami was Southern Illinois, a team it defeated by identical 6–1 scores in two March matchups and scored 25 runs in two wins the previous year. The Salukis were formidable and the Canes

possibly overconfident after beating mighty usc. Miami looked list-
less and, despite rallying to tie the game late, dropped a 4–3 decision.

The loss meant the Hurricanes squandered an opportunity to force
usc to defeat them twice in the double-elimination format. Three
teams, Miami, usc, and Southern Illinois University (siu), all with
one loss, remained. Rain wreaked havoc on the schedule and forced
a blind draw to decide final matchups. An ncaa official set out three
envelopes, each containing a paper marked "home," "visitor," or "bye,"
for the coaches to select. Fraser drew the bye and awaited the winner
of usc vs. siu.

A Trojans win set up a one-game championship rematch against
the upstart Hurricanes. The two schools could not have been further
apart, both geographically and in athletic history. usc had fifty-four
ncaa championships to its credit, not including five more in football.
Its baseball team alone owned nine. Miami, meanwhile, had no ncaa
championships in any sport. Fraser called the game the "biggest thing
that's ever happened [to Miami] athletically."

Playing the underdog role, Fraser referred to his team as the little
kids on the block challenging the big guys. He admitted he would
have been happy playing in the final game five years later because his
program's growth was ahead of schedule. Fraser kept things low-key
with his team to avoid additional pressure.

"Fraser wanted his players to have fun and didn't want them tight,"
recalled Marty Connors, who called games for wvum. "In talking to
him before the game, he was as calm as ever. He said, 'We worked
our butts off to get here, so we're going to do our best and see how
things fly.'"

Fraser pulled the right strings all season. In the College World Series
final, Kim Siepe moved to center field for defensive purposes. The
corresponding move meant sacrificing some offense by leaving Phil
LoMedico, owner of the team's second-highest batting average, out of
the lineup. On the mound, Fraser believed Jakubowski was his best
shot and opted to send his ace and a sixteen-game winner out on two
days rest rather than rotating through four other available pitchers.

An early miscue put Miami behind. With two usc runners on and
two outs in the first inning, a controversial call on a close play at
first base resulted in both baserunners scoring on the play to make

it 2–0. The Trojans built on their lead, and although the Hurricanes chipped away and put men on base, they stranded too many runners in a 7–3 loss.

Coming so close to winning the national championship was disappointing. Yet, it gained Miami notoriety and respect and was a springboard for the program. Fraser remarked at a team reunion years later that after entering Omaha as an unknown, the team left with everyone knowing "who the hell Miami was" and that "they took us serious from then on."

"The 1974 College World Series catapulted the program," recalled Connors. "You knew Miami was now a power and a team to beat. Fraser got so much respect from the other coaches."

Southern Illinois coach Richard "Itch" Jones told media during the College World Series that Miami "will be a national power" and predicted it would be "as well-known as Southern Cal and Arizona State."

The Hurricanes etched their place on the Miami sports scene. All College World Series games aired on wvum radio in Coral Gables, the only way to follow the games during an era when televisions had just three channels and were not in every household. Each win fueled further interest from the university, the Coral Gables and Miami communities, and across South Florida.

"I was playing center field in a Little League game, and parents sitting in the outfield were listening to the Miami games on the radio," recalled Joe Zagacki, who began broadcasting with the Hurricanes in 1985 and later assumed play-by-play duties. "I could hear the College World Series broadcast while I was playing my game. That was the first time I remember um baseball really taking off."

When the team returned home, eager fans greeted the Hurricanes and celebrated their College World Series run and national runner-up finish.

"When we came back to Miami, we had fans waiting for us at the airport like we had won. It was great," recalled González. "It was a big deal to reach No. 1 in the nation, and we were starting to get notoriety and be on the front of the sports pages in Miami."

Fraser recognized the College World Series win over usc as the program's turning point and a driving force for years to come. The university now realized the value of its baseball success and further backed Fraser's program. "Once we got a taste of that atmosphere, how good it could be, once the university got a taste of it, that's what drove us all to get back," Fraser said.

Reaching the College World Series, defeating mighty USC, and being on the cusp of the school's first national championship of any kind was a significant milestone. Belief prevailed that the program stood at the brink of greatness. A series of events in the coming years positioned the Hurricanes as the Southeast's top team and among the nationally elite.

With departures of assistant coaches Bill McClain and Red Berry, Fraser sought to fill their roles with one hire and selected Polk, whose Georgia Southern team ended Miami's season just two years prior. Polk was a Miami native and became good friends with Fraser while he spent four years guiding Miami Dade–South.

The up-and-coming coach was thought to be a potential heir apparent to Fraser, who was rumored as a candidate for Miami's athletic director position and had overtures from the Major Leagues. When Fraser was offered a Major League front-office position, Director of Athletics Pete Elliott called Polk into his office and told him if Fraser were to leave, he wanted him to take over as head coach. Fraser continued mulling over his Major League offer and had not reached a decision. Meanwhile, Polk, who had only been in the role for three months, was offered the head coaching job at Mississippi State when it suddenly opened in December.

"I finally went into Ron's office and said I can't wait any longer," Polk recalled. "I told him he was going to have to pull the trigger and that I was going to Mississippi State if he was going to stay. If not, it looked like I was going to end up in his seat."

Days after their conversation, Fraser decided to remain as Miami coach, and Polk accepted the position in Starkville. Finding an assistant coach with mere weeks remaining before the season, and doing so for the second time in a handful of months, was less than ideal. Another up-and-coming coach, this time from a nearby high school, came to the forefront, and Fraser replaced one future legend with another.

Enter Stanley Bertman, better known as Skip. A catcher for the Hurricanes from 1958 to 1960, Bertman spent eleven years as head coach at Miami Beach High School, winning a state title, finishing as state runner-up twice, and earning Florida High School Coach of the Year three times. Many considered him the best high school baseball coach in the state.

Bertman's wife, Sandy, had helped Fraser's wife, Liane, land an interview for her teaching position, and the two taught together at Tropical Elementary in Miami. When Fraser spoke about potential candidates for his open assistant coach position, Liane brought up Bertman.

"Ron said he would be great, but that he had a good job at Miami Dade–North [Community College], and with their coach near retire- ment, he was likely to get the head coaching position there. It was a good situation, and he doubted that Skip wanted to be an assistant coach at Miami," Liane recalled. "I said, let me check on that. I remember meeting [Skip's wife] Sandy in the hallway going back and forth with our classes and asking if she thought Skip would be interested in the assistant coach job. She said he would, so I told Ron to go interview him. It turned out that Sandy helped me get a job, and it worked out that Sandy and I got Skip and Ron together."

When Bertman came aboard, he said, "Ron [Fraser] is so charming and nice, I took the job for $14,500 and a car so I could work with him."

Bertman's decision had lasting effects on his career and Miami's history. No one could possibly have known at the time that Fraser's hiring of Bertman would forever change the college baseball landscape.

The generosity of George Light continued. After initial donations surpassing $100,000, Light provided another sizeable gift to complete the first-class stadium Fraser envisioned.

The new project, announced in 1974, included concrete stands spanning dugout to dugout behind home plate. Additional bleacher seating down the foul lines raised capacity to five thousand. Groundbreaking came in June 1976, later than the original timeline, and inflation nearly tripled the original construction costs to $250,000. Light's sizable donation only covered part of the bill. When overall funding came up short, a team of donors and Light, himself, added more. Local concrete, construction, tile, and hardware companies donated materials and provided labor at cost.

Much like Disneyland was to Walt Disney, the renovated Mark Light Stadium that opened in 1977 was a product of Fraser's imagination and vision. His hard work in hustling to finance his dream resulted in college baseball's first cathedral. Widely considered the premier facility in the sport, the stadium was the envy and aspiration of other schools.

How does an early 1970s malt liquor commercial factor into the history of Mark Light Stadium? It inspired Fraser to create the most expensive fundraising dinner to date.

Colt 45 began airing its bullfight commercial in 1970 that featured a gentleman sitting at a table in the middle of a bullring. From that inspiration, Fraser came up with an idea to hold a dinner on the infield turf—not just any dinner, a $5,000 per-plate dinner called "An Evening with Ron Fraser." Couples contributing $10,000 or more, or $5,000 per plate, toward the stadium complex received invitations to an eleven-course dinner. Fraser determined the cost after hearing that the Kennedys once held a $5,000-per-couple dinner. The mission was to raise enough money to retire the outstanding debt on the stadium's construction.

"It's the highest-priced dinner in the history of mankind," Fraser claimed while wearing an orange ruffled and brown tuxedo at an introductory news conference. "I don't even know if any president has had a dinner like this. I just hope we don't get any flaming brandy on the rug."

High-end donors personally received invitations delivered by players and Sugarcanes, chauffeured in a 1938 Cadillac. Upon arrival at the invitee's door, the player read from a scroll that stated the donor was cordially invited to an on-field dinner presentation by Ron Fraser and the baseball program.

The soiree brought the baseball program, and the university, its greatest worldwide publicity yet. News crews from CBS and NBC; writers from *Sports Illustrated*, the Associated Press, and United Press International; and magazines from as far away as Sweden, Japan, and Germany came to cover the event. Every newspaper, magazine, and television and radio station from South Florida attended. Media received an eight-page guide detailing the spectacle.

"It was the very first time in Miami television history that a local TV station broke away from primetime programming to give a live, up-to-the-minute report about what course they were eating in the meal and what wines they were drinking," said Dave Scott, an assistant coach of Fraser's staff at the time.

Antique cars drove guests from the faculty club to the stadium. Scott met them on the track outside the center field fence, helped them out of the car, and escorted them through the center-field gate. Fraser waited there to greet them, and Scott introduced the guests to the coach. After chatting, the guests hopped a tram to the bullpen for a drink before strolling around the infield and stopping at each base. At first base was champagne and caviar. Second base displayed the collection of Miami's NCAA baseball trophies. Dinner was served at third base. Guests stopped at home plate and completed the cycle by receiving a bat inscribed with their name.

Fraser flew in chefs from around the world. The menu was extravagantly prepared by Wolfgang Diehl, Eastern Airlines' top chef, who reportedly asked, "Who in the hell thought up this idea?" Each course seemed like a meal of itself with a list of exotic dishes, truffles, and top-shelf drinks.

The thirty-four guests dressed in tuxedos, evening gowns, topcoats, and fur. Each couple had its own waiter or waitress. An internationally famous harpist dressed in a white tuxedo at the pitcher's mound and violinists around the infield played music. Lavish floral arrangements, goldfish swimming in free-form pools, parrots, and other exotic birds in tropical trees adorned the field. An ice sculpture flown in from California stood in the dugout.

Fraser said he would not be able to top the lavish event. "A stadium is such a special thing for college baseball that we had to do something like this to recognize it," he said. Fraser's original idea involved chartering a Concorde jetliner for an evening in Paris with guests instructed to bring their passport without knowing their destination. An inability to gain permission to land in Miami nixed the plan, and the $5,000 per-plate dinner had to suffice.

The runner-up finish at the College World Series motivated Fraser and his team to solidify the program as a perennial national contender. Most Sun Belt schools did not prioritize baseball, including those in the Southeastern Conference, which had very few good teams. Florida

State, the state's flagship program, long stood as king of the Southeast, but Miami appeared ready to overtake it. FSU fans became noticeably more hostile toward the Hurricanes and ratcheted up the rivalry by declaring their intrastate foes as enemy No. 1.

The intensity reached crescendo during the 1975 matchup in Tallahassee. A standing-room-only crowd awaited, complete with truck beds filled with fans stationed beyond the outfield fence. The raucous environment took an ugly turn at the end of the opening game. After an 8–0 FSU victory, fans were berating Miami players from behind the team dugout. When Fraser stepped out of the dugout, a fan heaved a large ice chunk that struck him in the back of the head. Fraser lost his balance, fell, and hit his head on the dugout step. An ambulance was called; Fraser went to the hospital.

"A bunch of us went into the stands, which was crazy, but that was a sign of how much he meant to us. He was our leader," Scott recalled of the incident.

The next day, on WVUM Radio, a young broadcaster named Roy Firestone interviewed FSU coach Woody Woodward before the game and brought up how some of his fans took the rivalry too far.

"I will never forget that moment," Firestone recalled of the Fraser incident. "I was pissed off. Fraser could have suffered brain damage from the fall. It was that bad. Woody Woodward was not happy with this young kid, me, who was asking him about security, the ramifications, and whether or not the fan was going to be prosecuted."

"It was a hard interview—Woody was put on the spot and probably didn't like the questions," recalled Firestone's WVUM broadcast partner Gary Chrisman. "Roy was what he would become, and I told him that was his first real *Up Close* [the ESPN interview show that made him famous] hard-hitting interview."

The Seminoles completed a two-game sweep of the Hurricanes. Miami rebounded and reeled off twenty consecutive wins to gain a No.1 national ranking for the first time in its baseball history.

"Coach had the guys on the field and said, 'I've got some news for you' while trying to play it like he was down and sad," said Firestone. "He told them, 'This might be tough for you to take' and was just putting them on before saying, 'Well, we're number one,' and the guys went nuts."

Miami again went to Starkville, Mississippi, for the district tournament and faced FSU in the opening game. After falling to their rival,
1–0, the Hurricanes won a pair of games to set up a rematch. This time,
the Seminoles plated a pair of runs in the top of the ninth inning and
rallied for a 6–5 win that propelled them to the College World Series.

After the 1977 season began with the Mark Light Stadium dedication,
Miami amassed a sparkling 41–11 regular season record and held the
No. 1 national ranking much of the year. The Hurricanes hosted a
regional for the first time, another significant step in defining Fraser's
program. He now had home-field advantage that could help his team
advance to the College World Series. It was the prime opportunity to
showcase his program.

"Miami wasn't spending on anything, and at the time you had to
guarantee the NCAA money for your regional to host," said Zagacki.
"Fraser got the Orange Bowl behind him, and he created a regional
with the same type of pageantry."

Fraser drew upon the Orange Bowl Committee to help put on a big
event. Not only was the Orange Bowl game one of college football's
premier New Year's Day bowls, but its parade tradition also dated
back to 1936. Fraser knew how to bring in baseball's biggest names,
and recruited Ted Williams and famous announcer Mel Allen.

Prior to the first regional game at Mark Light Stadium, Williams
rode through the center-field gate and onto the field on a motorized
baseball-glove float furnished by the Orange Bowl Committee. As he
approached the infield, there was a high-kick routine at second base
performed by dancing girls wearing oversized vinyl baseballs on their
heads. Fraser strolled out to the pitching mound to greet Williams,
and instead of throwing out a ceremonial first pitch, Williams delivered the regional's ceremonial first hits.

The Splendid Splinter, seventeen years retired and fifty-nine years
of age, took off his windbreaker and wore an open neck sport shirt to
take his swings. Four pitches from Fraser produced four frozen rope
line drives to right field, including one that reached the fence on one
hop. The over four thousand fans attending went wild. As part of the
ceremony, Fraser presented each team with one of the balls hit by
Williams. Allen acted as the emcee before heading up to the press box

to join WINZ radio to call the Hurricanes games. The extravaganza earned mention in *Sports Illustrated*, which called it "just another day in the life of college baseball's most unusual coach."

The spirited atmosphere continued as Miami won its first three games. The Hurricanes needed just one win to reach the College World Series for the first time since an inaugural appearance three years prior. Clemson played the role of spoiler, taking a commanding early lead before withstanding a home-team rally in a 10–9 win that forced a deciding game. The start time for the final game was pushed back to 8:00 p.m., and at 9:15 p.m., with the game in the second inning, a line of fans still waited to buy tickets. Despite watching the Tigers cruise to a 7–2 win, many fans stuck around to salute the Hurricanes, and the players gestured back with appreciation.

The support showed throughout the regional tournament cemented Miami baseball's status. Dade County was abuzz after nearly thirteen thousand fans poured into Mark Light Stadium over three days, including a record 4,477 on Sunday. A *Sports Illustrated* feature story celebrated the regional's pageantry and electricity.

Miami pulled in a stellar recruiting class the following season, but the talent was too good—ten players, nearly the entire list of signees, chose professional offers instead. Left with literally half a roster, Fraser scrambled to recruit leftovers players in July, long after standouts and good players went elsewhere. He admitted he was in "deep trouble" with the situation and desperately called contacts for recommendations on any serviceable player still available. The list was extremely short, even with lowered standards.

Fraser found Tony Brewer, whose success as a state wrestling finalist in California limited his baseball season to about six weeks, leaving few to see his diamond success, and Mike Kutner, a National Hockey League draft pick from New Jersey. He brought in Wes Robbins, a Miami product who could hit and run but couldn't throw because of a bad arm. And he added Augie Ruiz from Kaiserslautern . . . Germany. Fraser liked the way he threw, but Ruiz didn't appear to know much about baseball.

In one of the most incredible single-season coaching jobs in college baseball history, Fraser's magic team produced separate fourteen-game and thirteen-game winning streaks, fifty victories, and a regional championship, and it ended up in the 1978 College World Series.

The overachieving team was memorable, but the death of the program's most significant benefactor overshadowed the season. Losing Light, Fraser's close friend, put things in perspective. While the on-field achievements were extraordinary, the team's most impactful effort came off the field.

Light was part of Miami's baseball family. Just before that season's regional, Light asked Fraser if he could speak to the team. He was eager to share news of his miracle eye transplant that helped him regain vision. Light told the team he had enough faith in them to make plans to go to Omaha and watch them play in the College World Series.

Suffering from the same crippling neuromuscular disorder that took his adopted son, Mark, and that was compounded by a rare blood type, Light developed a severe bleeding problem following abdominal surgery. Fraser received a late-night call after a game at Georgia Southern and told his team that Light's health had taken a turn for the worse. Light was in need of strong blood and platelets. Fraser asked his players to help when they returned from their road swing that included one remaining game in Georgia and two at Jacksonville. Instead, the players offered to split the team, leaving behind half the roster to play in the next game while the other half made a long overnight drive to Coral Gables to provide immediate help. Hurricane players continued donating blood and platelets throughout the regional tournament even though it meant weakening themselves and jeopardizing their pursuit of the College World Series. Their moving response showed how much Light meant to the program. The team decided to keep its efforts private to avoid publicity, and more than a decade passed before anyone mentioned them.

Miami played poorly and committed five errors in an 8–5 loss to Clemson in the regional opener. Postgame conversation centered upon how much their performance would have disappointed Light. Miami turned things around, proceeding to win four games in a row and advancing to the College World Series, just as Light said they would.

It was close to midnight before the championship game concluded and Fraser rushed over to the hospital to share the news with Light, who was unresponsive and in intensive care. Fraser told him, "We're going to Omaha, just like you said we were." Light died a few hours later.

Light believed that building a stadium and aiding Fraser's plan for the program could help Miami's players grow into young men and provide a lasting impact on their lives. Light, just like Fraser, was passionate about families attending the games and believed in inspiring the young fans through the experience.

Fraser told the *Miami News* in 1987 that Light "told me never to forget the family, and I think our program is based on it." He also credited Light's impact by telling the *Miami Herald* in 1988 that "Miami wouldn't be the program it is today without George Light."

Following his final regular-season home game in 1992, Fraser told the crowd "George Light was such a special friend, and without his help and generosity, I would have never had my dream. George believed my story and gave us the money for the lights and gave us the money to build those stands, and we were on our way."

The 1979 schedule featured a robust slate of sixty-one games that read like a who's who of college baseball. Fraser guaranteed season-ticket buyers a refund at the end of the season if the Hurricanes did not post a winning record. The promotion won the UM Athletic Department's best-promotional-concept award but, in typical Fraser form, was announced with twenty-seven games remaining on the schedule and the Canes just three wins away from a .500 record.

Miami reached the College World Series for the second straight season, marking its first back-to-back appearances in program history. Each trip, however, ended with 0-2 records and losses to West Coast teams. Despite successful seasons, Fraser and Bertman, both great baseball minds, knew changes were necessary to win an elusive first national championship. Miami needed more power hitting to close the gap. Its reliance on pitching, defense, and speed, all staples of Fraser teams, did not match up with the championship teams.

"To get there was one thing, but to win there we had to do some things a bit differently," said Dan Canevari, an assistant coach at the time. "You were going to win in Omaha with home runs. Everyone had good pitching, and it was hard to get hits. Everyone had a good catcher and could hold runners on, so the short steal game didn't work out there."

As the decade ended, Fraser added another crown jewel with a new locker room, clubhouse, and offices at Mark Light Stadium. Fraser upgraded to an office three times larger than his previous location, and Bertman and the baseball secretary had their own separate office space. The building upgrade provided Fraser additional facilities superior to other schools and added another selling point for recruits.

Even with the on-field success and facility improvements, Fraser continued to battle university funding issues. Football is the financial engine of college athletics, but in Miami's case, limited wins and insufficient attendance meant continued budget cuts. Concerned with the financial trends, Fraser was about to venture into unchartered territory to fund his program and, in the process, transform college baseball.

4

Business Decision

Defying logical cause and effect, the more success for Fraser's program, the more cuts the university made to the baseball budget. After eighteen consecutive winning seasons and three-straight College World Series appearances, Fraser saw his baseball budget cut for the third-straight year. Following the 1980 season, it dropped a whopping 69 percent from $100,000 to $31,000.

The news surprised Fraser, who instead thought he might be getting a raise and a small budget increase. His program, despite gaining unprecedented national notoriety for the university, suffered more budget cuts than the swimming, tennis, golf, or soccer programs. Fraser saw the writing on the wall.

"At that point, the program was going down the tubes," Fraser told the *Los Angeles Times* in 1992. "I figured, if it's going out, it's going to go out its own way."

Fraser argued his case with Director of Athletics Dr. Harry Mallios. Everything appeared stacked against his program as the pieces of the financial pie became smaller. Football scuffled along and was incapable of financially supporting other programs. There was no men's basketball program to offset some of the income gap. The nation was suffering through an inflationary economy. Title IX federal mandates were in play. As a private school, the University of Miami received no state aid for its athletics or facilities.

Fraser told Roy Firestone in a 1983 episode of ESPN's *Sports Look* talk show that "we were in a situation where we were probably going to lose our program or our program would be watered down to such an extent that it wouldn't be nationally competitive."

Financially handcuffed by the Athletics Department, Fraser asked Mallios to let him run the baseball program like a Minor League Baseball team. Fraser was betting on himself to be a self-sustaining business. He proposed being left alone by the Athletic Department to raise all his own money, salaries included, and make his own budget.

"Ron went up to argue with Dr. Mallios about giving us more money for our budget," recalled Skip Bertman. "Dr. Mallios said, 'Alright, you take it,' and Ron was in charge of raising his own money. He did much better than Mallios. I thought that was really cool. I don't think you could do it today."

Fraser set out to run his program like football or basketball at other schools. The thought of turning a college baseball program into a revenue producer was inconceivable. The sport had a modest, mainly geographical, following. There were pockets of popularity, but no school came close to the interest enjoyed by football or basketball. Fraser's risky plan was about survival.

Fraser told *Sport* magazine in a 1982 article, "We decided to go into business; it's the only way to survive. Even if you don't make money, at least you can lose less than you're losing."

In previous years, Fraser developed a reputation for hustling to raise funds and finding ways to cut costs while on a shoestring budget. In his early seasons, purchasing new baseballs was too much of a luxury, so Fraser found sponsors to supply the game balls. In exchange for giving the sponsor in-game announcements, a ceremonial photo, and an autographed ball, he never had to pay for baseballs again.

"He'd get a box of baseballs for about $25 a dozen in those days, and if someone was willing to give him that amount, they would be recognized over the loudspeaker as providing that night's game balls," recalled UM athletics historian Holmes Braddock. "He'd sell the deal to two or three different guys and have announcements in the third and sixth innings. The first few years, he had to hustle for everything."

In the early 1970s Fraser found unique ways to gain attention for the program. He started with Bat Night and Hat Night giveaways when neither was done in college baseball. Fraser wanted to provide unique experiences that brought people to the ballpark repeatedly. Fans enjoyed the low-cost fun atmosphere and family entertainment while watching winning baseball. In a 1973 article titled "UM Is Selling Baseball Not Gimmicks," the *Miami News* called the approach a circus atmosphere and imagined Fraser going into the parking lot and yelling, "Step right up, folks. Get your tickets. See the flashiest baseball show on earth."

Fraser built the right connections to secure agreements and donations. He formed a coach's committee of twenty-five prominent Miami CEOs and businessmen to help plan promotions and provide financial assistance, calling the group instrumental to his success. The team flew to road games, including intrastate trips, when nearly all other schools bused long distances. Miami had an unrivaled multitude of uniform combinations. At games, the team sold an annual baseball yearbook filled with advertisements. Fraser secured an agreement with a local car dealership to receive a car to drive every few months on a rotating basis. He did commercials and worked on the board of directors for First American Bank & Trust. Fraser struck deals with anyone and everyone to help his program.

"He had a lot of people in the community who financially supported the program and his projects and loved coming to the games," said Liane Fraser, his first wife.

To provide competitive salaries for his coaches, Fraser and Bertman started a summer camp in 1976 that grew to become a wildly successful financial windfall. One of the first youth camps run by a college sports program, now commonplace for all sports nationwide, it drew more than three hundred kids per week. Though Fraser's name was attached to the camp, he let Bertman direct it. Camp revenue alone brought them each approximately $40,000, which was more than their annual salaries at the time—Fraser at $30,000 and Bertman at $14,500. "He split the proceeds fifty-fifty with me, which was very generous," said Bertman.

"Looking back, the bulk of the wealth my dad built was from the sports camp," recalled Fraser's daughter Lynda Armitage.

The Ron Fraser Sports Camp focused on baseball while including an array of sports experiences each day of its three-week session. High school–aged attendees focused on baseball. Younger campers divided into groups and spent time roller skating and bowling at the Student Union, swimming in the Olympic-sized Hurricane Pool, and playing basketball, soccer, and other games. There were daily hot lunches in the university's Ibis Cafeteria. Fraser's friends in the Coral Gables

Fire and Police Departments drove firetrucks and police cars onto the field with flashing lights and sirens.

"I remember the firemen would blow the fire hose onto the artificial surface, which meant the kids could slip and slide," said Bertman. "We taught them how to slide that way, and they had so much fun doing it. We had a lot of kids there and a lot of fun."

Age-group leaders were typically coaches, whether a Miami assistant or an area junior college or high school coach. Future Division I coaches Paul Mainieri and Jim Hendry once led the prep division. Instructors, mostly made up of current players, oversaw smaller groups. Each day ended with the final fifteen minutes devoted to awards presentation, complete with prizes ranging from baseball cards and patches to trophies.

"Each coach, the division or group leader, would announce and introduce who won," said Fraser's daughter Liz Kraut, who helped sell T-shirts and refreshments at the camp as a youth. "They would be very animated and screaming the announcement, almost like a pro wrestling announcer. The kids would go crazy. They gave out twenty-five-cent, six-inch-tall plastic trophies with titles made by a label-maker. On Friday, you had the Player of the Week. That was the big one."

"I remember at the end of camp, they would give out these little trophies that were everything to us as kids," recalled Gino DiMare, who attended the Ron Fraser Sports Camp from an early age and later played as an outfielder for him. "The awards weren't just for participating; you had to earn them by standing out in some capacity—for sportsmanship, hard work, best player, best this or that. It was really neat."

To help parents, a private bus service transported kids to and from Miami Beach and other areas. Long, but coordinated, carpool lines formed during drop-off and pick-up times.

"Camp was the 'it' thing, and that was before the Metrorail and public transportation," recalled Dan Canevari, who helped run the camps, both as an assistant coach and while coaching at other schools. "Anybody who was anybody went to camp. It was amazing."

Kids across South Florida knew about the camp and looked forward to it as an annual summer highlight. Many years saw waiting lists reach into the hundreds.

"It was the camp in the city of Miami, and it was packed," said

DiMare. "I remember always looking forward to it. Everyone talked about camp at the end of the school year—'Are you going this summer? What week are you going?' It was such a huge thing."

Fraser recognized the value the camps held beyond the significant financial boost. They spread the word across South Florida and in baseball circles nationally. The camps grew prestige, gained the team new fans, and even developed future college players.

"Both Ron and Skip knew the camps would increase our attendance," said Canevari. "You want to get the kids to come to the game, because they'll bring the rest of the family."

"You'd ask a kid where he was from, and he'd say Kentucky or California," recalled Danny Smith, who worked as a camp counselor during the offseason while a pitcher for the Hurricanes. "Some probably attended in hope of being recruited to play there. Every time Coach Fraser came out to camp, he was in uniform. Everyone would stop and run over, get down on one knee, and listen to him speak to them."

Some of the camp alumni ended up playing for Fraser at Miami. Luis "Wicho" Hernández was one of the campers turned Hurricanes and remembered the impact it had on him. "Coach Fraser had such an amazing aura to him and made everyone feel special by speaking to every kid there," said Hernández, who began his Miami career in 1991. "Just being on that field in front of him and the other coaches was incredible. There wasn't a playground, a water park, or anything that came close. For local kids, Disney World couldn't compete with Mark Light Stadium."

Even to this day, adults share fond memories and stories about the Ron Fraser Sports Camp experiences of their youth. "If I go anywhere in Miami wearing a Ron Fraser Sports Camp T-shirt, someone is going to say something to me," said Fraser's daughter Cynthia Fraser.

"When you mention you played for Coach Fraser, one of the things you hear a lot is, 'Oh, I went to Coach Fraser's baseball camp when I was a kid,'" said Joe Nelson, a Hurricanes infielder from 1984 to 1987. "Everyone aspired to play for the Hurricanes. A lot of people I talk to remember attending Coach Fraser's camp and the profound impact it had on them as kids."

Fraser, always one for publicity, recognized opportunities for the camp to make news. One summer, a university security official alerted

Bertman about a potential kidnapping risk for a camper whose father was a politician. Bertman informed Fraser of the situation and assured him they would keep close watch. Fraser responded in jest that if there were a kidnapping, every newspaper headline would mention Ron Fraser's Sports Camp.

Focused on providing family entertainment, Fraser involved area youth baseball leagues in various ways. He and his assistant coaches conducted offseason clinics for youth baseball players. With the clinics came an invitation to attend Hurricane games on Local League Nights at Mark Light Stadium. Kids were invited to run the bases after the game, a standard promotion at all levels today. Youth players attending in uniform were recognized in the stands. The Hurricanes were one of the first teams to bring young fans onto the field to stand alongside position players for the national anthem.

"We all know a Little Leaguer isn't coming to the game by himself," said legendary Florida State coach Mike Martin. "That was Ron's idea. He didn't get that from someone else."

Fraser wanted Mark Light Stadium to be a place to take the kids for a night out, so he marketed to each person in the family, from clowns and toy giveaways for kids to facials and dress giveaways targeted to women. Having good food options so families could eat dinner at the ballpark was part of the allure. "You have to make it entertaining, like a circus. Kids have to want to go for their parents to go. You have to get the wives to come out to the park with the guys," Fraser said.

Fraser's commitment to making his program self-sustaining required exponential growth and revenue streams. He hired Rick Remmert, an employee of the school's Sports Information Department, as college baseball's first dedicated promotions director. Starting in 1981, the two teamed up to create a nightly menu of promotions and giveaways that were fun and often downright zany.

In 1980 Miami began offering season tickets and sold an NCAA record 1,600. Two years later that figure ballooned to 2,742. The abundant variety of Miami baseball merchandise sold at games rivaled souvenir stands at professional venues and included three different T-shirts, hats, jackets, and wrist bands. In 1981 alone, the team sold more than 1,500 hats and 300 jackets during games. Business was good.

The volume of giveaways ramped up so much that Fraser promised anyone who didn't get something free in 1981 would be in the minority. Giveaways occurred at all forty-six home games, and as often as each inning. Miami set an NCAA attendance record with 163,261 fans that season. By comparison, the football team drew just 120,007 to the Orange Bowl for its five home games the previous fall.

Fraser admitted that baseball could get boring at times and wanted to keep the excitement level high for the crowd. Each game featured a lucky-number drawing, a promotion commonplace at nearly every game today. Scorecards sold for twenty-five cents in 1981 and featured a number that, if drawn, instantly provided the fan a chance to win a used car, a diamond, record albums, up to $5,000 in a Money Scramble, Major League Baseball World Series Tickets, and more. Among the theme nights that season were the nationally televised East vs. West Classic against USC, the first-ever appearance by the San Diego Chicken at a college baseball game, and a Maine lobster bake.

The Cruise to Nowhere was one of Fraser's successful fundraisers. For $125 per person, guests enjoyed wine, dinner, and entertainment aboard a luxury ocean liner. The four-hour trip stayed near Miami without an actual destination. The initial event drew six hundred people. The following year, in 1982, the event tied in with Miami's football game at the Orange Bowl and included a shuttle bus service from the stadium to the dock. Over nine hundred people attended with sixty more having to be turned away; it raised more than $80,000 for Miami's baseball-scholarship fund and the International Seamen's Park.

The promotions became wilder at the ballpark. A bathing-suit manufacturer approached Fraser and offered to provide its latest animal-print suits if the Sugarcanes would wear them on the field. Fraser quipped that fans taking photos or bringing binoculars to Bathing Suit Night would be charged extra. They weren't, but the shtick added to the pregame publicity. A dozen bat girls clad in bathing suits and escorted by the designer company's representative stood on the field for the ceremonial first pitch. When repeated the following year, the promotion included free admission for fans wearing a bathing suit.

"If I could say one thing about Ron Fraser, it was that he had an enormous knack for promotion," said Firestone. "No idea was silly to him. Even if it started out silly, he could shape it and make it an idea."

Fraser earned the moniker of "The P. T. Barnum of college baseball." One car giveaway night featured nine sets of keys drawn from a hat. All the cars were used and most barely made it off the lot to the stadium. Nonetheless, fans enthusiastically cheered the excited prize winners.

"They sold raffle tickets all season long for a Cadillac to be given away at the last home game," recalled Braddock. "They drew the number [and] opened the center-field gate, and in comes a Cadillac about twenty years old. Everybody wondered what the heck was going on. The ticket said Cadillac, but not the year or model. The stands erupted in laughter, and the guy who won did too."

"I'll never forget they gave away this old Cadillac with big wings on it and everything," recalled former New Orleans head coach Ron Maestri. "It was putt-putt-putting along, but it shined. They must have spent forty days shining that thing. The visual of the winner getting into that car and driving it out to center field and out of the ballpark while it was putting and shaking was something else."

Another favorite was the money grab. Fraser, who sat on the Southeast Bank board of directors, arranged to have small bills placed around the infield. Two contestants selected from the lucky-number drawing had thirty seconds to pick up as much money as possible. A Brinks Security truck drove onto the field, and police with dogs stood on the foul lines for effect. Sugarcanes went to the bank, folded all the bills, and placed them on the field.

"I was amazed at how little they [contestants] collected given the time frame," said former Sugarcane bat girl Tracy Cardwell. "It was basically all $1 bills with a large denomination mixed in. There was a one-time $10,000 event, and the person ended up with about $200."

For the Trip to Somewhere promotion, Fraser got Eastern Airlines to donate a half-dozen trips to Puerto Rico, Acapulco, New York, and Las Vegas. Fans came to the ballpark with a packed suitcase, not knowing the destination. Upon entering the stadium, fans received a raffle ticket, made to look like a baggage-claim ticket, from an Eastern Airlines baggage handler. The winner, announced midgame, took his or her suitcase down to the field, got in a limousine, and went directly to the airport from the stadium.

Fraser was willing to try anything. And the promotions were never taken too seriously. Fraser became a frequent guest of Hank Goldberg, one of Miami's most-renowned sports radio stars, to talk about upcoming series and giveaways to lure in fans for the weekend. Even the opposing teams got caught up in watching the promotions during games.

Perennial college baseball power University of Texas and its legendary coach Cliff Gustafson played in Coral Gables four times during Fraser's tenure. The Longhorns, a traditional, buttoned-up program, only traveled to Miami or Arizona State for nonconference road series. Ty Harrington, a former player and assistant coach under Gustafson, remembers how his teammates got caught up in the excitement.

"If your lucky number was drawn and someone hit a home run, you won something," recalled Harrington. "A bunch of our players bought numbers, and the guy hit a home run. They were all in the dugout checking their numbers to see if they won. No one wanted to admit it. When the pitcher came back into the dugout, he checked his number too. I'm sure that story has been embellished, but the reality is we were not used to that and thought it was the coolest thing. It was fun for us."

One 1981 promotion factored into the actual game itself. Sam Sorce, a pitcher and outfielder, made college baseball history by becoming the first player to play all nine positions, plus designated hitter, in the same game. Promoted as 10 Night, the event included an invitation to famous model and actress Bo Derek, star of the 1979 romantic comedy film *10*, to attend the game. She never made it to the ballpark, and, as Fraser later stated, the key word was *invited*.

"Coach Fraser told me if I did this, they'd fly Bo Derek in for the game," recalled Sorce. "That's the only reason I did it. He thought there was a better chance of people showing up if Bo Derek was going to be there than watching me play ten positions."

Other memorable themed promotions included Tax Night and Open Heart Surgery Night. On Tax Night, anyone who brought his or her 1040 forms got into the game free. Tax experts were stationed in booths atop each dugout to answer questions and assist in completing the forms. A mail truck parked on site to accept completed forms and deliver them to the post office before the midnight mailing deadline. On Open Heart Surgery Night, also known as General Hospital Night after the popular television soap opera, the winner received a complimentary open-heart surgery, if needed, redeemable within the next five years. The prize was nontransferable.

When the University named Edward Thaddeus "Tad" Foote its new president in 1981, Mark Light Stadium hosted Big Foote Night. A tracing of the president's foot was placed at the stadium gate, and any fan whose foot measured larger received free admission.

Fraser often spoke to groups about how promotions could enhance their program. Miami was ahead of many of the Minor League Baseball teams, both in popularity and promotional gimmicks. Unlike today, only a handful of Minor League Baseball teams used promotions at that time.

"Minor League Baseball really took off in the early 1980s," recalled Danny Knobler, who covered both college and the Minor Leagues for *Baseball America* magazine from 1983 to 1988. "College baseball in some locations had already become a big deal, but their promotions were not the same as what Miami did. Miami was ahead, or certainly on par, with some of the Minor League teams."

With interest and attendance down, Minor League Baseball was considered a dying industry in the 1960s and through most of the 1970s. Teams in Nashville and Columbus led a renaissance, and a handful of other franchises followed in putting on promotions that brought people to the park. The sport relied on gate revenue, which made attendance figures critical. At that same time, Miami mirrored this approach, acting as the outlier in college baseball when no one was actively promoting the game to fans.

"Miami and Fraser galvanized college baseball with all the pro-motions," said Allan Simpson, who started *Baseball America* in 1981. "No other college program was doing things to that degree. Winning is almost incidental in Minor League Baseball, so they have to have a bigger reason to put people in the park, and some of it was through promotions. You win at the college level and can swing the fans that way. I think Fraser proved you could do it much more quickly if you brought people into the park with promotions."

Nationally renowned news and sports publications described Miami's baseball promotions like they were reviewing the latest block-buster movie:

"Miami's promotions would be the envy of a successful minor league team," wrote the *New York Times*.

Dan Shaugnessy of the *Washington Star* said, "As a promoter, Fraser knows no bounds. He makes Bill Veeck seem predictable and boring."

NBC Nightly News stated that "baseball at Miami has the look of a TV game show" when it aired a story about the program's promotions.

The *Orlando Sentinel* called the program "nothing more than a big league farm club with a campus" and described the ballpark, crowds, and promotions as "better than most Minor League teams."

"Ron probably promoted his program better than the Minor League teams did," recalled Jim Callis, who wrote for *Baseball America* from 1989 to 1997. "It was like going to a Triple-A game in terms of electricity, even between innings. It seemed like there was always something going on."

From 1981 to 1985, more than seven hundred thousand fans went through the Mark Light Stadium turnstiles, a figure that outpaced 80 percent of U.S. professional teams during the same span. Professional teams played seventy to eighty-one home games, depending on Minor League or Major League status, significantly more than the forty-five to fifty-five the Hurricanes typically hosted. The Hurricanes home stadium, with five thousand seats, better lighting, more concessions, and a $1 million scoreboard, surpassed many Minor League ballparks, especially as the 1980s began.

Major League Baseball commissioner Bowie Kuhn invited Fraser to speak to team owners about the value of promotions. Today, the thought of having a college baseball coach advise Major League teams on how to conduct their marketing and promotions is unfathomable.

Fraser laid out his approach in a chapter titled "Marketing and Promoting Your Program," which he wrote for the American Baseball Coaches Association's *The Baseball Coaching Bible*, published in 1999. In it, he described the need to gain respect for college baseball and its potential as an entertainment option on campus and in the community.

Fraser's first step was "cleaning his own house" by providing an attractive and welcoming environment. From parking and traffic to staff appearance, knowledge, and demeanor, Fraser believed in emphasizing every detail, even the smallest ones that could be taken for granted.

He described his family-first approach with a simple question of preference. Would you rather direct your marketing at someone who buys tickets and concessions one at a time? Or would you rather court the entire family and double, triple, or quadruple the payoff? Fraser used market research to help formulate his clean, G-rated family entertainment brand. Every day was family day or night at the ballpark. His surveys showed that mothers represented 40 percent of the primary baseball fans. If a mom finds the ballpark's restrooms clean, its food to be of good quality, and the kids having a good time, then Fraser knew he was successful.

For all his notorious giveaways and theme nights, Fraser may have been most proud of the 1981 game against Florida State, and it was not because of his 14–6 victory. Instead, he was elated with the record crowd of 7,268 fans, well beyond the listed capacity of 5,500, who crammed Mark Light Stadium on a May Saturday night. With seats completely filled, a roped-off portion of the field outside the foul lines and adjacent to the bullpens served as standing -room only.

"I got on base and advanced to third in the first inning," recalled Doug Shields, Miami's center fielder at the time. "Coach comes over [from the third base coaching box], looking up and talking about how the stands are packed and [how] he's got to figure out a way to get more people into the gate. My buddy [Rick Figueredo] is playing third for Florida State and says, 'Hey, coach, just rope off the bullpen and put them on the field.' Coach says, 'That's a great idea,' and leaves. In the middle of the inning, Coach goes through the dugout, out the back gate, and I'm standing at third base. Figueredo says, 'Who's going to coach?' and I said, 'I don't know.' Next thing you know, they're roping off the third-base bullpen area where our pitchers warm up, and another five hundred to seven hundred people are on the field in that corner. I'm thinking, *This is hilarious*."

"Coach Fraser asked us if it was alright to rope off sections of foul territory down the line, and we said, 'Sure,'" recalled Jim Morris, then an assistant coach on Mike Martin's FSU staff. "The fans were packed ten feet deep. It was the most incredible thing I've seen in college baseball."

The crowds literally overflowed. A record 8,277 turned out to see Miami open the 1986 season against Texas with seats and aisles jammed and fans standing outside the outfield walls. It spurred action from Coral Gables fire chief Phil Sistek, a former Hurricanes pitcher in the 1940s and a friend of Fraser. He told Fraser and the athletics department that they had to cap future attendance at six thousand fans, based on Mark Light Stadium's listed capacity of five thousand, with standing room for an estimated one thousand. Sistek told Fraser he would have to arrest him if they did not abide by that figure, though he was only half-joking about the offense.

Fraser thought an overflow crowd leading to his arrest would be the penultimate accomplishment and joked that he would retire immediately afterward. "Imagine the headlines 'Coach Arrested for Putting Too Many Fans at a College Baseball Game,'" he quipped.

In 1983 Fraser announced that he had been a coach too long and would call himself the first manager in college baseball. He also held the unofficial titles president of University of Miami Baseball, Inc. and college baseball's Mr. Promotion.

Fraser was the program's CEO and took on roles and responsibilities beyond his coaching peers. He frequently wore two hats—one as GM of the team and its promotions and one as coach and manager. Fraser often missed practices and teaching fundamentals during the week to secure deals and build relationships to help the program.

"I talked bunting for 15–20 years and we won and the bunting was good, but I didn't generate a lot of revenue or people in the stands," Fraser once said.

NCAA record attendance in 1981 produced $363,000 in revenue and made the program Miami's first profitable sport since football thirteen years prior. A year later that figure jumped to a combined $426,000 from gate, concessions, yearbook advertising, and sales, with over a dozen promotional events. No other school came anywhere close to those figures. The *Sporting News* ran a headline "Baseball Is a Big Draw at Miami U." Its National League beat writer Bill Conlin wrote that Miami's attendance "would be a terrific year for a Triple-A club." Fraser said in 1982 that sowing a profit at the end of the season was as important as winning because "if you don't make money, you may not have a team to field next year."

By the time he retired, Fraser's "business" was pulling in $500,000 for long-term scoreboard advertising agreements. The outfield fence featured forty advertisements at $6,000 per season. A per-game skybox sold out for the entire season's forty-plus home-game schedule and brought in over $80,000 annually.

"I remember when he brought out a spreadsheet and showed me the bottom line," recalled Canevari, who was coaching at Gables High School after serving as an assistant coach at Miami. "He said, 'We made over a million dollars. That was my goal. Nobody thought we could do that.' He created over a million dollars of revenue from signage, ticket sales, donations, everything. He was so proud of that."

5

Roaring Eighties

As the 1980s began, attention focused on the CEO of Miami Baseball, Inc. and his achievements in Coral Gables. Fraser's teams consistently sat near the top of the national polls. His promotions made national news and raised his own budget. A national championship was the lone missing piece.

"Ron had his juggernaut going. Programs emulated Miami and wanted to be Miami," said Segreto. "They wanted a stadium like Miami's. They wanted a promotional vehicle like Miami's. They wanted to create an entertainment-based value proposition for their fans and give them not just a game but also a whole form of entertainment."

Miami set a school record with an .833 winning percentage and 55-11 record in 1979. A year later, the Hurricanes went 59-12 (.831), spent ten consecutive weeks atop the national polls, and won their first two games in Omaha before finishing fourth. After three consecutive College World Series appearances, Miami began 1981 owning the nation's longest active streak.

The *Miami News* wrote, "Miami has become to baseball what Notre Dame is to college football. The Hurricanes may not have a national championship yet, but this is where the good players are and the hot prospects want to be."

The loaded 1981 roster balanced offensive power with speed, pitching, and defense. Pitcher Neal Heaton, coming off an All-American season, expected to be a high draft choice. Mike Pagliarulo anchored third base, a position he would play eleven years in the Major Leagues following his Miami career.

A highly anticipated series at Mark Light Stadium against Southern California opened the season. Dubbed the East-West Classic, upstart cable sports channel ESPN televised the showdown in its entirety.

Fraser pitched the idea that by bringing USC to Miami, ESPN would draw viewers from both coasts and everywhere in between. The historic broadcast launched college baseball's national visibility.

Before a crowd of 4,911, Miami twice rallied for a 7–6 opening-night victory. A 6–1 win the following day put the Hurricanes in position for a sweep. Down eight runs in the fifth inning of the series finale, Fraser implored his team to keep the pressure on. By the ninth, the Canes had chipped the deficit to two at 9–7 before a popup caught by the shortstop appeared to be the final out. While USC celebrated, the home plate umpire motioned to first, pointed to the catcher, and called interference on the swing. Miami had new life and the tying run at first. Frank Castro, a first-round MLB Draft pick four months later, promptly blasted a game-tying home run and sent the controversial game to extra innings. Miami had a pair of runners reach base in each of the first three extra frames but was unable to plate the winning run. In the Miami thirteenth, a walk, an error, and a bunt single filled the bases with no outs. Bill Wrona then took four consecutive balls to walk in the winning run for an improbable 10–9 victory and an impressive three-game sweep. Fraser called the win the most exciting game he had ever seen and basked in a sweep of the sport's biggest name as millions of cable TV viewers watched.

Sweeping USC was a springboard. Miami won the next eighteen games to start the season 21-0. When the streak ended in mid-March, the Hurricanes began another eighteen-game winning streak and boasted a gaudy 39-1 record on April 8.

Miami finished the regular season 56–8 and swept through four regional games in Coral Gables to reach Omaha for a fourth straight season. Considered one of the favorites to win the national championship, Fraser's team dispatched Maine in the CWS opener. The Canes fell, 12–6, to Oklahoma State, then dropped a one-run decision to Texas and were eliminated. Despite all their success, the season again ended in disappointment.

Fraser took note of a character in a South Carolina uniform at the 1981 College World Series. The Gamecocks brought their mascot, Cocky, to Omaha and a casual conversation between games involving Fraser,

Remmert, and John Routh, the student inside the costume, sparked an idea. Fraser wondered why Miami's baseball team couldn't have its own mascot.

The famous San Diego Chicken, the first traveling mascot, attracted fans at games coast to coast. Full-time baseball team mascots were scarce at all levels, and only a handful of Major League teams employed their own.

When Fraser brought the Chicken in to perform during a midweek game against Biscayne College, it marked the first appearance at a college baseball game for the feathered performer. The widely popular Chicken, not necessarily the game matchup, was responsible for drawing 5,600 fans. The mascot made at least one annual appearance from 1981 through 1983, performing routine acts such as coaching first, putting a hex on the opposing pitcher, and stealing home at full speed and again in slow-motion instant replay. Enthusiastic reaction to the Chicken's appearances inspired Fraser and Remmert to pursue their own mascot.

The university was hesitant about adding another mascot since it already had the Ibis, known in folklore as the last wildlife to take shelter before a hurricane and first to reappear after the storm, at football games. Since Miami baseball ran its business separately from the university athletic department, Fraser moved forward with local businessman and booster Jeff Werner, who financed the pursuit.

An avid Phillies fan, Werner drew inspiration from his favorite team's mascot—the Phanatic. The new Miami baseball costume weighed fifteen pounds, stood 6 feet, and featured a big snout, a large belly, and baseball shoes. A baseball uniform, complete with the number ½ on the back, topped the primarily orange fur with green accents. Like the Phillie Phanatic, the proposed Miami Maniac name used alliteration. Fraser went to the Coral Gables Chamber of Commerce and pitched an idea that his newly created mascot could help the city's image. Despite some consternation about using *maniac* following the 1980 riots in Miami, chamber members settled on using the suggestion, in part because no other name came to mind.

Mascots are only as good as the performer inside the costume, and the first two were lackluster. During a 1982 road trip to South Carolina, Fraser and Remmert recruited Routh and convinced him to come to Miami for a tryout. Routh debuted during the Florida State series and immediately won over the crowd with choreographed routines.

"I went out on the field prior to the game and the crowd was wondering what was going on," recalled Routh. "Our pitcher began warming up, and I went behind the catcher and began calling balls and strikes. I did my regular skits and a couple of dance routines all weekend."

Routh became the full-time Maniac in 1983, and Fraser called him the best recruit he ever landed. The Maniac's performances became an attraction. Kids followed him around the ballpark. Routh originated the well-known "C-A-N-E-S—Canes!" spell-out cheer. Musical artists inspired material for dance routines, like moonwalking to Michael Jackson songs. The Maniac did a *Rocky* spoof that began with the theme song, one-hand pushups, and shadow-boxing, before running up the stairs only to be "knocked out" by one of the kids following him. The Maniac even went streaking by peeling off his jersey top and running through the infield to celebrate victories.

Some of the most memorable Maniac skits came during the two weeks coinciding with the 1988 Winter Olympics. He mimicked speed skating by racing the Ibis on roller skates around the warning track and figure skating by wearing a dress and attempting to jump into the arms of an umpire and instead landing on the turf. The pinnacle came during an ESPN nationally televised game against Texas when the Maniac simulated ski jumper Eddie the Eagle on a plywood ramp—though admittedly, not well made nor the safest construction. Fraser advised Routh not to get hurt because he did not want bloodstains on his turf. Routh stuck the landing in his "half-dozen" practice attempts and repeated his success for the game night crowd. Olympic theme music played, and a batgirl put a gold medal around the Maniac's snout at the skit's end.

Fraser set the bar high when it came to ideas; the ultimate Maniac performance came in 1985. During an ESPN Sunday Night broadcast against Maine, the Maniac got married in the first mascot wedding. Pitched to the network as a three-minute event between the fourth and fifth innings, ESPN agreed to air the ceremony live rather than cut away to commercial break. It turned into a fourteen-minute spectacle.

A well-choreographed script began when the bride entered through the center-field gate riding in a vintage 1920s car, while the Maniac sat on a throne carried in by Miami's batgirls. The "Right-On Reverend

Rabbi" Rokeach was wedding officiant. Sebastian the Ibis served as the Maniac's best mascot and Freddie the Flamingo, from nearby Hialeah Racetrack, was the maid, or mascot, of honor. Grandpa Maniac was there. The wedding party included Maine's Black Bear, the Bud Man, Grimace and the Hamburglar characters from McDonald's, Sparky the Fire Dog from the Coral Gables Fire Department, the Sports Hound from local radio station WIOD, and four winners from a Maniac and Mrs. Maniac look-alike contest held two nights prior. It was a memorable night for the 4,217 guests and fans, but the game did not go as scripted. The No.1 Hurricanes saw their lead evaporate after the delay, and a twenty-four-game winning streak ended.

The notoriety eventually led to over two hundred Maniac guest appearances per year at ballparks in forty-nine states, plus Europe and Japan. During a 1985 Alaskan Summer League game in the coastal town of Kenai, Routh realized how famous the Maniac had become.

"The Maniac goes and sits in the stands and puts his arm around a young lady," Routh recalled. "About four rows behind me I hear this kid's voice: 'Hey, Maniac, I'm going to tell your wife.' I'm thinking, *How in the world? I'm five thousand miles away*. It showed with the reach of television what a small world it was that this kid saw the Maniac's wedding."

The 1982 Hurricanes figured to take a step back after heavy losses from the previous season's roster. Miami made dubious history early on by losing a game to Division II Florida International University. It dropped three-consecutive home games for the first time, in the process recording its longest home losing streak since 1969. The Hurricanes fell to twelfth in the *Collegiate Baseball* poll, a dramatic drop after spending the entirety of the previous three seasons ranked first or second. Fraser told his team the results were not bothering him because the team was giving its best but just did not have it that season.

That message sparked a turnaround. The Hurricanes posted a sixteen-game winning streak and defeated the Baltimore Orioles for the first time in seven exhibition meetings. Miami swept through its own Coral Gables regional, winning all three games by a combined 42–9 score. The toughest opponent that weekend may have well been Mother Nature.

Monsoon rains flooded the Mark Light turf and reached knee-deep level in the outfield. For some fun, the Maniac jumped in a raft and paddled across the outfield. As the flooding subsided, Fraser called in a helicopter to have the spinning blades help expedite drying the turf to get the team back on the field. Never one to miss a publicity opportunity, he invited media out to film the dramatic scene.

Miami entered the College World Series as a distinct underdog in a field that included the sport's giants—Texas; California State University, Fullerton; Oklahoma State University; Wichita State University; Stanford; University of South Carolina; and fellow underdog University of Maine.

"We didn't have guys who were physically great, throwing ninety-nine miles per hour or hitting 15 home runs," recalled Wrona of the 1982 squad. "We scrapped. We had dirtbags."

Behind Sorce's pitching and a three-run home run by Omaha native Phil Lane, the Hurricanes topped Maine and future Major League pitcher Bill Swift, 7–2, in the opener. Next up was No. 2 Wichita State, a game producing one of the most famous trick plays ever executed in any sport.

The Shockers featured a prodigious running game, stealing 338 bags while being caught just 48 times in 87 games. All-American Phil Stephenson, brother of head coach Gene Stephenson, set an NCAA record with 87 steals in 93 attempts. Fraser, concerned about neutralizing the stolen base, discussed an approach with assistant coaches Bertman and Dave Scott, who described a trick play he saw executed by an American Legion team. Needing to loosen his own team up a bit, Fraser decided to have some fun. He tried the modified play out with his team at practice and put it in his back pocket for potential use at just the right time.

"When our pitcher turns around and throws to first base, I want a player to come in front of the dugout and scream, 'Down there!' and I want the right fielder to run towards the field and the first and second basemen to run down there [to the bullpen], and I want bat girls out there in the bullpen," Fraser described his instructions in a later interview. "When the ball comes rolling up, I want the girls to jump on the bench so they wouldn't get hit. Our first baseman dives over the runner upset and starts running."

Proper execution required a list of meticulous details. It had to be twilight, precisely between 8:15 and 8:30 p.m., because the setting sun over Rosenblatt Stadium caused a glare directly toward first base. There had to be a player, not a full-time coach, coaching first base. The baserunner must take an aggressive lead, dive back on pick-off attempts, and likely attempt a stolen base.

After Miami took a 4–3 lead, Stephenson led off the sixth inning with a walk and was certain to be on the move. Pitcher Mike Kasprzak made multiple throws to first base to keep him close. Fraser called for the play, and Bertman stuck his finger in his ear, the signal to put it on, and Kasprzak repeated it on the field. He stepped off the rubber and turned to throw to first again. Stephenson dove back into the bag, first baseman Steve Lusby leaped over him, cursed, and took off toward the bullpen along the right-field line.

Miami's relief pitchers and catchers sitting on the bullpen benches jumped up and scattered, as did the nearby Sugarcanes. Second baseman Mitch Leone and right fielder Mickey Williams dashed toward the bullpen. Players in the Hurricanes' dugout yelled, "Go! Go! Go!" and "There it is!" as Stephenson, seeing the chaos, got up and ran toward second base. About halfway to the bag, Kasprzak, holding the ball the entire time and only acting like he threw it to first, lobbed it to the shortstop Wrona, who tagged an astonished Stephenson.

"I missed practice because I wasn't feeling well, and one of the guys told me I wouldn't believe the trick play we were going to do," said Wrona. "I'm thinking, *This is going to look stupid, and we're going to look like fools.* I'm watching the play develop, and all I'm thinking is *Catch the ball.* When I did, Phil looks at me and goes, 'Oh shit' and stops. I tag him, and the rest is history."

Miami won, 4–3, seizing all momentum after pulling off the most improbable play on college baseball's grandest stage. Even the umpires were confused. The first base umpire ran toward the bullpen for a few steps, and the second base umpire, who had been demonstrative with his calls, simply put up his thumb when signaling the out. The home plate umpire asked catcher Nelson Santovenia what happened in case someone asked.

In an era before the twenty-four-hour news cycle, the highlight led coverage on every sportscast, including ESPN's *SportsCenter* and *This*

Week in Baseball. Fraser credited Scott and called it one of the biggest plays in baseball history. "They say there is nothing new in baseball. That was new. It was a very special play," he said. More than three decades later, former Miami player Preston Mack created a documentary titled *The Grand Illusion.*

Miami headed for a showdown with top-ranked Texas, which sported a gaudy 59-4 record and sixteen-game winning streak. Texas sent fireballer Roger Clemens, whom Fraser described as the best college pitcher he ever saw, to the mound. The Longhorn ace was 12-1 with a 2.06 ERA and threw ninety-five to ninety-six miles per hour, while the Hurricanes countered with Sorce, who threw in the low eighties. The starters went toe-to-toe, with Clemens yielding 7 hits and 2 runs and Sorce, combining with Danny Smith, allowing just 5 hits and 1 run.

With the Hurricanes leading 2–1, Texas had runners at first and second with no outs. To preempt a likely bunt, Fraser called for a pick-off attempt at first. Instead, his pitcher, Rob Souza, overthrew second when the ball slipped out of his hand. As the ball went into center field, Texas's lead runner froze and remained at second as coach Cliff Gustafson screamed at him to run. Rather than easily advancing to third, the runner feared the Hurricanes were using another trick play. Miami induced a double play, thwarted the rally, and held on for the 2–1 victory.

"Their runner stayed on the bag with his arms folded, and I asked him, 'What are you doing?'" recalled Wrona. "He said, 'I thought he threw the rosin bag into center field after seeing that play the other day.' He should have been standing on third and instead folded his arms like, 'No, you're not getting me on television.'"

After defeating Maine, Miami was one win from a national championship and faced a rematch with Wichita State, which needed to win twice. This time the Hurricanes cruised to a 9–3 victory without any trick plays, behind a three-run home run by Lane and another strong outing from Kasprzak. Fraser won his first College World Series in a year that seemed improbable.

"It was a very competitive team, and we played well at the end," recalled Dan Canevari, a graduate assistant coach that season. "We were full of baseball-savvy guys with high baseball IQ and had the right amount of elements to win in Omaha."

Miami's national championship was the school's first in any major sport and the first NCAA Division I title for the state of Florida. Fraser took great pride in that achievement, especially at a private school. The championship provided a morale boost to Miami and Dade County, which was labeled as the Drug Capital of the World at the time.

Approximately two hundred fans greeted the national champions' return at the airport. A celebration rally drew more than five thousand fans to Mark Light Stadium, many waiting more than two hours to enter. National championship T-shirts sold out in just fifteen minutes. Fraser praised the fan support and popped a bottle of champagne as a toast to the crowd.

The 1982 championship defined team effort. Not one Hurricanes player earned All-American honors. Despite a 3–0 regional record on its own turf, no Miami player made the All-Regional team. Only catcher Nelson Santovenia reached the Major Leagues. Pitcher Danny Smith earned College World Series Most Outstanding Player honors but emphasized the teamwork involved that season: "I told our guys at our twentieth reunion that if I had a trophy or a plaque for that award, I would have cut it into twenty-five pieces and given one to every player and the top of it to the coaches. It was an MVP team. The baseball, the atmosphere, the aura, the organization—Ron Fraser created all of it."

Winning fueled interest in Fraser's program nationwide. The multicolored orange-and-green striped jerseys worn at the 1982 College World Series became very popular. The following year, three high schools and two junior colleges wore similar jerseys, and Miami's uniform supplier received inquiries from teams as far away at Tupelo, Mississippi, and Wausau, Wisconsin, looking to mirror the trend.

Fraser received a new five-year contract replacing his deal that still had two years remaining. Believed to be the largest salary in college baseball, rumors placed the contract above several college football head coaches. Fraser's compensation as head coach and assistant athletic director, plus summer camp, clinics, and endorsements, approached $90,000 annually. His deal included a weekly television show, unheard of for a college baseball coach.

Expectations remained high, but Miami did not return to Omaha until 1984. Although the Hurricanes achieved a No. 1 ranking, the team finished 48-28 and lost more games than any season in school history. It was the first season without Bertman, who became head coach at Louisiana State University (LSU), on staff. Media blamed Bertman's departure for the team's struggles, and pressure built.

With only his starting first baseman and right fielder returning to the team, the 1985 season appeared destined for the same fate. Miami needed to rely on little things to win, perhaps more than in any other season. The team lacked individual stars, but its unheralded players made the most of their opportunities. Different heroes, sometimes multiple ones, emerged on a game-to-game basis.

"You knew someone was going to make something happen," recalled Chris Magno, the team's starting catcher. "You didn't have to worry if someone was having a bad game because someone else was going to come through."

Speed was the roster's strength, and Fraser put pressure on opponents with stolen bases, hit and runs, and moving runners over. Miami played with an intense competitiveness and found ways to win. After eighteen-straight victories, Miami owned a 28-5 record in March and later posted a separate twenty-four-game winning streak.

The galvanizing moment came during the April 19–20 series at the University of Florida. Miami won the opening night game, 11–0. Fraser went out to dinner and returned to commotion in the hotel. Some players broke curfew and were caught drinking. Fraser instructed his team to meet on the bus at 6:00 a.m., and most had no idea why. They rode to the field for "a bit of distance running" with wind sprints, a few hundred bear walks, cartwheels, and grass rolls for approximately two hours. The hot muggy weather and physical exertion had players vomiting on the field.

After a brief pause, Fraser informed his team it was halftime and sent them back out for more running, bear walks, and grass rolls. Even complete exhaustion did not break their spirit. Catcher Julio Solis was so fatigued that teammates carried him while whistling the theme song from the war movie *The Bridge on the River Kwai*. Fraser finally dismissed the team at noon, but when they headed toward the bus, he said, "Coaches ride; ballplayers walk" and left them with a three-mile trek back to the hotel by foot.

While addressing the team before that night's game, Fraser accepted blame for the likely loss. Down 4–2 entering the ninth, his players showed the same resolve as that morning and rallied for four runs and a 6–4 victory. On the ride back to the hotel, Fraser told them they must be the happiest team in America. He printed T-shirts with the slogan and placed them in player lockers on Monday morning.

"He could have just taken the three or four guys who missed curfew and disciplined them, but he put the entire group together," Rick Raether recalled. "I was like the movie *Miracle*—again, again, again [the scene where U.S. hockey coach Herb Brooks repeatedly had his players skate sprints]. We were going to put up with our punishment, but we were not going to lose to coach that day."

After a 56–14 regular season, Miami dropped to the Coral Gables Regional elimination bracket after a loss to rival Florida. In the rematch against the red-hot Gators, and with a College World Series berth at stake, the Hurricanes completed an improbable rally. In more Mark Light magic, the Canes scored seven runs in the final two innings, keyed by the drop of a lazy fly ball and a Chris Hart three-run home run, for a 12–9 win. Fraser created the Miami mystique, and his belief rubbed off on his players.

As the No. 8 seed, Miami finished last in a poll that asked competing coaches their predicted College World Series champion. The field was so stacked that no one even considered the Hurricanes as a dark horse. Fraser played up the underdog role, and his players had confidence after playing a difficult regular-season schedule.

The Hurricanes rolled to a 17–3 opening win over Stanford, which featured five future Major Leaguers. After a loss to Texas, Miami needed three-straight victories while facing elimination. Up 2–1 on Oklahoma State, Rick Raether struck out Pete Incaviglia, whose NCAA-record 48 home runs were nearly as many as Miami's 58 that season, to end the game.

Again with their backs to the wall, Miami met Mississippi State University, arguably one of the most talented college baseball teams ever assembled, with four future Major League All-Stars in Will Clark,

Rafael Palmeiro, Jeff Brantley, and Bobby Thigpen. Trailing 5–3 in the eighth, the Hurricanes drew within a run entering the ninth. Jon Leake led off with a walk before the unlikeliest of heroes delivered a fairy-tale ending.

Greg Ellena, a walk-on bullpen catcher, had seventeen career at bats in two seasons. Placed in the lineup with two catchers out, he started hitting and never stopped. Now facing Thigpen and with his team down to its final strike, Ellena, known as "The Bull" for his strength and weightlifting prowess, belted an unlikely two-run walk-off home run that knocked out the Bulldogs.

The win propelled the Hurricanes to a rematch with Texas, but they needed two wins for the national championship. With Miami down one in the sixth, Magno tripled and nearly scored on an overthrow that almost went off the tarp and into the dugout; instead, he retreated to third. When Hart, one of the team's top power hitters, stepped to the plate two batters later, Fraser walked over to Magno and put a play on just as Longhorns ace Greg Swindell toed the rubber.

"I had my hands on my knees still huffing and puffing and Swindell is about to wind up. Coach says to me, 'Mags, he may lay one down here,' and I'm thinking, *Holy shit*, because he's never bunted a day in his life," recalled Magno.

Hart's bunt went into the air on the right side of the infield, causing Magno, with his vision obscured by the lefty Swindell, to freeze. When he saw Swindell was not going to catch it, he bolted for home. All-American second baseman Bill Bates charged in, barehanded the ball, and threw a rope to the plate.

"I do this kind of hook slide, but it's a head-first slide, and just got my hand in around the tag," said Magno. "That was one of those Fraser . . . calls."

Magno's dash tied the game, and an RBI single by Rick Richardi in the eighth made it 2–1 and propelled the Hurricanes to a winner-take-all title game against the Longhorns. Rain paused the game's start, and Texas players waited tensely in their dugout. Miami players, meanwhile, were loose and dancing to their favorite songs in the locker room. Fraser told his team Texas was "tight as a drum," which furthered the Canes confidence. The rain never stopped, and the game was postponed to the next evening.

Texas sent future big leaguer Bruce Ruffin to the mound, while Miami countered with Kevin Sheary. The Longhorns committed five errors, including four in the first three innings. The Hurricanes built a 6–0 lead and never looked back in a 10–6 victory for their second national championship in four seasons. Fraser even donned his lucky shoes from 1982 for the championship, despite foot pain caused by the shoes being two sizes too small.

Magno had to be hospitalized with a blood clot prior to the deciding game. After the win, the team went directly to hospital, trophy in hand, to celebrate and present him the game ball. After hitting .480 with 3 home runs during the College World Series, Ellena earned Most Outstanding Player honors. Sheary won all three of his starts in Omaha, accounting for nearly half his season total of seven.

"I never played with a group of players who better defined the word *team*," said Dan Davies about the 1985 team during his UM Sports Hall of Fame induction.

The 1985 College World Series featured thirty-two players who went on to the Major Leagues. Miami had just two future Major Leaguers, but they were the mascot (Routh) and public address announcer (Rokeach), who reprised their roles with the expansion Florida Marlins in 1993. Not a single player on the team played Major League Baseball.

"It was special. It was magical. They earned it," said Barry Leffler, who broadcast games for WVUM. "It wasn't just luck; it was about clutch performances over and over again."

A crowd of ten thousand fans celebrated at Mark Light Stadium, and a separate downtown Miami rally was held. Fraser received keys to the cities of Coral Gables, Miami Beach, and Miami. The Florida state senate honored him. Major League Baseball commissioner Peter Ueberroth sent a congratulatory telegram that called Miami an outstanding program and model for others. There was talk of visiting President Ronald Reagan at the White House, like professional championship teams did, but that never materialized.

National championships, College World Series appearances, exciting promotions, and a sizeable following drew more attention to Miami than anywhere else in college baseball. Fraser's iconic program became one of the most identifiable in all of college sports.

"As the 1980s came along, they were sort of this new program that was taking over," said Allan Simpson, founder of *Baseball America.* "Miami, almost by storm, overran college baseball. A lot of it was Fraser. He had the vision [and] a persuasive personality, was creative and outgoing as could be, and sought media to help him build the program."

Miami became an ESPN favorite and appeared on the network more than sixty times during the 1980s, far more frequent than any other team. Additional games aired regionally, and the Hurricanes had more local media coverage than any program in the country. In many ways, the interest level resembled a Major League team. Three major newspapers covered the Canes beat at a time when it was unusual for a college baseball team to have any dedicated reporters. Miami television stations provided coverage throughout the season, frequently leading their sportscasts with Fraser's team.

"Our television station used to do pregame and postgame coverage of their games," said Hank Goldberg. "They covered it as a major part of the sports coverage. They had reporters at every game. They sent a crew to Omaha every year. It was remarkable. They had a good PR staff at the U, but Fraser was the one who generated everything."

Fraser was the only coach with weekly radio and television shows, normally reserved exclusively for football and basketball coaches. All games were broadcast on radio, uncommon at the time, and even the college radio station drew large audiences throughout the area.

"The coverage of the team around the city was huge," said former assistant coach Turtle Thomas. "We were on the front of the sports page every time we played—big articles, TV, radio. It was an event when Miami baseball played at home."

"If you wanted to play at the pinnacle of college baseball, you wanted to come to Miami," said Paul Hundhammer, who came from California to play for the Canes in 1979–80.

The Hurricanes finished every season of the 1980s with a top-ten national ranking and were in the top six nine of those ten years. They played in eight College World Series during the decade, winning two in four years. Miami won nearly 75 percent of its games and averaged 53.4 wins per season from 1980 to 1989. Winning was expected, and so was finishing the season in Omaha.

Miami's 1982 national championship extended the college baseball map to the East Coast. The Hurricanes became the first College World Series champion in sixteen years from east of the Mississippi River. USC and Arizona State had won eleven of the fifteen titles during that span, with Arizona winning twice and Cal State Fullerton and Texas once each.

Collegiate Baseball named Fraser its coach of the decade for the 1980s, a selection made by a committee of college baseball experts. "There were some very talented coaches nominated, but Ron Fraser—for his contribution to college baseball—has set the path for other coaches to follow. Amateur baseball will always be indebted to him," publisher Lou Pavlovich said in the announcement.

Baseball America chronicled college baseball's history from 1981 (the year of the publication's inception) in its 2020 book titled *Head of the Class*. Using a point system incorporating on-field success, number of All-American player selections, and player evaluation, including Major League top-ten draft choices and players reaching the Majors, Miami ranked as the No. 2 program of the 1980s, behind only the University of Texas.

Miami recruited nationally during the 1980s, and its rosters were dotted with players from coast to coast and from north to south. There was never a shortage of players interested in coming to Coral Gables, playing for Ron Fraser, and appearing on national television.

"Miami is known everywhere," said Thomas, Fraser's recruiting coordinator from 1987 to 1992. "You have a better chance from the beginning because everyone knows Miami. The weather's great, the program's great, and of course, there's Coach Fraser."

One of Fraser's top recruiting victories came in 1988 when he landed Alex Fernandez from nearby Hialeah. A first-round draft pick (No. 24 overall) of the Milwaukee Brewers, Fernandez became the first player drafted in first round since 1979 to turn down a professional contract to play college baseball. Negotiations went down to the wire; Fernandez had to decide whether to attend the first day of classes at Miami or sign professionally. He chose to attend Miami, and Fraser, a major factor in that choice, met Fernandez in his classroom. "He was pumped when I walked into class. He gave me a high five," Fernandez recalled.

The following year, Charles Johnson, the No. 10 overall selection in the 1989 draft, spurned professional baseball to play for Fraser and the Hurricanes. In 1991 Fraser brought in his third first-rounder in four years when Kenny Henderson, drafted No. 5 overall, chose Coral Gables over signing professionally.

"Of all the schools in the country, Miami was the place if you wanted to be on a team where you could actually be seen and have some national presence," said Fraser's daughter Cynthia. "It was a really big deal to be at Miami."

"Not only did Fraser have his own knowledge, but he put together great staffs. When you recruited good players, coached them up, and had all the others things with promotions and people in the stands, you had the premier program," said Ron Maestri, who coached at New Orleans from 1972 to 1985. "He recruited everywhere. With the popularity he established, who wouldn't want to go to Miami?"

6

End of an Era

Fraser needed to field powerhouse teams each season, which would sustain attendance to fund the nation's premier baseball program. College World Series appearances were expected and often seemed a foregone conclusion. Fraser reached a level where it was increasingly difficult to top his own achievements, be it postseason success, attendance marks, or unique promotions.

In the past, reports had Fraser coming close to leaving his role for professional baseball or even the athletic director chair at Miami. Those opportunities either never materialized or he turned them down. As the 1990s began, talk of retirement became the most prevalent other option. Speculation became an annual rite as the decade turned, yet Fraser never talked about it publicly to avoid hurting recruitment. In 1989 he addressed his future in an interview with the *Miami Herald*, saying, "If I went another two years, or maximum three years, then I think it's time to go."

Despite reports, Fraser disclosed that he had not signed a contract extension after the 1989 season. He later hinted that he might retire after the final two years remaining on his current contract. "I have a contract with Miami, and I hope to fulfill that, but that might be the last contract I sign," he said.

His contracts were by far the best of his career. Fraser was among the nation's top-paid baseball coaches; his salaries began to correspond with the income and notoriety he brought the university.

"He was starting to get rewarding contracts," said Jerry Reisman, who helped negotiate his final agreement. "I told him he was finally making some money, the money he earned."

While attending a January 1992 awards banquet, Fraser fell five feet off a dais while walking along a narrow line from where he sat. The incident chipped a bone in his heel and bruised his back, shoulder, ankle, and knee. Fraser walked with a resulting limp afterward, and one of his knees needed replacement.

X-rays on his back injury detected another health concern—an abdominal aortic aneurysm. If the aneurysm were to grow, it could burst his aorta. Fraser had to wear a wire-and-box contraption to monitor blood pressure and notify him when his blood pressure sky-rocketed. One time, a notice came at 10:45 p.m., and he was asked by his cardiologist what happened. Fraser quipped that he must have given one hell of a postgame speech because the reading nearly went off the meter. Fraser remarked that other alerts came when one of his players missed a sign.

Whispers already began about the 1992 season being Fraser's last, especially with additional coaching duties for the U.S. Olympic team after the college season. He talked about retirement for a while, but never with a certain decision or timeline. Fraser's pride and desire to finish at the top meant he did not want to overstay and risk the program's decline. The offseason fall and resulting health news moved up his decision to retire, which he announced just before the season began.

"He wasn't sure until he was sure," said daughter Cynthia of his decision to retire. "If it was not for his health, I think he would have stayed."

"I do think it was health-based. There was no other way," recalled daughter Liz of his retirement decision.

At Fraser's retirement announcement, university president Edward Foote stated, "There will be a successor to Ron Fraser, but there never will be a replacement for Ron Fraser."

Fraser spent thirty years achieving incredible success coaching, promoting, fundraising, and running his program as a business. He took on a list of additional duties well beyond those of his coaching peers while still fielding teams consistently among the nation's best.

Fraser told media he wanted to retire a year later and would have liked to coach another year or two, but it was time to move on. He forecasted that "walking out of those gates [at Mark Light Stadium] for the last time will be the hardest thing I'll ever have to do."

He went through the entire 1992 season and Olympics before his aneurysm was surgically repaired more than a year later. He never disclosed the situation publicly because he did not want his fitness questioned as coach for the Olympic team.

Nearly two years after his retirement, Fraser admitted he did not have much choice in his retirement. His doctors recommended he give up coaching because of high blood pressure and health.

Fraser's retirement announcement created a last-dance feel to the season. Expectations were high, and Miami sat atop the preseason national rankings. The roster included eight returning position starters and five pitchers plus the nation's No. 1 recruiting class. Fraser compared the depth to his 1974 team that enabled a B-squad to play its own twelve-game schedule. Catcher Charles Johnson told media before the season that the team went three-deep at every position and had the potential to go all the way.

"We had overwhelming talent," recalled Wicho Hernández. "The intrasquad games were tougher than [those against] some of the opponents we played. It was just incredible."

Despite the retirement announcement, the season was mostly business as usual. Interviews, photo shoots, and other engagements pulled Fraser away from practices more frequently. He never emphasized the final time with anything he did, but he made additional time for his players and coaches while further appreciating those daily interactions.

Every road trip featured some form of special presentation honoring Fraser. He told his players that there would be "some stuff" before the game but not to pay attention to it. They were there to play a game and take it to the other team. Tributes from rivals Florida and Florida State particularly touched Fraser, who admitted to being a bit choked up. At FSU, where Fraser finished his college playing career, Coach Mike Martin organized a special ceremony for his contributions to college baseball. Fraser paraded around the field in the backseat of a convertible while fans cheered him. Saluting the school's archrival coach showed tremendous respect and sportsmanship.

"He was one of those guys loved by everybody, even to this day," said Thomas, an assistant coach during Fraser's final season. "The farewell tour and the gifts and accolades were amazing. You just sat there with your mouth hanging open because he's almost like a baseball god."

"The amount of respect given to Coach Fraser was amazing and the recognition he got from other big-name programs and coaches was unbelievable." said Henderson, a freshman pitcher on the 1992 team.

The mightily talented Hurricanes boasted the nation's best record and top ranking. Miami seemed destined for a trip to Omaha complete with a national championship. It was the storybook script Fraser deserved. Those expectations, however, came externally, not internally. Fraser downplayed his retirement and rarely talked about it with his team, often saying he was simply along for the ride. His players wanted to win for their legendary coach, and that motivation added to their commitment and competitiveness.

Led by a battery of Johnson, who became the first draft choice in Florida Marlins history, and consensus All-American pitcher Jeff Alkire, the Hurricanes compiled an impressive 55-10 record (a remarkable .846 winning percentage) and spent most of the season ranked first. The Canes won twenty-seven of their last twenty-nine regular-season games, including a nineteen-game winning streak, and ranked among the national leaders with a sparkling 2.92 team ERA and .973 fielding percentage. There was some Miami Magic along the way—twenty-one comeback victories, a 14-3 record in one-run games, and a 5-0 mark in extra innings. A ten-run rally gave Miami a final at bat win over the University of Tampa. A 5–4 April walk-off against Florida State came when the catcher dropped a called third strike that would have ended the game and wildly threw to first, allowing the winning run to score.

More than 161,000 fans came to Mark Light Stadium during Fraser's final season. As the home schedule wound down, the regular season's final series marked "Ron Fraser's Last At-Bat." Fraser was unsure about his readiness for the emotion and admitted he would be a mess if he thought about it. He had given up coaching at third because of his health issues that season, but in the final game of the series, Fraser took the field for the bottom of the eighth inning and the Hurricanes last at bat. The crowd cheered him wildly in one of the top goose-bump moments in Mark Light Stadium history.

The win completed a sweep of Georgia Tech, coached by friend Jim Morris. Most of the six thousand fans made their way to the field for a forty-five-minute postgame ceremony emceed by Jay Rokeach and filled with entertaining stories and humorous anecdotes. Fraser took the microphone and addressed the crowd:

"You've been the greatest fans any coach could ever have because without them and without you, we don't have a baseball program. And I thank you from the bottom of my heart. I will miss this. I will miss these young people who really make your life worthwhile. I will miss all you fans. Thank you. I love you all."

Fans lined up along the base paths and formed a corridor from second base to center field. Starting at home plate, Fraser methodically circled the bases, pausing to shake hands and give a personal comment to well-wishers. After returning to home plate, he made his way back out to second base and down a red-carpet surrounded by fans to the center-field gate, while Frank Sinatra's "My Way," a Fraser favorite, played over the loudspeakers. A shiny Rolls Royce awaited him for his grand exit.

"Funny, they're all thanking me," Fraser told media afterward. "I'm thinking I should be thanking them."

Fraser's fanfare included the Coral Gables City Commission announcement naming the block of Ponce de Leon Boulevard running along the south side of Mark Light Stadium as Ron Fraser Way. University president Foote provided Fraser back pay for the nine years he spent as a part-time coach at the beginning of his career. "That's how good he was. . . . They wouldn't have done that for anybody [else] in the world. He really deserved it," said Bertman.

The following weekend, Miami hosted the NCAA Regional as No. 1 seed. After winning the opener, it dropped a 6–3 decision to Notre Dame. Facing elimination against North Carolina State, the Canes blew a 3–0 lead and entered the eighth inning tied, with their season hanging in the balance. Fraser uncharacteristically told his team, "You've got to win this game for me" before adding, "If we lose, it's my last game. I won't get paid anymore, and tomorrow's a holiday [Memorial Day], and I get paid time and a half."

With a runner at third and the score tied at four in the bottom of the ninth, Fraser pinch hit for Hernández, who was hitting .330. In his place, Keith Tippett, batting .213 on the season and 0 for 8 as a pinch hitter, singled to right field to give the Canes a walk-off win over

North Carolina State to stay alive. Once again, Fraser had a knack for making the right move in the right situation.

The regional was down to three remaining teams, each with one loss—Miami, Notre Dame, and South Carolina. The Hurricanes needed two wins on the final day to advance to Omaha. A 17–2 rout of the Gamecocks set up a winner-take-all rematch against Notre Dame. A healthy respect existed between the baseball programs, but the recent football rivalry triggered the Miami crowd. Win or lose, the game marked Fraser's last at the ballpark he built. He pulled out his lucky shoes worn while winning the 1982 and 1985 College World Series championship games, and his pregame message to the team was simple: "You guys better not send me off in my last game with a loss."

With nearly five thousand fans in the stadium and another five hundred watching through the outfield chain-link fence, Fraser jogged out from the dugout and received a standing ovation that lasted more than a full minute. Alkire took the ball, and on two days' rest, turned in a legendary complete-game performance in a 5–1 victory that never appeared in doubt.

"About the fifth inning, I started to realize these guys are playing with passion and purpose. It was more than just a game," recalled then Notre Dame coach Pat Murphy about Miami that night. "They knew this was their coach's last stand. The energy from the crowd made a huge difference. It was pretty special."

In the clubhouse celebration afterward, Fraser told the team he had a special guest who wanted to say a few words. His team waited in a heightened state of exuberance and anticipation. Given Fraser's connections, it could have been just about anyone. Football coach Dennis Erickson, coming off his second national championship at Miami, walked in, and the team started clapping. He began walking around while looking at everyone without saying anything. The players began to wonder what he was doing. Then, in typical football coach delivery, Erickson yelled out, "Way to beat the goddamn Irish!"

"We went nuts. We were so fired up," Alkire recalled of Erickson's poignant statement.

It was fitting and ironic that two legends in their respective fields, both with Omaha ties, made final appearances on their home turf that

Memorial Day evening. Shortly after Fraser secured Miami's trip to the College World Series, the final episode of *The Tonight Show Starring Johnny Carson*, hosted by a Nebraska native, aired.

A line in the *Miami Herald* read, "If you come away understanding nothing else about Monday night, please understand this: Mark Light Stadium will not be the same without Ron Fraser."

Fraser's final appearance was the lead storyline throughout the 1992 College World Series. Cameras, media, and fans followed him everywhere he went in Omaha, from the moment he got off the bus and headed inside Rosenblatt Stadium to the locker room. To help align his obligations and provide a buffer when needed, Fraser asked his former pitcher Danny Smith, the 1982 College World Series Most Outstanding Player turned police officer, to accompany him in Omaha.

"I don't ever recall him saying that he had enough [of the attention in Omaha]. If anyone wanted to speak to him or wanted an autograph or an interview, he would stop for them," recalled Smith. "Part of that was Ron Fraser being Ron Fraser. It was like being with a movie star and the paparazzi storming him. It was overwhelming, but an amazing thing to watch."

The top-seeded Canes needed thirteen innings to secure a 4–3 win over a scrappy University of California squad in the opener. Two days later, they posted another 4–3 win, this time over Augie Garrido's Cal State Fullerton team. Miami sat in the driver's seat and needed just one win to reach the championship game.

In a rematch against the Titans, Fullerton jumped out to an early 7–0 lead. Miami fought its way back and had the tying run at the plate before making the game's last out in a 7–5 final. The teams met three days later with a CWS championship game appearance on the line.

In a Friday night game played less than eighteen hours before the scheduled title contest, the Hurricanes fell behind early, and a steady rain began. There was no stoppage of play, and the decision was made to play through the precipitation. At one point, the first base umpire started sprinting down the foul line to make a fair or foul call and fell down on the wet grass. Pitchers and infielders were slipping on dirt that turned to slick mud. The infield became so slick that the teams were called off the field for a brief delay. Fraser told the umpires, "All these years we've worked hard to get this game to where it is, and you guys have just set it back by what you're doing here tonight."

One Hurricane player said he had never seen anything like what happened that night, adding, "Fortunately no one was injured because it could have easily happened. They would not do that nowadays."

Because the field already had puddled, no tarp was put out, and the teams were sent back out to finish the game in the downpour. Renowned for its remarkable work, the Rosenblatt Stadium ground crew tried to keep up on the field conditions after each inning, sometimes between outs, as the game went on. Fraser was in disbelief that the game continued in dangerous conditions. Miami lost 8–1 in a contest that was part tragedy, part irony.

"That game was probably the saddest moment in College World Series history that I can remember," said Jim Callis, covering the College World Series for *Baseball America* at the time. "I remember that as Fraser's last game. It was an unfitting end to his college coaching career."

Ironically, by bringing college baseball to television, Fraser in a way was victim to his own success. CBS aired the single championship game Saturday at noon local time. To accommodate that timeline, the Friday night semifinal game could not be postponed and was instead played out in the abysmal conditions. The logistics of postponing and resuming later would have resulted in a rescheduled championship game.

Despite the disappointment and finality of coaching his final game at Miami, Fraser was as cordial and accommodating as ever. He showed pride and hid sadness when walking off the field, speaking to his team, and answering media questions in the postgame press conference.

As the rain continued falling, Fraser walked out of Rosenblatt Stadium for the final time. A young boy waited outside for an autograph, and Fraser gave him his game hat. As Fraser began boarding the bus in front of Rosenblatt Stadium, he gazed back at the hallowed college baseball ground where he coached forty-seven games and won two national championships in twelve trips.

"I remember when he got on the bus, he took a step up to board, then stepped back down and looked at the stadium," recalled Smith. "I got tears in my eyes when he did that because I knew he was looking for the last time. You knew that was it. He wasn't coming back. He got on the bus and told everyone, 'Good job' and went on with the rest of his life." After thirty seasons and over 1,700 games as coach, Fraser's Miami career came to an end at age fifty-six.

Fraser's retirement created the most attractive job opening in college baseball. He left the program on top and had a salary on par with many football coaches, along with supplemental income from both television and radio shows.

Speculation about successors grew as Fraser's final season wound down. Rumors focused on pitching coach Brad Kelley and Notre Dame coach Pat Murphy. Names initially mentioned included Bertman, Polk, former assistant coach Jerry Weinstein, and Long Beach State's Dave Snow. Media reported that North Carolina State's Ray Tanner interviewed with Director of Athletics Dave Maggard and that Tennessee's Rod Delmonico expressed interest. Murphy was a strong candidate but pulled out at the last minute to remain at Notre Dame before later succeeding the legendary Jim Brock at Arizona State in 1995. He eventually worked his way to Major League Baseball and became the manager of the Milwaukee Brewers.

"That was one of the handful of programs that were really trying to bring in money, make money, and be the very best," Murphy said of Miami baseball. "They looked at baseball as something really important in the athletic department. Being in a great city like Miami with the great fan base and tradition they had, it was easy to see it as a premier job."

Kelley was awarded the job by Maggard, who touted his promotion as an opportunity to maintain the rich tradition established by Fraser. Fraser called Kelley one of the best young coaches in the country and someone who knew what it took to run a successful program. However, it soon became apparent that neither the continuation of tradition, nor success, went as envisioned.

Described as a brilliant baseball mind and a hard-nosed baseball guy, Kelley had a personality completely opposite of Fraser. He was neither a promoter nor a public relations figure and did not sell the program to the media and fans. Despite Kelley's high regard and respect as pitching coach, moving into the head coaching role for college baseball's most visible program appeared too much.

Fraser threw out the first pitch at the 1993 opener but stayed for only two innings before leaving. He attended just three games that season, not staying more than a handful of innings at any. "I didn't really feel like I was welcome," Fraser later told media about the 1993 season. "He wanted to change everything. Why fix it if it's not broken? I sort of divorced myself from the program. I didn't feel comfortable and I didn't come around."

Kelley removed Mark Light Stadium's artificial turf, despite the advantage it served for many years, and replaced it with grass. He had the office furniture changed and walls repainted. Each decision symbolically wiped away the Fraser era in exchange for a new beginning. Kelley, however, lacked the warmth and ability to engage fans, and his changes angered the program's support network built by Fraser. Season-ticket sales dropped 40 percent and overall attendance by one hundred thousand, accounting for nearly $500,000 in lost revenue.

Ranked second in the preseason, Miami started 16-10 and was swept at Texas, Florida, and Florida State during the season. Team chemistry fizzled. Players were left uncertain where they stood with their coach and afraid to make mistakes for fear of being removed from the lineup. Pitching decisions were often taken out of pitching coach Lazaro "Lazer" Collazo's hands. It was a one-way-or-the-highway culture. The Hurricanes ended the season with five consecutive losses, including two at the South Regional, for a 36-22 mark. Everything that could go wrong did. Further complicating Kelley's situation was allegations of drinking with players at an airport bar during a late-season road trip. The university investigated the matter, and in September, after just one season, Kelley resigned.

"I get upset talking about it. The program was damaged," Fraser later said in an interview.

After Kelley's removal, Fraser became involved in helping new AD Paul Dee with the coaching search. Speculation centered around Morris, Tanner, Snow, and Weinstein. Fraser believed in Morris, whom he knew for nearly two decades and coached alongside for the 1987 U.S. Pan American Games team. When Morris received a call about the job, he immediately called Fraser and came down to visit with him and learn more. For Morris, Fraser's backing of him as the right guy for the job was vital. Dee called two people for their opinions on whom to hire—Fraser and Bertman.

Fraser's approval meant the world to Morris, who would not have accepted the job without it. Morris told Fraser he wanted him at his side for his introductory press conference. Fraser had recently undergone the procedure to repair his abdominal aortic aneurysm, yet on the same day he was discharged from the hospital, he went directly to the press conference in an ambulance and sat in a wheelchair next to Morris. "We have the right guy," announced Fraser.

Morris, who had the consensus No. 1 team entering the 1994 season with future Major Leaguers Nomar Garciaparra, Jason Varitek, and Jay Payton, said at his hiring that he left the top team in the nation for the top program in the nation. After building a junior college program and his Georgia Tech program from virtually nothing, Morris quickly found out how high expectations were at Miami. "You come to Miami where you're not supposed to lose any games. It was a totally different situation to step into to," Morris said.

During his tour while interviewing for the position, Morris noticed the 1974 national runner-up trophy sitting on the ground to keep open the door to the clubhouse bathroom open while being cleaned. "Basically, the national runner-up trophy was a doorstop in the toilet is the way I took it," recalled Morris. "I thought, *Man, this is a tough place to coach.* It kind of set the standard for the expectations."

Soon after starting the job, Morris received an introduction to Ethel Light, widow of program benefactor George Light, as "Coach Morris, who is replacing Ron Fraser."

Mrs. Light looked Morris directly in the eye and told him, "No one will ever replace Ron Fraser."

"Mrs. Light, you are exactly right. I agree with you," Morris responded.

Morris had characteristics comparable to Fraser. He understood the value of promotions and fan interaction, played a similar style of baseball, and related well to his players. Unlike Kelley, Morris sought advice and input on a regular basis, often asking, "What would Ron do?" about details from scheduling to fundraising. He opened the program up to Fraser, giving him a key to his office and a standing invitation to attend games, practices, and meetings. Fraser declined the invitation to sit in the dugout during games so as to not interfere but offered support for anything Morris needed. He made it clear he would not be looking over Morris's shoulder or telling him how to run the program.

"I told him I have your office in your building [the Ron Fraser Building], so you are always welcome to use it," Morris recalled. "I'd come in after practice or something, and Coach Fraser would be making a speech. Or I'd walk into my office not knowing he was in there, and he might be on the couch asleep. I'd quietly get my stuff, get out of the office, and close the door back up."

Much of the Miami baseball magic returned. Attendance grew by over 20 percent after falling to its lowest point in fifteen years in the year under Kelley. At the first home game, Morris and Fraser made a ceremonial entrance via helicopter, landing in the Mark Light Stadium outfield. Fraser became a fixture as an analyst for Sunshine Network game telecasts.

"I've got the most influential coach in the history of college baseball right by my side," said Morris. "Anytime I wanted to do something, I felt I could run it by him. He's probably already tried it and could tell me whether it was going to work or not.

"I had his total loyalty, and vice versa, and he would only tell me something that was going to help me and the program, *loyalty* being the most important word with capital letters and underlined. I knew that there was a mutual feeling of loyalty."

Fraser's presence had a positive impact on the players, some of whom he had recruited. "It was nice having him back around," said Henderson. "He'd come in and just hang out and chat with us in the clubhouse. When Frase showed up, everyone had a smile on their face."

Morris went on to an extremely successful twenty-five-year run at Miami that nearly mirrored Fraser's on-field accomplishments. Morris went to thirteen College World Series and won two national championships, while Fraser made twelve appearances and also won twice. Each coach's first national championship came on his sixth trip to Omaha, and both finished with more than one thousand Miami victories. With their longstanding success, it is easy to think of the program's transition as a direct passing of the torch from Fraser to Morris despite the one-year gap in between.

Fig. 1. George Light (*left*) and Ron Fraser at the dedication of Mark Light Field in 1973. Light, an instrumental benefactor and friend, made Fraser's ballpark vision a reality with his contribution. A second donation three years later helped upgrade the stadium, named after his late son, to the nation's premier college baseball facility. Photo from UM Libraries (n.p.).

Fig. 2. Ron Fraser hoists the 1982 NCAA Championship trophy with his team. The eight teams in the College World Series field that season combined to send thirty-two players to the Major Leagues. The Hurricanes had one. Photo by Ken Lee.

Fig. 3. One of Ron Fraser's greatest legacies at the University of Miami was creation of the Miami Maniac, the first mascot specific to a college baseball team. The Maniac, originally portrayed by John Routh, served as the official mascot of the College World Series and made guest appearances at Minor League games and International baseball events during the summer. Photo from UM Sports Hall of Fame archives (n.p.).

Fig. 4. OPPOSITE TOP: After leading the charge to get college baseball on television, Ron Fraser's Miami teams became a fixture on ESPN broadcasts. The Hurricanes became network darlings and had multiple games air from Mark Light Stadium each season during the 1980s. Photo by Ken Lee.

Fig. 5. OPPOSITE BOTTOM: No coaching tandem in college baseball history attained the level of success achieved by Ron Fraser and Skip Bertman (*left*). Following eight seasons as Fraser's top assistant at Miami, Bertman became head coach at LSU, where he won five national championships in a ten-year span and was instrumental in the SEC rise to baseball prominence. Photo from UM Sports Hall of Fame archives (n.p.).

Fig. 6. ABOVE: Ron Fraser throws batting practice in Omaha, Nebraska. Fraser, a former pitcher, also took great pride in his fungo hitting and the ability to place pop-ups close to the plate. Photo by Ken Lee.

Fig. 7. OPPOSITE TOP: Ron Fraser and Maine's John Winkin teamed up to promote college baseball on several occasions. When Fraser took his team to Orono, Maine, for the first time in 1984, the two teams held a public lobster bake to kick off the weekend series. Photo by Ken Lee.

Fig. 8. OPPOSITE BOTTOM: ESPN's Irv Brown interviews Ron Fraser and his team during the 1985 College World Series. While facing elimination, the Hurricanes posted three consecutive one-run victories over Oklahoma State, Mississippi State, and Texas before defeating the Longhorns a second time, 10–6, to win the national championship. Photo by Ken Lee.

Fig. 9. ABOVE: Mike Fiore (*right*) was the quintessential Ron Fraser type of player. Fiore was a Freshman All-American and earned first team All-American honors two years later. He set several Miami records and played for Fraser on Team USA at the 1987 Pan American Games. Photo by Ken Lee.

Fig. 10. OPPOSITE TOP: The Miami Maniac's 1985 wedding ceremony aired live to a Sunday-night national television audience on ESPN and was the most extravagant and unique mascot event of its time. Photo from UM Sports Hall of Fame archives (n.p.).

Fig. 11. OPPOSITE BOTTOM: Ron Fraser is interviewed following a Team USA game in Cuba during a pre–Pan Am Games tour in 1987. His squad was the first American team to play on Cuban soil since Fidel Castro took over; it won two of the five games played in Havana. The team defeated the Cubans during a memorable round-robin game in Indianapolis and finished as Pan Am silver medalists after the championship game rematch. Photo by Barry Leffler.

Fig. 12. ABOVE: Ron Fraser stands in front of St. Basil's Cathedral in Moscow's Red Square. Fraser and his Hurricanes team became the most prominent U.S. team to visit the former Soviet Union when Miami played in the Peace in the World baseball tournament during the Fall of 1989. Photo from the Fraser family personal collection.

Fig. 13. Ron Fraser talks with legendary Texas coach Cliff Gustafson prior to a meeting between two of college baseball's most historic and successful programs. Fraser and Gustafson met twenty-five times, including a 1988 meeting that marked the first between active coaches with 1,000 career wins. Photo by JC Ridley (Caneshooter.com).

Fig. 14. Ron Fraser speaks with Alex Fernandez (*right*) at third base. Fraser was known to calm his players in tense situations, often asking baserunners how many fans they thought were in the crowd or how many hot dogs were sold at that particular game. Photo by Rhona Wise (www.rhonawise.com).

Fig. 15. ABOVE: Ron Fraser visits the mound during his final season at Miami. Catcher Charles Johnson (No. 23, *left*), whom Fraser called "Charlie," was the first-ever draft choice of the Florida Marlins in 1992. Johnson attended Miami after turning down a lucrative professional contract offer out of high school to play for Fraser and what he described as "without a doubt the best baseball program in the country." Photo by JC Ridley (Caneshooter.com).

Fig. 16. OPPOSITE TOP: Ron Fraser addresses adoring fans during a post-game celebration after his final regular-season game, dubbed Ron Fraser's Last At-Bat, at Mark Light Stadium in 1992. Photo by Rhona Wise (www .rhonawise.com).

Fig. 17. OPPOSITE BOTTOM: Ron Fraser takes a trip to the mound during a rain-plagued elimination game against Fullerton at the 1992 College World Series. Ironically, the man who put college baseball on television coached his final game in heavy rain, in large part because of the next afternoon's nationally televised championship game. Photo by JC Ridley (Caneshooter.com).

Fig. 18. Ron Fraser retired as the NCAA's second-winningest all-time coach with a 1,271-438-9 (.747) record, and his teams set an NCAA record with twenty-consecutive postseason appearances. *Collegiate Baseball* magazine named Fraser its Coach of the Decade for the 1980s. Photo by Rhona Wise (www.rhonawise.com).

Fig. 19. ABOVE: Ron Fraser established the blueprint for running a successful college baseball program, both on the field and as a business. He frequently shared his knowledge with fellow coaches in an effort to help grow the sport nationally. Photo by JC Ridley (Caneshooter.com).

Fig. 20. Ron Fraser and University of Miami president Tad Foote talk in front of the dugout before a game. When Foote was hired, Fraser held a Big Foote Night promotion for which a tracing of the new president's foot was placed at the front gate and any fan whose foot was bigger entered free. At Fraser's retirement, Foote gave Fraser back pay equal to a full-time salary during his early years on a part-time salary. Photo by JC Ridley (Caneshooter.com).

Fig. 21. TOP: Miami baseball retired Fraser's number on April 24, 1993. Fraser and six of his players, plus Assistant Coach Skip Bertman, have their numbers on the outfield fence at Alex Rodriguez Park at Mark Light Field. Photo by Rhona Wise (www .rhonawise.com).

Fig. 22. RIGHT: Ron Fraser coached the United States to the 1969 Amateur World Series Championship, silver medals at the 1971 and 1987 Pan American Games, and a fourth-place finish in the 1992 Olympics. He coached Team USA in baseball's first Olympics (1992) as an official medal sport. Photo by Rhona Wise (www.rhonawise.com).

Fig. 23. TOP: Ron Fraser with his daughters (*left to right*), Lynda, Cynthia, and Liz, on Christmas Eve in 1995. Photo from the Fraser family personal collection.

Fig. 24. BOTTOM: Ron Fraser with his grandchildren (back row, *left to right*), Fraser Poorman, Kyle Gonzales, (front row, *left to right*) Brett Kraut, Andrew Kraut, and Amanda Gonzales, during his 2006 induction to the National College Baseball Hall of Fame in Lubbock, Texas. Photo from the Fraser family personal collection.

Fig. 25. ABOVE: Ron Fraser's first wife, Liane, stands next to his statue in front of Alex Rodriguez Park at Mark Light Field. Unveiled in 2015, Fraser's statue was the first for a sports figure at the University of Miami. His likeness portrays Fraser the way he dressed for work each day—wearing a coat and tie. Photo from the Fraser family personal collection.

7

International Influence

While deployed to West Germany during his U.S. Army service, Fraser started coaching as a player-coach for his military team. When their German opponent needed a fill-in, Fraser offered to step in and ended up coaching the team. That experience led to a stint as German National Team head coach. Fraser inherited a squad that had been banished from the European Baseball Championship for throwing beer bottles and threatening an umpire. His German team took bronze at the European Championship and, more remarkably, won the tournament's sportsmanship trophy just one year after its incident.

Upon returning to the United States, Fraser finished his degree at Florida State and served as freshman baseball coach. The Netherlands took note of Fraser's work and sought him to lead its national program. Major League Baseball Commissioner Ford Frick and Vice President Richard Nixon encouraged Fraser to accept the Dutch offer, which he did.

Baseball in the Netherlands was a work in progress. Fraser started from ground zero and began teaching the basics. The Dutch coach who introduced baseball to Holland learned from a book and never attended a game. His interpretation that a pitcher had to keep his toe in contact with the pitching rubber at all times was taken literally. Dutch pitchers did not follow through in the windup and instead maintained contact with the rubber even after releasing the pitch.

Fraser saw an opportunity to further develop the sport. The Netherlands won three consecutive European Championships since beginning competition in 1956 as part of the six-country European Baseball Federation. Soccer dominated the country's sports culture. The growth potential intrigued Fraser because, at the time, baseball was not much more than a weekend-only sport played during the summer months.

He began staging clinics across Holland to teach fundamentals and develop interest.

"He was a rookie coach and didn't have any experience, but he worked very well with the players and adjusted quickly to a different culture and baseball setting," said Charles Urbanus Jr., who later played for Fraser and whose father, Han, was Holland's legendary baseball pioneer and starred on Fraser's Dutch teams. (Charles Urbanus Sr. is actually Charles Jr.'s uncle.)

Led by the trio of Han Urbanus, Joop Geurts, and Herman Beidschat, the Dutch won their fourth-consecutive European Championship and first under Fraser, in 1960. Afterward, the Netherlands prime minister summoned Fraser to his home and asked what it would take to retain him as leader of the national baseball program. Fraser, caught off guard, came up with a number he admitted was fantasy—$19,000, a large sum at that time, plus a few months back in the United States. The prime minister agreed.

After winning a second European title in 1962, Fraser earned a ten-year contract offer. By then, Fraser was set on returning to the United States and eventually landed the head coach position at Miami.

Just three years into his tenure at Miami, the NCAA appointed Fraser to its four-man committee promoting world baseball and assigned him to Europe and South America. He made international baseball a part of his program's outreach and began a series of annual trips later that year. An initial roster of fourteen players included eleven Miami players—five from the freshman team and six from the varsity—took its first goodwill trip to Colombia as part of Coral Gables's annual People to People International program for its sister city, Cartagena.

Fraser taught fundamentals and distributed bags of bats, gloves, and baseballs, which had been collected in Coral Gables, to the children attending clinics and games. He also gave away souvenir bats and T-shirts, records by Stan Musial on how to hit a baseball, and sheets, blankets, and utensils for hospitals. At night, the team played exhibition games, often drawing large crowds, with all profits donated to underprivileged children. The trips provided unique and memorable learning experiences for the players and allowed the Hurricanes to play additional games against top local or national squads.

From localized power outages to sitting on fruit crates in the back of a cargo plane while flying between cities, there were many eye-opening experiences during the South American tours. Townspeople and dignitaries welcomed the team with open arms. One of the most interesting meetings came in 1971 in Managua, Nicaragua.

Fraser told his team about a breakfast invitation, with the trip including a bus ride to the top of a mountain. He instructed players to dress well, including sport coats, for the event. The team knew nothing about who was hosting the breakfast, except that the host's son was attending the University of Miami and had been playing tennis.

After arriving, the team learned that the lavish and ornate mountaintop residence was the presidential palace. It had a throne befitting a king, and many of the players took turns taking a seat before the host entered the room. In walked General Anastasio "Tachito" Somoza Debayle, dictator and president of Nicaragua.

"He came out in a [Che] Guevara shirt, and we're all making fun of him—the guy looked like my barber—and we had a few jokes with that," recalled Joel Green. "I hope no one there spoke English."

Somoza was friendly in greeting his guests. He gave them glasses of orange juice and held conversations with several attendees. The players thanked him for his generous invitation and for hosting them. He told them to think nothing of it, as his son was also a University of Miami student.

Randy Olen then asked the president, out of genuine curiosity, about the depth of the large lake hundreds of feet down from the backside of the palace.

"My friend, that lake is very deep," responded Somoza.

Olen and his teammates later learned that Somoza lined people up on the wall, which had no screen, and had them executed by gunfire; they would roll down the hill into that lake.

"To this day, there is no intimidation to anything that could happen to me after having breakfast with General Somoza," recalled Olen about the lessons learned on the trip. "Meeting really important people was like nothing to coach. I thought, *You've got to be kidding me*, because no one else in college baseball was doing things like this."

A memorable umpire controversy occurred in the final inning of a game in Colombia. The home plate umpire refused to call a strike, and Fraser went out to protest. On his trip back to the dugout, the first base umpire stopped Fraser and told him there was a problem. He informed him that the home plate umpire was gambling on the game's outcome and bet against Fraser's team. He then told Fraser not to worry because he was betting on his team. The umpire added an instruction—after a walk, throw the ball to first base.

The batter walked, Fraser's pitcher threw over to first, and the first baseman applied the tag to the runner, who was standing on the bag. The first base umpire called him out, and Fraser's team won the game.

The South American experiences extended beyond incredible stories. Games and practices provided additional reps to ready for the season and drew attention to the program. When recruiting, Fraser promised players that they would travel. He took teams to five different Latin American countries in the first seven years of international tours.

In terms of international competition, USA Baseball was far from the national governing organization it is today. Officially instituted as the U.S. Baseball Federation in 1978, the organization had prior national teams that were put together basically by a handful of college coaches, who selected a team, arranged a schedule, and then managed. USC's Rod Dedeaux is credited with first facilitating international baseball by taking his college teams to Hawaii and on to Asia in 1955, two years after the Korean War. He was instrumental in getting baseball into the 1964 Tokyo Olympics and served as the American head coach. Other college coaches showed interest in growing the sport, but no formal national governance existed, and very little money was available.

Fraser was among the top coaches who helped expand Dedeaux's international work. His strong ties to Holland and the European Championship helped grow European national programs, and summer trips to South American opened doors in Latin American countries. Whereas other college coaches aided amateur baseball's evolution into international competition, the momentum began with Dedeaux leading West Coast and Asian efforts and Fraser heading into Latin America and the Caribbean after establishing his roots in Europe.

"They were the founding fathers of USA Baseball, there's no doubt about it," said Mike Gaski, who spent two decades as USA Baseball president. "Before the Amateur Sports Act officially formed USA Baseball, it was the interest Coach Fraser and Coach Dedeaux had in having teams represent our country. They were our resource and the guys we went to for guidance."

In 1969 the United States sent a team to an Amateur World Series (later known as the Baseball World Cup) for the first time since 1942. After serving on the committee selecting the previous year's Olympic team, Fraser was chosen as coach in a late replacement for Arizona's Frank Sancet, who suddenly was sidelined by a medical issue. Santo Domingo, Dominican Republic, hosted the series amid anti-American sentiment after U.S. military involvement four years prior. At the opening ceremony, U.S. players were roundly booed and had urine-filled bottles hurled at them. Despite the hostile environment, the Americans reached the championship game and faced Cuba in a matchup of undefeated teams. Physical threats were made at the U.S. team, and everyone attending the game was checked for weapons, long before there was any type of security check at sporting events. Fraser told the team their lives were threatened and they may not play the game.

"We are all twenty-one or so, and we wanted to play this game," Fraser's Miami shortstop Joel Green recalled. "It was probably the most exciting game I ever played in."

A U.S. Embassy representative assured Fraser that the two to three thousand marines stationed in the Caribbean could be there in twenty-five minutes. Fraser laughed in response, telling him that may be true, but he and his team would all be dead by then.

Two armored trucks, much like those delivering money to banks, picked up the U.S. team from its hotel and took it to the stadium. Very few vehicles were on the road because protestors had littered the path to the stadium with glass. The trucks arrived safely but were unable to get into the stadium to drop off the team because of congestion on the streets around the stadium. An estimated fifty thousand people were inside the stadium and another ten thousand waited outside, unable to get in.

Police formed a barrier, and an officer would cock his revolver and run each player into the stadium one-by-one. Once inside, a policeman would again cock his revolver in the tunnel, peer around the corner, and lead players onto the field. As a precaution, the Americans warmed up in center field instead of near the stands. A machine gun sat atop the dugout, with approximately seventeen soldiers with AK-47 automatic weapons in the dugout for additional security. On the field, the United States scored the game's first run before Cuba plated the game's final two runs in a hard-fought 2–1 decision. After the game, the U.S. players returned to their hotel, awakened at 2:00 a.m., and snuck out of the country to return home.

After serving as an assistant coach for the silver-medalist U.S. team at the 1971 Pan American Games, Fraser returned to the Netherlands the following summer and coached the Dutch National Team to another European Championship. Despite a decade between his work there, Fraser's fame and reputation grew during his absence.

"Everyone knew he was a big-shot coach because he coached the University of Miami," said Charles Urbanus Jr. "He came back with a little more professional style of coaching and a blueprint for building up the Dutch program. It was really an amateur sport still in development, and he was able to have high standards and adjust without lowering them."

Dutch baseball became more refined and skilled, consistently winning European titles and representing the continent at the Olympics and the World Baseball Classic. Fraser offered Urbanus, a member of the national team at age sixteen, a scholarship at Miami. Urbanus turned down the opportunity due to distance and later went on to a successful playing and coaching career of his own, carrying on the legacy of his father Han and Uncle Charlie, a family considered as Dutch baseball royalty.

Fraser provided guidance that helped the sport expand its reach in Holland with better facilities, media coverage, and player development. The country built a national stadium capable of staging top-level tournaments in Haarlem. Dutch National Broadcaster NOS televised a European final against Italy, a first for the Netherlands. Fraser helped position national team coach Charles Urbanus Sr. to lead the program forward.

In 1985 Fraser became the first American inducted into the Honkbal (Dutch for "baseball") Hall of Fame. Beyond leading Holland to its first three European Championship titles, he helped start the Haarlem Baseball Week, a tradition held annually 1961–72 and then in alternating years through 2018 before restarting in 2022. Even after leaving the Netherlands, Fraser made occasional guest appearances, even once coaching the Dutch entry himself.

Fraser remained involved in Dutch baseball as a remote advisor for the country's national program. Each year, the nation's most promising youth player, as nominated by the Dutch national coach, is presented with the Ron Fraser Award.

The U.S. National Team tabbed Fraser as head coach for the 1973 Amateur World Series. His squad included four of his Miami players— Kim Siepe, Wayne Krenchicki, Orlando González, and Bob Bartlett. Having only a few days to set a team and prepare, Fraser decided to employ what he called a "gimmick"—a roster featuring only lefthanded hitters and pitchers meant to confuse opponents. The ploy worked. The Americans won their first nine contests, including a 4–2, eleven-inning win over Taiwan, to reach the title game against host Nicaragua. Fraser's team clawed out a 1–0, ten-inning victory over future Major League All-Star Dennis Martinez to claim the first U.S. gold in seventeen years of the Amateur World Series.

U.S. baseball continued to develop and grow international competition as Fraser continued in various roles. By 1984 the sport returned to the Olympic stage in Los Angeles, coached by Dedeaux. Fraser seemed the natural choice as next head coach, and in September 1985 USA Baseball offered him the position for both the 1987 Pan American Games and the 1988 Olympics. Without assurances regarding his role and autonomy in selecting assistant coaches and players, Fraser committed only to the 1987 Pan American Games.

The United States owned just one Pan American Games gold medal and one silver in its history. A fourth-place finish was its best in the previous three Pan American Games. Cuba, the reigning World Amateur Champion, was an overwhelming favorite and featured a loaded roster that included Luis Casanova, Victor Mesa, Lourdes Gurriel Sr., and Omar Linares. Fraser remarked that the Cubans "could probably finish third in the American League East."

Fraser chose his Miami assistant Brad Kelley, former assistant Jerry Weinstein, and Georgia Tech head coach Jim Morris as his assistant coaches. His roster was talented, but very young—"I've got to get special permission from their parents to play a night game," Fraser quipped about his squad. One-third of the team was not yet born when

Cuba last lost a Pan Am baseball game in 1967. Notable future Major League standouts Jim Abbott, Ed Sprague, Gregg Olson, and Tino Martinez, whom Fraser had recruited out of high school but elected to play alongside his brother at the University of Tampa, mixed with top college underclassmen, including Miami outfielder Mike Fiore.

International baseball was a different game. Fraser planned to combat veteran rosters and conservative styles of station-to-station baserunning and home runs with a riverboat gambler approach featuring an attacking offense of hit and run and stolen bases. It was the same recipe he used at Miami—and an occasional trick play was not out of the question. Fraser planned to rotate pitchers every few innings, regardless of performance, to keep opponents guessing. *Sports Illustrated* wrote, "The U.S. baseball coach in the Pan-American Games is crazy, but then he has his reasons."

The Americans started their pre–Pan Am Games tour 17-1 before a five-game series in Cuba, the first appearance by a U.S. team in four years. The Cubans intimidated opponents with a pregame routine of arriving late rather than taking batting practice (they took it elsewhere) to give the appearance it was not necessary. The state-sponsored team made a grand entrance and walked in from right field while laughing and acting if the upcoming game was no big deal. During games, the Cubans demonstrated aggressive play and did things like stepping on an opposing baserunner's foot.

"We'll intimidate right back," Fraser said. He understood the political dynamics of the many Cuban immigrants in South Florida. Facing Cuba, and beating them, was important to him, and he emphasized it to his players.

Much like a big party, a boisterous crowd packed the fifty thousand–seat Estadio Latinoamericano singing and dancing to music two hours before the game's first pitch. The Cubans won a one-run contest that night and a 7–3 decision the next night, though the atmosphere was vastly different.

The Americans noticed increased Cuban security and more restrictions when they arrived at the stadium for Game Two. The crowd again packed the stadium two hours prior, but it was almost eerily silent. A government official informed the Americans that Cuba's leader, el presidente, would be in attendance. The reference, of course, was to Fidel Castro, the dictator, who saw beating the U.S. team soundly on Cuba's home turf as a great propaganda opportunity.

With action ongoing during the first inning, the crowd behind the plate rose to their feet with polite applause as Castro, dressed in shiny, silk-like fatigues, made a grand entrance down the aisle to his front-row seat. The Cuban team stopped and rushed over to greet him as the crowd cheered wildly. When Cuba's players returned to their dugout, a delegate came over to Fraser and told him he could go over to meet el presidente.

Castro was a hot-button topic and not one for discussion with South Floridians who had recently come from Cuba. They hated him, and it was downright blasphemous to even speak his name. Knowing the political ramifications back home, Fraser told the Cuban delegate that he was not there to meet the president, he was there to play baseball. The delegate pleaded, and the lack of movement by Fraser and his team created awkward and tense anticipation as Castro waited.

Fraser told his players to stay right where they were. Castro would have to come to them. They were not going to him. Castro stood up walked back through the stands and came down to the U.S. dugout. Fraser was not going to shake his hand. Castro politely grabbed Fraser's arm in greeting and began shaking hands with the team, telling them it was a pleasure to have them in Cuba and, although the two countries did not see eye-to-eye politically, the Cuban and American people love sports.

"He had that little wink in his eye," recalled longtime Miami trainer Vinny Scavo, who was serving as the U.S. team trainer. "I'm thinking this guy [Fraser] is the best. That was unbelievable. I knew that was for Miami—all the people that struggled. He wasn't going to let them see him go up and meet Castro. He could come to meet him."

Fraser told USA Today in 1999 that he considered Castro's invitation "an intimidation thing," adding that "I don't want to be intimidated."

"He [Fraser] was politically astute and knew how to thread the needle between not offending and upsetting his countrymen at home but at the same time not causing an international incident by being disrespectful," recalled Barry Leffler, a former Miami student radio baseball broadcaster traveling with the team for a local television assignment and standing in the dugout at the time. "It was tense, but Castro relented and went along. If you think about life lessons, it was a perfect example of how to handle that situation properly."

The third game, played the following night, was also noteworthy. Fraser sent Abbott to the mound. Well-documented as being born without a right hand and adapting to switching his glove quickly to his throwing hand after each pitch, Abbott was a curiosity to the Cubans. Local newspapers were not so kind and labeled him "a freak."

Mesa led off the game with a high chopper off the plate. Abbott came off the mound, kept his glove on his arm, and waited before catching the ball and throwing out the speedy superstar at first. Fraser called it "one of the great plays ever, whether he had one hand or five hands." The crowd was in disbelief but cheered his outstanding play.

Thousands of fans remained outside the stadium well after the game's completion. Fraser and Abbott were the last Americans to head to the bus, and the large crowd was cause for concern without any context for their intentions. Fraser told Abbott they should go say hello and advised him to tip his hat as they made their way through the crowd. Fans cheered a new foreign hero, and Fraser later described the scene as giving him chills and the greatest show of respect he had seen.

"I didn't really know him [Fraser] that well, but we sort of bonded in that moment," Abbott said. "It was a striking moment and one that he and I loved sharing."

The United States won two of the first games, proved they could play with the mighty Cubans, and "got them thinking," as Fraser put it. Without ever admitting it, the Cubans were leery of Fraser's aggressive play and gamesmanship.

Great anticipation surrounded Pan Am Games baseball competition in a time when the Olympics were king of sports programming. Holding the games on U.S. soil just three years after the Los Angeles Olympics drew significant media attention, even though baseball round-robin games seemed inconsequential until the United States and Cuba clashed with 4-0 records.

Team USA took a 2-0 lead in the first inning before Cuba scored the next 4 runs for a 4-2 lead. Ty Griffin's seventh-inning solo home run cut the American deficit in half. A manufactured run, on Fiore's sacrifice bunt, knotted the game one inning later, setting the stage for one of international baseball's most dramatic finishes.

Tied at four in the bottom of the ninth and with two outs and the winning run at first, Griffin belted a two-run walk-off home run that sent 13,500 fans at Indianapolis Bush Stadium into a frenzy. Cuba's incredible twenty-year, thirty-three-game Pan American Game winning streak abruptly ended. The CBS national broadcast was baseball's equivalent to the Miracle on Ice, complete with similar storylines—a team of young American college players, on their home soil, defeating a communist state-run powerhouse amid Cold War political tensions.

"The Pan Am Games in a lot of ways were more special than the 1988 Olympics because the Cubans were there (Cuba boycotted the 1988 Seoul Olympics)," recalled Danny Knobler, who covered the games for *Baseball America*. "I don't know if there was ever as much attention paid to any international baseball game as U.S.-Cuba in 1987. The idea of kids playing against the Cubans was like the U.S. versus the Russians in basketball at the 1976 Olympics and hockey in 1980."

Just like Herb Brooks and the Miracle on Ice team, Fraser deserved a lot of credit for taking an underdog team, building its confidence, and executing an unconventional plan that led to victory. In another parallel to the famous U.S. hockey team, the memorable victory was not for the gold medal. Fraser joked after the game, "Do we get any kind of medal for this?"

After compiling a 7-0 preliminary-round record and a one-run win in the semifinal, the United States and Cuba met again for gold. Good fortune was not on the Americans side this time, however. After taking an 8–5 lead, they eventually fell, 13–9.

Winning two games in Cuba, waiting for Castro to come to his team, and the Pan Am Games victory over the Cubans were breakthrough achievements in USA Baseball's evolution. One year later the U.S. team won gold at the Seoul Olympics.

"That moment (with Castro in Havana) helped propel the U.S. to win in Korea in 1988," said Fiore, who later served as USA Baseball's collegiate general manager. "Nobody will connect the dots, but if you ask players on the team that night who went on to play in the Olympics the following year, they all felt what Fraser did when he said, 'We're not going to him, he'll come to us' was one of the best things ever. There was a confidence that all of us felt by waiting back and letting him come to the Americans. I think coach deserves a lot of credit for the way we played the Cubans and the way we played the Japanese, the two best teams in the world at the time. We went toe-to-toe with them and had a lot of confidence doing it.

"I give Ron a lot of credit for it because I was there in the dugout. His message and themes and ability to understand circumstances and pass it on to his team through psychology was part of the many things that made him great."

Two years after the Pan Am Games, Fraser broke through another political wall by taking his Miami team to the Soviet Union. Invited as the lone U.S. representative in the Peace in the World baseball tournament, the Hurricanes joined university teams from China and Japan and host Moscow University in opening the nation's first baseball stadium. Just the second U.S. collegiate team to compete in the USSR, Miami was the biggest name to appear behind the iron curtain.

Fraser predicted the Russians to be a force in international amateur baseball in less than a decade, citing that they had not played ice hockey until after World War II and developed into a dominant team. Fraser told Steve Pivovar of the *Omaha World-Herald*, "By 1996, I can see them winning a medal in the Olympics. It might not be gold, but they're capable of getting that far that quickly."

American entertainment was just beginning to reach the Soviet Union at the time. News of Miami's trip even elicited a call from Jon Bon Jovi, who had made a trip two months prior, to relay tourism tips.

"I don't know who Bon Jovi is, I should, but I don't," Fraser told media about the call. "I asked him if he was a baseball player and he said, 'No, man, I have a band.' I think he was a little upset I didn't know him."

The team stayed at the Hotel Moscow, the country's largest hotel and within walking distance to the Red Square. Each room had microphones to overhear conversations, and some team guests, including Fraser, had fun taking advantage of them. Fraser once said he didn't have ice in the room, and a few minutes later ice arrived.

Miami held its first workout next to the thirty-six-story Moscow State University building from the Stalin era. Just forty-eight hours before the first game, players practiced on a nearby asphalt track because construction of the new stadium was still ongoing. Fraser arranged a team photo in front of Saint Basil's Cathedral, the iconic Moscow building with ornate, multicolored spirals, and their appearance drew rock-star-like attention.

"He made sure we had a team photo in Red Square with the Kremlin in the background," said Kevin DiGiacomo, a rising sophomore on the team. "We didn't know how significant that experience would be in our life, but he recognized those things and made sure it was captured."

Much of the competition, however, lagged far behind a U.S. college program the caliber of Miami. Moscow State's baseball team was in its infancy. Their players stepped with the same foot when they threw—right-foot step for a right-hand thrower—much like some young kids do when first starting to play baseball. Fraser instructed his pitchers to throw only fastballs and changeups, no breaking balls. China's representative had technical skill, but lacked athletic strength and speed. Their players smoked cigarettes in the dugout, a significant cultural difference from a Miami team that wasn't allowed to chew tobacco. Even the game presentation was vastly different. The PA announcer was giving play-by-play accounts like a broadcaster, such as, "He's in the windup, here's the pitch" in Russian over the loudspeaker with play ongoing.

Facing Japan, Miami's closest competition, and tied in the bottom of the ninth of the final game, a Miami leadoff triple put the winning run at third. To entertain the crowd while scoring the walk-off run, Fraser called for a suicide squeeze with no outs—an unconventional decision in the situation. The play backfired, the runner was out at the plate, and the ninth inning ended in a tie. Not knowing that extra innings would not be played until informed following the inning, Fraser explained to his players what transpired. With a twinkle in his eye, he rationalized the situation: "What better way to end a World Peace tournament but in a tie."

"Coach Fraser took it upon himself to tell us you represent the U.S., and if you think about the time, it was the end of the Cold War. It was still Communist, and the wall didn't come down until the following spring," said Hurricanes pitcher Jim West. "When the tournament started, we were all standing in the outfield as teams, and they played each national anthem. I remember thinking that I never felt more proud. I looked around, and there were guys on the team with tears in their eyes as they played our national anthem."

Named as Team USA's 1992 Olympic coach in July 1990, Fraser called it the greatest honor ever bestowed on him and "as great an accolade you can have as a coach."

The U.S. team still needed a top-three finish at the 1991 Pan Am Games to qualify. Mississippi State's Ron Polk coached the team, and Fraser eagerly awaited the verdict despite full confidence in his colleague. He traveled to Cuba as television commentator for the games but forgot his passport and, despite talking his way into the country, could not enter the stadium. Eventually, a bronze-medal game victory put the Americans into the Olympics.

"He was a wreck down there because his job was on the line," recalled Polk. "Without his passport, he couldn't get into the games, so it made him more nervous. He listened to the games on radio from his hotel but didn't know enough Spanish, so he had to piece it together."

The 1992 Olympics was extra special for Fraser for a number of reasons. After previous demonstration-sport status, it marked baseball's first time as a medal sport—a goal he and Dedeaux worked toward for nearly twenty-five years. It also marked Fraser's return to Barcelona, where he began his career leading the Netherlands to the European Championship, making a fitting bookend after announcing his retirement that spring.

Fraser prepared thoroughly. A year prior, he visited the competition venues, including one cavernous stadium that measured 420 feet to center field and that he described as "looking like the Grand Canyon." He worked with the U.S. Baseball Federation to compile the initial list of ninety invitees, including five of his own Hurricanes, who tried out for the team during a ten-day November camp in Homestead, Florida. With its draft coinciding with the start of Olympic preparation, Major League Baseball allowed Fraser to protect twenty players from pressure to accept contract offers and turn pro until after the games concluded. Fraser wanted a roster featuring speedy contact hitters who could handle pressure and were easily coachable.

Morris, then coaching Georgia Tech, pushed his shortstop as a roster candidate. Fraser told Morris he would not take a freshman to the Olympics. After Georgia Tech played at Miami that spring, Fraser changed his tune and said, "That's my shortstop." Who had Morris suggested? Nomar Garciaparra, a future first-round pick selected twelfth overall before six All-Star selections during his fourteen-year Major League career.

Drawing on prior experience, Fraser knew his team of nineteen- to twenty-one-year-olds would face fierce competition from much older and experienced opponents. Cuba led the field and remained the most dominant team on the planet with a big, strong, and experienced team full of speed and power. The Cubans won the last twelve major international tournaments it played while amassing an incredible 67-1 record (the lone loss coming to Fraser's 1987 Pan Am team) and averaging more than 10 runs per game and allowing fewer than 3.

Leading up to the Olympics, Fraser repeatedly spoke to the media about Cuba's talent, once drawing a comparison between their team and his own as a "thoroughbred racing a donkey." He stated that Cuba was "better than Cleveland"—drawing the ire of Indians manager Mike Hargrove, who didn't find the comment amusing—with six or seven players on its roster who could be playing in the Major Leagues.

Japan's players came from the country's Industrial League, which compared to AA or AAA level in the United States. Employment in other jobs for companies like Mitsubishi and Nissan allowed retention of their amateur status for the Olympics. Puerto Rico and Taiwan were strong, veteran teams and played together for years. Nicaragua and even Costa Rica fielded underrated teams.

Fraser told *Sports Illustrated*, "If we win, it'll be a miracle—bigger than Jesus giving sight to the blind man, but smaller than Moses parting the Red Sea."

Fraser tried to temper expectations of U.S. media not in tune with international baseball competition. When he spoke about the expectations to win a gold medal, he compared the task to the 1980 Olympic hockey tournament where young U.S. college kids faced teams often ten years older and playing together throughout their careers.

Fraser's U.S. team had only been together five weeks but had talent. There were sixteen first-round picks, fourteen of whom reached the Major Leagues, looking ahead to pro contracts and big league pursuits.

The Olympics were not the ultimate prize like it was for players from other countries.

"It had to be a monumental challenge because we had guys making a lot of money in the draft," recalled Fraser's own Miami standout Jeff Alkire. "A lot of them were on the phones with agents, and a lot of business was going on while we were trying to gel as a team, which made it tough. We had guys trying to cut deals, get signed, get bonus money and shoe deals. I'm sure it was a challenge to keep us in line."

A grueling pre-Olympic barnstorming schedule featured exhibition contests in Major League ballparks nationwide. A daily publicity onslaught of luncheons and press conferences produced questions about the team and its gold-medal pursuits and drafted players' million-dollar contract negotiations. As media savvy as Fraser was, it was a lot to manage.

"The way he handled all the distractions, deflected it all away from the players and other coaches, was remarkable," said Mike Gaski, who served on the 1992 staff and later became USA Baseball president. "He was locked in and probably more competitive than I've ever seen anybody in my life."

In Barcelona, Fraser led the baseball team into Montjuic Stadium just ahead of the initial basketball Dream Team that featured the Hall of Fame roster of Michael Jordan, Magic Johnson, Larry Bird, and others. The International Olympic Committee fined Fraser's team $600 for allowing Bird, a former baseball player himself, to exceed the number of uniformed personnel sitting in the dugout when he attended during a basketball off day.

The Americans started 3-0 in the Olympics before their matchup against rival Cuba. Just like Fraser experienced with his 1987 Pan Am team, the Cubans badly wanted to beat the U.S. team. Cuba scored 5 runs in the first inning of a sloppy four-hour game that saw a combined 9 errors in a 9–6 final, won by Cuba.

The United States finished the round-robin with a 5-2 record, good for a second-place tie with Japan and Taiwan, behind 7-0 Cuba. The tiebreaker meant another matchup with Cuba, this time in the medal-round semifinals. The Americans fell, 6–1, to the eventual gold medalists and lost to Japan in the Bronze Medal Game. Despite not medaling, a fourth-place finish was quite an accomplishment, though not the result Fraser wanted in his final coaching role.

"If you asked anyone abroad in the 1960s, '70s, or '80s, who they thought of when they think about baseball, Fraser's name is in the top two or three," said Ish Smith, USA Baseball president from 1980 to 1989 and International Baseball Federation president from 1981 to 1993. "He certainly put the U.S. on the map internationally and was so well known throughout Europe. His name was gold."

"He basically got Holland's program started, and now they're the best program in Europe, no doubt," said Jerry Weinstein, Fraser's former assistant coach at Miami and with USA Baseball. "He was the godfather of baseball in the Netherlands."

The biggest influences on USA Baseball came from Dedeaux and Fraser. "They were really at the forefront of the game internationally," said *Baseball America*'s founder Allan Simpson. "In Fraser's case, he had a successful program in Holland, had a natural inclination to promoting the game internationally, and became quite involved in the U.S. Baseball Federation. Dedeaux helped bring it to life, and Fraser came behind him and was on the forefront of things that were happening in the 1970s. The two of them have to be the most prominent, from a college standpoint, in their roles in developing international baseball."

Fraser once summed up his world travels in baseball by saying, "I've met presidents, I was introduced to the queen of Holland, I had an audience with the king of Belgium—all because [of] my work in baseball."

8

Coaching Wisdom

Once described as a mix of Casey Stengel and Bill Veeck, Fraser compared favorably to both. No college baseball coach ever wore so many hats. Fraser could have earned Hall of Fame recognition strictly as coach or promoter and businessman.

Fraser's ability to connect with each person he encountered was a special gift. He knew his players well and listened to his assistant coaches, allowing him to push the right buttons at the right times. Fraser coached everyone fairly while treating everyone differently based on individual personalities.

Fraser often said, "There are two ways to go—first class and no class." He preached that anyone can do something, but better is to raise oneself up and do it with class. That was more than words. Fraser exuded class in everything he did in his program, from the way he handled people to how his team played, traveled, and appeared off the field.

Another piece of Fraser's advice was to "out big 'em" and "out last 'em," explained as "Be bigger than them and outlast them. They'll go away, and you'll still be standing." He also conveyed a similar and more common theme: "It's not how you start; it's how you finish."

Fraser had an unmistakable aura. He weaved his colorful anecdotes into any moment and teachable lesson he wanted to emphasize. The stories often included humor and almost always had listeners at the edge of their seats even when they heard the story before. His speeches had warmth and impeccable timing. He stopped midsentence to look around, give a smile, and tie it all together with the next words. When Fraser spoke, every word was heard.

"I remember being blown away listening to Coach Fraser's stories," said Joe Nelson, a middle infielder from 1984 to 1987. "By the time you were a senior, you had heard the story, but it had a new twist. You got to see the freshmen sit there completely starry-eyed at Coach Fraser. That was always fun to watch."

Fraser excelled as a psychologist long before teams at any level dedicated staff to the role. He believed people operated with their minds rather than physical reactions. He held a firm belief that no one functioned well under pressure. Hard work was the root of his philosophies. Fraser likened baseball to a classroom final exam, sending his team out on the field to test the opponent.

"He rarely talked through that night's scouting report. That was not him," said Mike Fiore, Miami's all-time hits leader. "What got him going was reaching his players through motivation, through psychology, and through comfort because as they understood the comfort and relaxation, he knew the players would go out and perform."

Whether speaking to the entire team, to smaller groups, or to a player one-on-one, Fraser had an incredible knack for communicating. He had a unique ability to make each person feel like he was talking directly to him or her.

He projected confidence that trickled down to his players. Pressure never bothered Fraser. No opponent or coach intimidated him. He was calm and cool regardless of the game score or situation and often joked about something to keep his players loose. Regardless of the score, Fraser was an optimist and never uptight in the dugout.

"I don't care where we played, Ron Fraser was the show," said Doug Shields, who played from 1981 to 1984. "When the coaches went out to home plate before the game, he glowed. The other coaches were all business. Frase was smiling and having a good time. His personality was bigger than all, and when he walked out it was a different tone."

Fraser had impeccable people skills and an ability to read each person and know what made him or her tick. He pressed the right buttons with Joel Green, a standout from 1969 to 1971, when mired in a sophomore batting slump.

"I was not doing so well, and he called me over to his house because I was sulking. I thought he was going to give me a pep talk," recalled Green. "He said, 'You've had a great career here at the University of Miami. I'll let you keep your scholarship, and you can stop playing.' Are you kidding me? It got me so pissed off I wanted to kill him." Green responded by going 10 for 14 at the plate and stealing 8 bases in the next series against Tulane.

Paul Hundhammer, who played a decade later, recalled the honest answers Fraser gave in meetings. After transferring in from a California junior college, Hundhammer found himself out of the lineup and asked Fraser about it. In a sincere straightforward response, Fraser simply told him to be better.

"I walked out of his office and really needed to look myself in the mirror," Hundhammer recalled. "I had to play better, so I got after it. It was just one of those moments that stuck with me for my entire life. You begin to understand what you need to do to be successful."

Players and assistant coaches witnessed firsthand the intuition Fraser exhibited during games. Sometimes a gut feeling prompted him to remove a pitcher before a big inning occurred. He always seemed to send the right pinch hitter up to bat in the right spot. Often, he was dead-on with his call for a particular play in a crucial situation.

"You could not make the mistake of trying to think ahead of him," said former Florida State coach Mike Martin. "You better be sure you have the right guy in the bullpen because he might have a pinch hitter getting loose in the clubhouse. He wasn't going to show his hand. He was one of those guys who was always ahead of you."

"He understood baseball," said Bob Bartlett, who pitched from 1971 to 1973. "He knew when to take out the pitcher. He knew when to bunt and when not to bunt. I think he was a master of the game and managed the game very well."

In a 1965 game, Fraser faced a critical late-game situation and without luxury of a deep bench. He sent Bob Sheridan, admittedly not a great hitter, in to pinch-hit with an instruction to get hit by the pitch. When Sheridan asked what he meant, Fraser told him to step in front of the ball and let it hit him because he wanted him to get on base.

"He called me back from the on-deck circle and said, 'Look we've got to get baserunners. Don't be afraid if he comes inside.' I told him I'd walk right into the pitch. He told me to do some pretty good acting, which I did," recalled Sheridan, who went on to a Hall of Fame career as a boxing commentator. "That tells you how good a player I was if he picked me to pinch-hit to get hit by a pitch. The funny thing was he probably never asked anyone else to do that."

Fraser had pronounced success using Randy Olen as a pinch hitter during the 1971 season. Olen reeled off eight pinch-hits in a row and finished the season 9 for 12 at the plate. With a .750 batting average, Olen's father asked Fraser years later why his son didn't play a lot more that season.

"I knew exactly when to use him," Fraser said matter-of-factly.

"My dad was astounded. That's the type of aura Coach had," Olen said.

Sometimes Fraser's personnel decisions were based on business. In 1989 highly touted Alex Fernandez pitched on Sundays, the day typically reserved for the No. 3 starter. His 15-2 record and 2.01 ERA indicated he was worthy of the top spot or at least a bump to No. 2. When Fernandez asked about the opportunity to move up in the rotation, Fraser told his young pitcher he needed him on Sundays because he brought in bigger crowds. The team already played to large crowds on Friday and Saturday nights, and Sunday afternoons typically drew less fans.

Fraser's teams played with energy and exuberance. Regardless of the setting—a midweek game in March, a rivalry game, a nationally televised Sunday night game, or an NCAA Regional Championship or College World Series—his team came prepared. That was a reflection of Fraser and his leadership. His team's preparedness started with the type of players he recruited—great baseball players but, just as important, quality people who understood they are part of a baseball family.

"You knew his kids were well coached, well mannered, and well behaved. They never argued with umpires and never created any problems with the other team," said Richard "Itch" Jones, who coached against Fraser during his thirty-six-year career at Southern Illinois and the University of Illinois. "You also knew his team would take advantage of any weakness you had, and they were not going to make mistakes. They beat you with good, sound baseball."

While Fraser had a long list of All-Americans and future Major Leaguers, he often featured rosters filled with smart, hard-working players and some who did not exhibit the most impressive natural skills. He built his teams with players who had baseball IQ and understood the game and its nuances.

Part of that roster construction came by need. As a private university, Miami did not receive state funds and had a very expensive tuition rate. It put Fraser at a disadvantage, which sometimes meant bare-minimum roster numbers. Few potential walk-ons were available, and many of those were not high school standouts. State schools might have a tryout attended by one hundred players, all of whom were prep stars. Fraser had to look deeper to find different types of players than the other schools recruited. He sought out grinders and emphasized character makeup. It was easy to find players who dominated at the high school level, but Fraser sought mentally strong players who responded to adversity. Fraser emphasized speed, pitching, and defense. Attention to detail was significant. Practice drills formed habits.

"We spent so much time doing the smallest tasks, whether it was an hour of reading pitches in the dirt or an hour working on one specific play you might use once in a season," said Wicho Hernández, who played on Fraser's final two teams. "His attention to detail was like nothing I've seen before."

If a player made a costly defensive error, Fraser typically did not address it because it resulted from effort made during a game. Mental errors were a different matter. If a player missed a sign, he came out of the game. Fraser stressed that mental mistakes had more effect on results than physical errors.

Describing his offense as "movement and pressure," Fraser employed a very aggressive style. He believed in putting pressure on the defense as much as possible because the team in the field likes to be in control. Fraser wanted his teams to create so much movement that the defense had to countermove, which took it out of control when the ball was hit.

"I always felt sometimes baseball gets a little boring so you've got to make it move and have excitement," Fraser once said in an interview.

Fraser's offense philosophy started with being a tough out. He took pride in players having more walks than strikeouts at the plate. He detested striking out. To him, great plays included a two-strike foul ball or drawing a walk. Miami played small ball, which perfectly fit its home artificial surface and large outfield dimensions. Players attacked, took the extra base, stole second and third, would use a hit and run on any count, bunted, and squeezed. Fraser's teams stole more than

175 bases seven times, and topped 200 stolen bases in four seasons, including a school record 231 in eighty games (2.89 per game) in 1985. In 1979, Miami set a school record by swiping 14 bags in a single game.

"When you played a Ron Fraser team, your pitcher needed to be within reason with his release time, your infielders needed to be on their toes, the catcher needed to have awareness that is off the chart, and your outfielders better have not relaxed in the least," said Martin. "If your second baseman or shortstop took a little nap because he was PO'd that he was 0 for 3 at the plate, their guys were going to steal third. If you threw to the wrong base or missed a cutoff man, they were going to take advantage of every mistake that you made."

Fraser continued to employ his style of scratching out runs even when the aluminum bat made home runs more prevalent and college baseball moved into its "gorilla ball" era. On several occasions the Hurricanes found a way to win despite being outhit on the scoreboard.

"Coach once told us at Texas that we may see a bunch of balls flying out of the ballpark but not to get down about it," said Kevin DiGiacomo, first baseman from 1989 to 1992. "'Keep scratching out runs, and we'll be fine,' he'd say. That was his philosophy, and it worked."

Fraser told his players to relax and have fun but instilled the need to perform so that fans would show up—translation: they had to take care of business and make the games exciting; otherwise, gate revenue would not cover the first-rate equipment and resources the players were accustomed to. He made a point to keep game times below three hours for fear of losing fan interest if games extended longer.

Fraser put his players in the best position possible to be successful. He laid his expectations out to his players, and it was up to them to meet them. He treated his team like grown men, much like professional players, and trusted them to act responsibly on and off the field. Fraser accepted nothing less. His players and assistant coaches did not want to disappoint him, just as they wouldn't a father. When Fraser spoke, his players were respectfully silent and listened closely. Discipline was important.

Jim Maler hit a dramatic go-ahead home run in a hotly contested 1977 game at archrival Florida State. As he rounded the bases, he gave a double-bird salute to the fans who were riding Maler and the Hurricanes all weekend. Fraser was livid and took him aside. He told

Maler that he embarrassed himself and the team and he never wanted to see him do that again. The verbal lashing was audible enough that many around the park could hear it.

"I received my correction very humbly," recalled Maler, who went on to a Major League career. "It quickly changed me from a cocky young ballplayer to someone who needed to learn and mature and show respect. I learned quickly from that one. He changed my life for the better."

Alex Fernandez generally arrived on time when he played at Miami but admittedly by just a minute or two. On one occasion he got to practice fifteen minutes late, and when he started to explain his tardiness to Fraser, the coach responded, "It's okay. No big deal. Just put your running shoes on." Fernandez spent the entire practice running. After practice ended, Fraser called Fernandez into the dugout. Thinking how thankful he was to be done, Fernandez was told he had another hour left and to turn off the lights when done. "I was never late for any of my coaches ever again," Fernandez recalled.

Fraser often sent messages to his teams in effective and memorable ways. There was no outwitting him. He devised a brilliant plan to track his players who had decided to leave the hotel and break curfew during road trips. There were multiple variations through the years, but a favorite method typically began by striking up an initial conversation about the team with hotel staff. In some instances, the employee was already a Canes fan; if not, he or she played the role.

When leaving the hotel for dinner, Fraser would give the employee a hat to wear and hand the person a brand-new baseball. He requested that the employee ask any player who came into the hotel after a specific time (11:00 p.m. or whenever curfew was set) to sign the ball. He asked to have the ball left at the front desk and provided a monetary incentive. Fraser picked up the ball the next morning and saw the names. When his team boarded the bus, he called out a list of names and asked them to get off the bus for some type of punitive running. The guilty players were left wondering how he possibly knew they broke curfew.

"Guys were writing their own name on their death sentence when they signed the baseball," said Chris Magno, the team's starting catcher in 1985 and 1986. "It was the most brilliant thing I ever heard and typical Coach Fraser."

Fraser did not anger often, but when he did, his team knew it. Running for hours after a game, until everyone had left the stadium, was the price often paid for not playing the game the right way. There were batting-practice sessions after night games and even a dawn scrimmage pitting the Early Birds against the Worms. (Fraser named the teams.) Times were different without NCAA practice limits.

"Ron could get very upset, but not yelling and cursing, when the kids played poorly at somebody else's ballpark," recalled Skip Bertman.

"At that time, you hated it, but you realized what it meant," said Dr. Marc Mestre, a freshman pitcher on Fraser's final roster who went on to become vice president and chief medical officer at Nicklaus Children's Hospital. "It wasn't a vindictive way or done in a manner to embarrass you. There was a certain expectation that was set. Don't embarrass the uniform because it means something."

Fraser told his players that when they put on the uniform, they no longer represented themselves, but the university. Once so upset at his team's lack of effort, Fraser told them they were embarrassing the university and had them wear their practice shirts inside out and put athletic tape over the M on their hats.

"You couldn't do that stuff now, but he did, and it worked," said Gino DiMare, who played four years under Fraser and spent twenty-four seasons on Miami's coaching staff, including five years as head coach. "The guys understood we weren't giving the effort we needed to give, and we weren't playing up to the standard the program stood for."

Typically, Fraser preached the big picture to his team after a loss. When not doing the little things resulted in defeat, it provided an instructional opportunity and learning experience. Fraser found the silver lining and positives to build his team back up and put them in the right frame of mind to be successful the next time out.

"I thought he did an excellent job of coaching us after a loss," said DiMare. "You've got to turn the page, learn from it, deal with it, and be able to bounce back the next day. He did that as well as anybody."

Fraser also reined his team back in when they won. If his players were giddy, he cautioned them about getting too far ahead of themselves or becoming overconfident. Fraser's expressions and tone of voice tempered the enthusiasm just enough so that his team remained focused on winning the next game.

On the rare occasion when Fraser needed a lights-out speech, he turned to his good friend Tommy Lasorda. The team needed a boost during a 35-24-1 season in 1987. Fraser thought it was time to bring out his big gun, and Lasorda delivered a pregame speech at a "win one for the Gipper" level. However, it did not provide the intended result.

"We're back in the locker room after the game, and Lasorda walks in and is like, 'Guys, I broke out my best stuff tonight. When I give a speech like that you're supposed to go out and win the damn game, not lose it!'" recalled Nelson. "He was so blown away that he gave his best stuff and we went out and lost. We felt terrible."

Renowned for his groundbreaking business work and promotions, Fraser took an innovative approach to coaching. Some of his visions produced on-field strategies adopted by other coaches.

Fraser established the closer's role in college baseball at a time when bullpens were not a priority for even the deepest teams. Following a bullpen-by-committee approach in 1973, Miami's relievers struggled to close out games. Fraser then brought Rick Floyd in when the game was on the line, sometimes for multiple innings, before saves were an official statistic. Floyd threw 61.2 innings in 24 appearances while compiling a 6–4 record and 2.47 ERA for the 51-11 Hurricanes, and a new trend began.

"Ron was a big believer that the role of the relief pitcher was becoming critically important in baseball at that point," recalled WVUM broadcaster Marty Connors. "He was ten years in front of his time in discovering that, and as the years went on, it really became more and more important."

Fraser employed an innovative sign system that was too complex for opponents to pick up during games. To make it easier to remember for himself and his team, Fraser assigned each position its own sign. All nine players corresponded to their position number on the field. Fraser pulled at his belt for the pitcher, number one. The catcher, number two, had a different sign, the first baseman, number three, and so on. Then he would start a sequence of signals. For example, if he pulled on his ear or the bill of his hat once, then the batter bunts; he could do nothing else. If Fraser pulled his ear or the bill of his hat twice, a hit and run was on. The runner could steal a base but had a different sign. If Fraser never touched the spot that corresponded with the position, the batter was free to do what he wanted at the plate. It made baseball's longstanding art of stealing signs nearly impossible.

"It was very unique, and I often wondered how the heck you could steal a signal because you never knew what was going on," said Warren Bogle, who later shared the system with friends coaching high school baseball. "They work very well, and no one can steal them."

Fraser's instructions could sometimes be confusing to his own baserunners. "If you were rounding second and on your way to third, he'd have his left hand up while his right hand was straight down by his knee," recalled Olen. "You'd come into third standing up, and if you were safe, he'd say, 'Good job,' and if you were out he'd say, 'Why did you miss the sign?' He was right either way."

Fraser employed a unique pregame infield regimen as fast as lightning. Fraser would hit one ball to get it started. Then he would hit a second ball and a choreographed two-ball infield warmup would begin. His players had to learn the routine and execute it because it was fast-paced action.

"It was really something else," said Mike Pagliarulo, who went on to an eleven-year Major League career. "Balls were flying everywhere, but it was done systematically. It was coordinated, so you had to be on time, and you were always moving. It was fun to watch for fans but was also a discipline of using your skill and getting ready to play."

Sometimes, the infield and outfield routine continued without baseballs; it was dubbed the phantom infield. Fraser told players they were going to be so good at it that the other team would wonder whether they used a ball or not. The Hurricanes performed it so precisely that it became an illusion to those watching. Fraser timed the routine to exactly ten minutes. It started with a ball hit to the outfield. The outfielder's throw came to second then to third, then to the catcher, who would throw to the guy standing next to the fungo hitter behind the mound. All the throws were timed perfectly, making it appear as though two baseballs were in use. Everyone moved with precision, and all throws appeared on target. When a slow roller was "hit" to an infielder, he pulled a baseball from his back pocket and threw to first to not give up the gig. Opponents thought it was crazy. The routine was typically used before the opening game of a series.

"It was like dueling banjos in the movie *Deliverance*," said Ron Scott, starting catcher on the 1974 and 1975 teams. "Coach thought it was great, and we were really good at it."

Fraser dared to be different with his team's uniforms and equipment. He created, developed, and designed distinctive uniforms utilizing Miami's orange-and-green combination. The Hurricanes were one of the initial teams to wear combinations outside of traditional home-white and road-gray uniforms, including an all-orange (jerseys and pants) uniform. Fraser outfitted the team in orange socks, a color uncommon at the time, and planned to use white shoes (when black was the only option) until the shoe company contract fell through. He came up with green gloves for the entire team, thanks to a deal with McGregor, for St. Patrick's Day.

Fraser tried using orange baseballs, at least during practice, before Charlie Finley attempted it with his Oakland Athletics. The color peeled off the balls, so they were never used in games. Fraser had the bases painted in the school's orange-and-green color scheme, but that did not last either.

In the late 1960s Fraser tried a peculiar approach to speeding up the pace of play. He thought players spent too much time between innings looking for their gloves before returning to the field. As a remedy, he had his players leave their gloves on the field after the inning, figuring the odds were slim that a batted ball would hit one. The idea did not catch on.

Fraser came up with an innovative defense to combat a sacrifice bunt intended to advance the runner from second to third. Typically, shortstop Joel Green would cover third as third baseman Bobby Flynn moved in to field the bunt. Fraser decided to create a diversion and attempted the idea at practice. Instead of charging in from third, Flynn stood directly in front of the pitcher, who threw the pitch over his ear to make it harder to see. Flynn asked Fraser if he was going to get killed in that fielding position. They tried the unique alignment before an umpire ruled it illegal.

Fraser kept his players loose and wanted them to play that way. In a one-on-one interaction during a stressful moment, he might go out of context and ask a player how many people were in the crowd or how many hot dogs or hamburgers sold that night. When the topic turned to business, it took the player's mind off the situation and put him at ease.

"If I'm standing at third against Florida State in what you'd think is an intense moment, coach would come over and say, 'Hey, Mags, how many people do you think we have here tonight? Looks like a pretty good crowd; I'm going to go with seven thousand. What do you think?' to loosen you up," recalled Magno.

Fraser interjected humor when his team appeared uptight. Fiore recalled a rain delay during a rivalry game against a high-powered Florida State team. Fraser's speech went something like this:

"Yeah, they're good, and we're going to have to play our best to beat them. I want you to understand why they have the record they have. It's not because they're talented. It's not because their coach is good. I want you to know they played really inferior opponents. Look, Mike Martin brings down these teams, and he gets a couple local yocals to take off the tires from their bus. They have to stay seven days, and they end playing this bad team for seven days."

"When he told the story, everybody just erupted," said Fiore. "There's nothing true about it, but the reality was he knew these games are meaningful and he sensed the team was a little anxious. He wanted his team to be relaxed, and what better way than to make them laugh, make them more comfortable, and make them at ease?"

Fraser knew how media relationships could mutually benefit his program. He was a savvy businessman who believed in the power of publicity.

"Ron would always take your call, and before I asked questions, he gave me three anecdotes because he knew they made a good story," recalled Jim Callis, who covered college baseball for *Baseball America* during Fraser's final seasons at Miami. "He understood perfectly what the media was trying to do and helped you do your job because publicity was good for the program."

Fraser embraced his student broadcasters from the campus radio station and treated them like part of the team. He knew that their broadcasts helped provide exposure to fans.

"He treated us as if we were ESPN," said Paul Frishman, who called games on WVUM from 1982 to 1985. "That's who he was. He made you feel like part of the team and part of the fabric of the program. He would spend so much time with us as students, giving us information so we could do our jobs and really tell the story of the program while on the air."

Fraser's vision included serving as the field manager, GM, and CEO. His need to hustle and financially support his own program more than anyone in the country meant missing practices and turning over many day-to-day coaching responsibilities. When he was at practice, oftentimes he had to step away to make calls promoting and selling.

Fraser surrounded himself with outstanding coaches and brilliant baseball minds. He put an immense trust in them to do their jobs while he handled the bigger picture. Bertman was his right-hand man for eight seasons and served as the nuts-and-bolts guy on the coaching staff. Fraser was secure and confident enough to publicly discuss Bertman's expanded role rather than claim all credit for himself. The two meshed perfectly and had a very unique arrangement in college baseball.

While Fraser met with key and influential people around South Florida, Bertman handled practice, preparation, and instruction. Fraser's appointment schedule never got in the way of his game coaching, but occasionally the duties collided. He always showed up to the ballpark in a shirt and tie, though sometimes his team was already taking batting practice, requiring a quick change into uniform.

"At times, he'd come running in, and somebody had to park his car," recalled Bertman. "He'd come zooming out to get the lineup card and go to home plate because he was playing tennis with some donor. Sometimes, he'd be on the telephone with someone even though the pregame was taking place."

Bertman was the pitching coach and had complete control over the staff. In his first season, he coached third base at his request and Fraser's insistence. Fraser had always coached third, and it was a difficult change for him. Fraser positioned himself in the corner of the dugout and smoked cigarettes at the time. When Bertman looked in for a signal, Fraser, who was not used to relaying them to a third-base coach, left him waiting. Other times, Fraser was engaged in conversation with someone who came up to the dugout. The arrangement did not last long.

"Skip was coaching third, and there were times he would come into the dugout and say, 'Coach, I'm looking for you to give me a sign whether you want to steal or hit and run. I look over, and you're standing in the corner of the dugout chatting with Tom, Dick, and Harry,'" recalled Stan Jakubowski about Bertman's first season under Fraser. "Coach Fraser could have success while showing more interest in other people than [in] what he was doing."

"Not his fault, he wasn't used to that," said Bertman about coaching third. "He came to me and said, 'I'll make you a deal—let me go back to third, and I'll give you autonomy with the pitchers,' and the deal was struck."

9

College Baseball Trailblazer

Fraser singlehandedly ushered in a new era of college baseball. While other coaches had more national championships on their résumé, Fraser's extensive contributions transcended the sport.

"I don't think you can overstate how important Ron Fraser is to college baseball," said Jim Callis, who covered the sport for *Baseball America*. "If you were ranking the most important people in college baseball over the years, I don't see how you could argue with Ron Fraser as No. 1. There are some great coaches and players, but I don't know how anyone could compare to what Ron did. He did it first."

What college baseball is today was nothing more than a dream in the 1970s. Fraser was bold enough to make Coral Gables the laboratory for growing the model college baseball program.

"Coach Fraser should be on the Mount Rushmore of college baseball because he helped promote the game to a standard many benefit from today," said Mike Fiore. "To me, that is his real legacy. In many ways, I think he might have known what was going to happen. That's the kind of guy he was."

Today's college baseball plays in front of large stadiums with raucous crowds. Almost every game is streamed or televised in some form. The sport continues to rise in popularity nationwide.

"Ron Fraser created the birth of college baseball as we know it today," said Dan Canevari, who coached under both Fraser and Skip Bertman. "He brought it up to a major sport. Skip Bertman, his disciple, took it to the next level. Ron's work was carried on with Skip, who learned all the other things besides baseball from him."

The impact and legacy that Ron Fraser left on college baseball is irrefutable. He accelerated the sport's growth by taking risks without fear of failure. Fraser's vision included bringing respect and dignity to

COLLEGE BASEBALL TRAILBLAZER 119

college baseball because he believed it was such a good product. The Associated Press wrote, "What [Ron] Fraser is doing with the Hurricanes program may set the tone nationwide for the future of college baseball." That bold statement foretold the sport's success.

Fraser held the unofficial commissioner of college baseball title during the 1980s. "Basically, he was the king of college baseball. What he did was a miracle," said Ron Polk. "He was the guy, and everyone said, 'This is college baseball, the guy that really started the big crowds, excitement, and the new stadiums going up.'"

Fraser merged his vision with his own personality and made a distinct effort to step beyond coaching and develop areas to build the foundation both for his program and the sport as a whole. His skill set, energy, and hard work set the bar and resulted in the blueprint for success.

When Fraser retired, *Collegiate Baseball* stated that "college baseball will never be the same again." The publication called him the "greatest showman ever to coach college baseball" and the one who "symbolized everything good that college baseball stands for."

Fraser used public relations, marketing, and sales better than anyone and well ahead of most in the sports world. He created a fan atmosphere beyond the game, and it spread nationally. Today, crowds of six thousand to eight thousand, and sometimes more, routinely pack the top college baseball stadiums during spring weekends. The trend began in Coral Gables before it caught on elsewhere.

"He'd bring in five thousand people in 1980," said Bertman. "He did for baseball what Arnold Palmer did for golf and what Muhammad Ali did for boxing. He was a superstar thirty to forty years ahead of his time."

Placing an emphasis on publicity, promotions, and a winning team, Fraser generated excitement. Fans flocked to Mark Light Stadium, regarded as the nation's premier college baseball facility and an inspiration for stadium construction. It was the place to be for baseball and entertainment.

For some visiting programs, Mark Light Stadium, with its large crowds and boisterous atmosphere, appeared to be a place from a different planet. An opposing coach voiced his disapproval of the raucous setting during the pregame umpire's meeting at the 1985 NCAA

Regional while music played, announcements bellowed across the public-address system, and the Maniac ran around on the field. The coach told Fraser, "You've got rock and roll playing, that loud guy on the PA, people in the stands, and that fuzzy rodent over there. That isn't college baseball."

Fraser promptly retorted, "Well, it's college baseball now."

Promotions turned games into events, which meant bigger crowds that generated more revenue. Miami's program was profitable and self-sustaining. Fraser showed athletic departments that baseball did not have to lose money. His work was an anomaly in a time when baseball drained the budget, no programs produced revenue, and very few broke even financially. As a visionary who ran his program like a business, Fraser formed the Coaches Committee to involve the area's leading businessmen in securing sponsorship deals and advising profit growth.

"If you want respect from your athletic department and from your athletic director and athletic community, you have to generate revenue," Fraser told *Collegiate Baseball* after his retirement. "As soon as we started generating income, it made all the difference in the world. At one time, we were making so much money for baseball that we were asked to give some of it back to the athletic department."

Fundraising was the pillar of Fraser's economic philosophy, which led to stadium and facility construction and upgrades. Miami led the way for other schools that took note and invested in their baseball programs and facilities.

"Coach Fraser knew if you want to attract the best players, you had to upgrade your facilities. You have to do all those little things," said Tom Baxter, who played for Fraser and became a longtime Division I assistant coach. "He changed a lot of administrators' minds and got them to think differently about what could be done with baseball. It certainly made the game better."

"He opened so many presidents' and athletic directors' eyes to say, 'Wow, college baseball could really be something,'" said Matt Tyner, who played for Fraser and later became head coach at Bellarmine University and Towson University. "The ones that have made the Fraser commitment and had the same vision . . . are self-supporting and make money."

Former Hurricanes players Ron Scott and Jerry Weinstein, a former assistant coach for Fraser, carried on his fundraising legacy in their own junior college programs. Scott, at Fresno City College, held annual dinner-dances that typically drew one thousand participants, a significant figure for a junior college and among the most successful at that level. Weinstein brought his Sacramento City College community together to build the flagship facility for California community colleges. Within two years, he had a two-thousand-seat stadium with batting cages underneath and an eight-thousand-square-foot locker room.

"Athletic Directors are figuring out what Ron Fraser showed them 30 years ago," Bertman told media at the 1994 College World Series. "If you can put a good baseball program on your corner, like a McDonald's, it will turn in a lot of money and turn out a lot of happy customers."

As revenues grew nationwide, so did coaching salaries. The need to win, draw fans, and bring in money added job pressure. At some schools, baseball moved closer to its football and basketball counterparts in the expectations for a return on investment. Those advancements connect back to Fraser's production at Miami.

His investment in a modern, first-class facility was well ahead of its time. While USC and Arizona State accumulated championships during the era of West Coast dominance, Mark Light Stadium set the bar for facilities and helped shift power eastward. Fraser's ballpark cathedral became the envy of the entire country. As college baseball's growth accelerated in the 1980s and 1990s, it produced a national construction boom and stadium arms race.

"Once you have the stadium, then comes all the marketing to get people into the stadium, and you provide them a good experience. It created a ripple effect," said Eddie Cardieri, University of South Florida head coach from 1986 to 2006.

Fraser opened doors with his impactful innovations. Earl Weaver compared Fraser's contributions to college baseball to what Babe Ruth did for growing Major League Baseball during his playing days.

He was among the first to institute fall baseball practice but took it a step further. Many schools, including some in the Southeastern Conference (SEC), held less than a dozen fall practices and simply sought players to fill out their rosters. Miami, meanwhile, played two dozen games against area junior college teams and drew crowds for

Friday Nights at the Light. Between fall, winter, and regular season, Fraser's teams played close to one hundred games during the academic year. The NCAA later imposed limits on the number of games teams could play and reduced the fall schedule to what amounted to a series of practices and intrasquad competitions similar to football spring practice. Eventually, the NCAA shifted back to allowing schools to play a limited number of fall baseball exhibition games.

At the 1992 College World Series, legendary Texas coach Cliff Gustafson summarized Fraser's contributions to college baseball by calling him "more responsible for the growth of the game in the last 25 years than any other one person," adding that "he has done so much for college baseball and done it in such a classy manner. He has been a pioneer in so many ways, made it so much easier for the rest of us."

Fraser spearheaded the most significant step in college baseball history when he went to ESPN headquarters in Bristol, Connecticut, in the fall of 1980. He set out to convince the one-year-old network to televise college baseball. Met with skepticism when lobbying by phone for several days, Fraser remained persistent. ESPN was unsure about the quality of college baseball or if enough viewer interest existed for a sport then considered obscure. Fraser countered that the sight of palm trees and baseball was enticing in February while snow covered much of the country, football season was over, and spring training yet to begin. Armed with Miami hats and jackets, Fraser walked through offices passing out souvenirs to everyone. He pestered them until the network, which needed programming, took the gamble and agreed to televise games.

ESPN agreed to air the entire 1981 season-opening series between Miami and USC. Initially, the network planned to air one game on delay, but Fraser persuaded them to show all three games live. The Hurricanes were gaining momentum, and the Trojans were considered the Yankees of college baseball after winning six national championships during the 1970s. Until its trip to Miami, USC had never played east of the Mississippi River. ESPN covered most of USC's travel expenses for the televised series.

"I remember my dad wanting to be part of it and talking about how big this could be for college baseball," said Justin Dedeaux, who was an assistant coach for his father at USC and worked as a color commentator on ESPN's College World Series broadcasts.

Fraser called ESPN the biggest factor in the development of college baseball's popularity and the sport's turning point. Prior to the agreement, televised college baseball was limited to occasional broadcasts of the final game of the College World Series on tape delay a week or two after its completion and often not in its entirety. Fraser believed College World Series attendance warranted live broadcasts and the exposure did not risk decreasing its crowds.

Placing any sport on television was challenging when only the national networks, ABC, CBS, and NBC, produced sports programming for national distribution at the time. Before ESPN, the chance for broadcasting college baseball was almost nonexistent. The sport was considered niche, and its interest compared more to college tennis than college football or basketball.

Starting with the Miami-USC series, the domino effect began when television ratings pleased the fledgling all-sports cable network. That led to a weekly game schedule that often included multiple Miami appearances. An ESPN rep told the *Miami Times* in 1982 that "everyone at the network loves 'em [Miami]. They're our team."

Television exposure catapulted interest in college baseball, especially among the schools appearing on the game broadcasts. Regular national television appearances sparked growth from obscurity to the big time. Overall national college baseball attendance was a mere 5.3 million in 1979, the year prior to ESPN's launch. By 1983, it more than doubled to 12.8 million. ESPN's regular-season game schedules grew to fifteen games in 1985, with most games airing on Sunday nights.

"People forget that Ron had college baseball as the Sunday Night Game of the Week long before Major League Baseball," said Fiore. "It's a great time slot. Those are the things that people do not really understand about his greatness. He understood how to take it to the next level. He was in a class by himself."

The ripple extended to the College World Series. ESPN began broadcasting every game, and the entire schedule aired live by the end of the decade. Television ratings grew. Attendance soared. The greatest explosion in popularity came during the mid-to-late 1990s, when the

College World Series became a focal point of ESPN's programming and a staple of summer's sports landscape. CBS became the first major network involved and forced the CWS to change its format from full double-elimination to a single-game championship from 1988 to 2002.

"The College World Series on ESPN was incredibly important in college baseball's rise to prominence," said Allan Simpson, founder of *Baseball America*. "When it went on ESPN, that's when college baseball really started coming of age. Miami was at the forefront of everything that was happening, and the reason was Fraser."

In 1979 the College World Series averaged 8,707 fans per session. A decade later, and after television helped grow the sport nationally, that figure nearly doubled to 14,762 by 1989. Today, average attendance routinely approaches 25,000 per game.

Polk told ESPN in 2016 that "Ron Fraser is the guy who woke this sport up. He's the one who turned the sport and the College World Series into what they are now."

Omaha, Nebraska, annual host of the College World Series since 1951, reaped rewards from college baseball's growth. In 2011 the CWS moved into a new $131 million, twenty-four-thousand-seat downtown ballpark that coincided with a twenty-five-year NCAA agreement to keep the event in Omaha. Baseball ranks second to men's basketball in the amount of NCAA Championship revenue produced.

"Fraser started the ball rolling, no question about it," said Polk. "If he was living today, he would be very proud of what college baseball is today, especially in the Southeast, with crowds and television coverage. These are the things he envisioned when he was at Miami."

Fraser developed the formula for creating a successful college baseball program. Bertman took it to LSU and carried it a step further.

When he took the job, LSU baseball was an afterthought, with just one NCAA Tournament appearance in its history. Bertman, despite averaging crowds of 918 fans his first season and playing in a facility he described as a "dump," began involving the community and creating G-rated family entertainment. He called his program a "Son of Miami" and used many of the same promotions, from San Diego Chicken appearances to money scrambles to garner interest. Every detail was important.

"I wanted to make sure seats were wiped clean, hot drinks were hot, cold drinks were cold, and the hot dogs were well done," said Bertman. "I told a group of LSU baseball boosters I wanted a clean women's restroom with a diaper-changing table. They thought I was crazy. I explained if Momma doesn't come to the game, nobody comes. If Momma can't enjoy the restroom and change the baby, nobody comes."

Bertman won the SEC Championship and achieved a top-five national ranking in his second season at LSU. By year three, he took the Tigers to Omaha for the first time. Bertman went on to eleven College World Series appearances and won five national championships to cement his reputation as one of the top coaches in college baseball history. In 2001, Bertman's final season as coach, the Tigers led the NCAA with over seven thousand fans per game, part of a stretch as national attendance leader in twenty-five of twenty-six seasons from 1996 to 2021.

"I got a lot of credit as a leader because I had big crowds at LSU, and now they have big crowds everywhere," said Bertman. "Ron was doing it ten years before me. I wouldn't have had the success I had without Ron Fraser."

While the modern-day SEC is college baseball's standard for on-field success, facilities, and investment in its programs, that was not the case before Bertman and Polk. When Polk arrived in Starkville in 1976, he was the first full-time head baseball coach in the SEC. Most of the league's head coaches were assistant football coaches filling their offseason in a part-time role. Teams played on dilapidated fields without any media attention, a far cry from the large stadiums and television appearances of today.

Considered the Father of SEC Baseball, Polk won more than 1,300 games and five SEC Championships, and he made sixteen trips to the College World Series over two stints at Mississippi State and stops at Georgia and Georgia Southern during his thirty-five-year career. He was adamant about growing the game across both the southeast and nationally. To aid the sport's development, Polk long advocated restoring scholarship levels with numbers capable of filling out a baseball roster rather than a golf or tennis squad.

Much like Fraser pioneered facilities and media growth, Polk and Bertman led the way in lifting SEC baseball from an afterthought to a top league in the 1980s. Athletic directors reached out to Mississippi

State and LSU to learn how they could make money from the sport. They poured resources into baseball and built new stadiums. Success brewed interest, and television coverage grew exponentially. Bertman told ESPN.com in 2016, "Anyone who has ever attended a game in Starkville or at Alex Box Stadium in Baton Rouge knows that Ron Fraser's fingerprints are all over those places."

The SEC won its first national championship in 1990. The following year, Bertman won his first of five CWS titles in ten years. SEC schools continued raising the bar and grew into the most competitive conference in the nation, annually fielding championship teams and leading attendance figures. Today, eight SEC stadiums seat more than six thousand, including four with capacities exceeding ten thousand.

"If he was alive today and saw the twelve thousand people at LSU or Arkansas or Mississippi State, he'd go bananas," Bertman said of Fraser. "He was the guy who did it. He was very underrated for what he did for the college baseball scene and getting people to watch the game."

Places such as Baton Rouge and Starkville, later Fayetteville, and most of today's other baseball-crazed locations are in places where the university is the focal point. By contrast, Fraser made college baseball a priority in Miami despite the endless entertainment and recreation options and well before the sport gained widespread popularity.

"You could definitely argue that Ron Fraser might be the most important figure in college baseball history," said Callis, "I don't think college baseball would be what it is today without him. He showed the template for building a program. And he did it in Miami, a big city, not an area where the university is king and there is nothing else to do."

Fraser openly shared his blueprint beyond his former assistant coaches. He encouraged fellow coaches to take the next step with their programs by sharing ideas and insights. Fraser never viewed other programs as a threat to his own success. His mission to help broaden the game's national appeal reached across Florida and nationwide, including areas not considered baseball hotbeds. Programs like those at the University of Maine and other northern schools benefitted from his advice and became better.

"The thing that is really cool is that he was so willing to share his vision, and when you're in the coaching business, there are a lot of guys who don't want to do that," said Rob Cooper, who went on to coach Wright State University and Penn State University. "Some of the best growth in college baseball was during the period when Fraser was at Miami. His willingness to share his vision and not just keep it in Coral Gables changed our game."

His vision and determination, along with his combination of charisma and wit, made him college baseball's national spokesman. In 1989 the American Baseball Coaches Association selected Fraser as recipient of the Lefty Gomez Award, an honor given annually to the person who has distinguished himself in amateur baseball. Fraser often presented at the ABCA Convention, explaining his recipe for success to peers from all levels.

"Coaches and administrators said I want to be like Miami," said Ty Harrington, who played for and coached under the legendary Cliff Gustafson at Texas before twenty years as head coach at Texas State University. "They needed a nice facility, a great atmosphere, and to put money into it. Look around at the stadiums—it's unreal. The SEC and ACC facilities are through the roof. Look at attendance in 1985 versus today. I think he's responsible for that."

Fraser advised his friend John Winkin about building his program at University of Maine. Based in the Northeast corner of the United States in a climate not ideally suited for a February–May schedule, Fraser regularly invited Maine to play at Miami and arranged games to be part of ESPN's schedule. The Black Bears gained unprecedented exposure, and their baseball program made six College World Series appearances before the school won its first hockey national championship. Winkin built the Northeast's top program, hosted six NCAA Regionals, and even brought warm-weather powers Miami, North Carolina, Oklahoma State, and UCLA in for series.

Sacrificing a home weekend for the cold of Maine, Fraser scheduled a 1986 series to help his friend's program. It was the first time a big-name program came to Orono, Maine, and the weekend became a major local event. When Miami flew in for the series, multiple marquees around town read, "Welcome University of Miami Hurricanes."

The teams held a joint lobster bake and autograph session as a fundraiser. Before the opening game, Fraser and Winkin boarded a two-seat Mercedes and waved to the crowd as a driver delivered them from center field to home plate. Miami players tossed fresh oranges to the crowd. Famous author Steven King, a Maine native, threw out the first pitch and provided copies of his newest best-selling horror novel to the players to commemorate the event.

"The atmosphere of having a team like Miami play in Orono was unbelievable," said Mike Coutts, then a Maine assistant coach. "I remember Wink and Ron talking about getting Miami up there and how great it would be."

Winkin often stated he wanted to be the "Miami of the Northeast," pinpointing Coral Gables as college baseball's epicenter. Fraser advised Winkin on how to grow his program with the right facilities while supporting and encouraging him to think big. Adding a new clubhouse and lights opened doors for Winkin to lure high-quality opponents and postseason games to Orono. Maine's improvements aided its recruiting in New England, allowing retention of players who typically left for southern programs.

"People across the country thought, *Wow, college baseball is really on the map now*," said Coutts. "[Hosting] wouldn't have happened if Wink wasn't able to build the clubhouse and lights, and that was spurred on by Ron Fraser. Every year we came back from Miami, Coach Winkin had new ideas based on his conversations with Ron. I think that kept him motivated."

Fraser scheduled a two-game fall exhibition series at Notre Dame in 1988 around the highly anticipated, nationally televised football game between the two schools, which ranked first and second in the national polls at the time. Dubbed the "Battle Before the War," the series featured Miami first-round picks Joe Grahe and Alex Fernandez and Notre Dame's future Major Leaguer Craig Counsell. The opening game drew more than five thousand fans, the largest crowd in Notre Dame history, despite 28-degree weather. Murphy, in his second season, wanted his team to play the best and called his two wins the turning point for the program. He expressed his appreciation by calling Fraser a class act and his program the epitome of college baseball.

"Ron taught me it's okay to help other programs. The other coach isn't an enemy, and you can work together," recalled Murphy. "He had a view of the big picture and cared about the college game like no other. Few have had the impact he had on college baseball."

Fraser helped grow college baseball in his backyard—Florida—without fear of the competition. While coaching at South Florida, Eddie Cardieri met with Fraser and Promotions Director Rick Remmert to get ideas how to get better crowds.

Miami traveled to play at Stetson University, Florida Atlantic University, and even Division II Florida Southern College. Fraser told coaches, "I'll put you on the roster" (referring to the schedule), though his team had everything to lose and nothing to gain by playing the schools. He scheduled the games to help provide exposure to their programs because he realized the challenges coaches faced. Fraser took Miami on regular trips to DeLand, Florida, knowing that playing Miami drew large crowds for Stetson.

"Ron didn't have to come up and play us as much as he did, but he made the commitment to make the trip every other year," said Pete Dunn, Stetson coach from 1980 to 2016. "He truly wanted to build and promote the college game, not just Hurricane baseball."

Dunn drew from Fraser's promotions and introduced them into his own program. When Stetson built a new stadium in 1998, it held a black-tie fundraiser that included dinner on the field and orchestra atop the dugout.

"I enjoyed observing and learning things from him that I could take and incorporate into my program," said Dunn. "People emulated [Miami] and copied the things he's done to promote their own program since he was there."

Florida Atlantic started its baseball program in 1981. One year later, FAU faced Miami for the first time after Fraser agreed to play at least twice each season. Merely getting a program of Miami's caliber on the schedule was a big step. FAU won three of the first eight meetings between the schools and gained instant credibility. Fraser praised FAU coach Steve Traylor and his program, earning the program further credibility, and recommended the school to coaches seeking games on trips to South Florida.

"I think it was the watershed moment of FAU baseball," recalled Traylor of the first win over Miami in 1983. "When Ron would talk to the media, he always gave kudos to our players and [me] and what we were building. That was huge, more than money could buy, just beyond belief in terms of what it meant for our program. It may have advanced the program by a decade."

Several successful college head coaches can trace roots back to the Wizard. "Every coach should be lucky enough to coach under the master," Bertman said of Fraser.

Scott, who caught for Fraser's 1974 and 1975 teams, took lessons from many experiences with him on the way to becoming the winningest coach in California community college history with over 1,000 victories in thirty-four seasons at Fresno City College.

"I am forever indebted. He was truly a special guy for me, and the more I was away from him, I realized how special he was," said Scott. "He let me run the game [as catcher] and asked me what I thought when he made a mound visit. We were coached in practice, and we got to play the game. That is a philosophy I learned from him. He let us play and offered little things during the game to help us if we needed it."

A 1974–75 teammate of Scott, Tom Holliday, got his start in coaching when Fraser offered him an opportunity after graduation. Gino DiMare played on Fraser's last four teams before spending nineteen seasons as an assistant coach under Jim Morris and five years as Miami head coach from 2019 to 2023.

Cooper began his coaching career as a student assistant with the help of his college coach, and former Fraser assistant, Jerry Weinstein. Cooper arrived on campus the fall following Fraser's retirement in 1992, but the influence Fraser had on his career was instrumental.

"He was invested in me and always made me feel like I was one of his guys," recalled Cooper, who pursued his master's degree in sports management while assisting with the baseball team. "He was really good about saying, 'That is a great idea, but you have to look at this also.' What I really tried to pick up from him is hire really good assistant coaches, let them coach, and don't micromanage. Free players up to play and perform, almost in an artistic way. When they struggle, you as the head coach shoulder the blame. That's what I've tried to do, and I draw that back to him."

In many ways, Morris is traced to Fraser, even though their only coaching experience together came when he was an assistant on the 1987 U.S. Pan American Games staff. The relationship began when Fraser befriended Morris as a young Red Sox farmhand working out on Miami's turf before spring training in 1974. As Morris went into coaching, he sought advice from Fraser. When Morris took over the Georgia Tech program in 1982, his home field had two sets of bleachers. A Coca-Cola machine was the only concession. He duplicated Fraser's approach to generating revenue from annual yearbooks and outfield-wall signage. Morris created a twenty-five-person coach's committee filled with successful Atlanta-area businessmen with Georgia Tech ties. Just like Fraser, he believed the more money he brought in, the more he would get to spend. If he did not bring in money, he was limited in what he could do. Morris credited Fraser as having more influence on his building Georgia Tech into a national contender than anyone else.

When Tulane hired Rick Jones, a former assistant coach under Morris at Georgia Tech, as head coach in 1993, he asked Fraser to attend his introductory press conference. Fraser, who had helped Jones in his candidacy, obliged and went with him to meet with influential donors and explain how he built his program at Miami. He told Tulane supporters they had the right guy and believed Jones could have similar success at a small private school with a modest baseball history situated in a major city.

"I had to raise money [and] put people in the seats, and we had to win," said Jones, who turned Tulane into a national contender, ascending to first in the polls and reaching the 2005 College World Series. "He had a blueprint for that. We followed it, and it worked. He showed—and we were able to do it at Tulane—that baseball can actually make money for your athletic department.

"Every opening day, I mean every year until he passed, I'd pick up the phone and call Coach Fraser and say, 'Coach, it's opening day, and I just want you to know I wouldn't be here if you hadn't made this happen for me, and I'll always be appreciative.'"

Fraser accomplished things no one else had done before him. Those achievements traced back to the fundraising-and-promotion seeds that eventually blossomed nationwide. Jay Rokeach, the most famous public-address announcer in college baseball, created Fraser's nickname "The Wizard of College Baseball" in the mid-1970s. It stuck and reflected the coach's contributions still felt today.

"Ron Fraser did not get enough credit for what he did for college baseball," said Mike Martin, friend and rival coach at FSU. "He was a great ambassador for the sport."

In 2001, *Baseball America* named Bertman No. 2 and Fraser No. 3, behind only USC's Rod Dedeaux, as the century's best college coach.

"While Rod Dedeaux had the most success in terms of championships, I think Ron had a greater influence on more programs," said Callis. "He was a resource who encouraged other coaches. If a coach was trying to build something, he could call Ron, and [Ron] would help them and give advice."

Like a genealogy tree, nearly every important advancement in college baseball links back to Fraser. Today's fan interest, stadiums, and broadcasts are better than ever across the SEC, in Omaha, and on most campuses nationwide. All share a common thread back to Coral Gables.

"Ron Fraser created what we know today as college baseball, whether it is television or the fans," said Luis "Wicho" Hernández, a former Miami standout and analyst on ESPN college baseball broadcasts. "To think that here's a guy who hasn't coached in over thirty years, who outside of Miami shouldn't really be known much, his impact on college baseball is incredible. When you look at what he did and where we are over thirty years later, it's really legendary."

10

Professional Baseball

A friend of seemingly everyone in baseball, Fraser was closest with Dodgers icon Tommy Lasorda. The two originally met in 1952 during a tryout in Brooklyn. Lasorda was a farmhand in the Dodgers' Minor League system, and Fraser aspired to play professionally while concluding his high school career in Nutley, New Jersey.

The two became friends in the 1960s after meeting at a party before a World Series game between the Yankees and Dodgers. Fraser, who had been coaching in Europe, had two extra box-seat tickets from then commissioner Ford Frick and gave them to Lasorda, a Dodgers scout at the time. Lasorda, who had upper-deck tickets, asked Fraser how a college coach had such good seats. The two formed a bond from there and grew as close as family until Fraser's final days.

Fraser and Lasorda were exceptional baseball promoters with bigger-than-life personalities. They treated people with respect, dignity, and class. Fraser bled Miami's green and orange. Lasorda, of course, bled Dodger blue. Fraser was much more low-key than the boisterous Lasorda. One sportswriter jokingly called Fraser a "more stable version of Lasorda" when comparing the two.

They spoke frequently about baseball and life and appreciated each other's company and friendship. Lasorda often called Fraser after victories, waking him up when neglecting the three-hour time difference between the two coasts. They visited each other as often as their schedules allowed. Lasorda typically made appearances in Coral Gables to speak to the Hurricanes team prior to starting spring training in nearby Vero Beach and was a featured speaker at the team's banquet. On occasion, Lasorda would sit in the Miami dugout during a game. In some ways, he was an extension of Fraser's staff, leaving his college players awestruck.

"Coach would get people every year to tell incredible stories to the team," recalled Chris Magno. "We'd have Tommy Lasorda hanging out in our dugout. You felt a bit like a movie star when you played for Miami. It was an unbelievable experience."

Phil Lane recalled a time he stopped by Fraser's office when the coach had just returned from playing tennis. Fraser was talking on the phone to a guy named Tommy. When Fraser went to change shirts, he told Tommy to talk to Phil, his third baseman, and turned the phone over. Lane had no idea with whom he would be speaking.

"I got on the phone and he's asking me about the team, and I'm like, *Holy shit, it's Tommy Lasorda,*" said Lane. "Not only am I playing for Coach Fraser, but I'm sitting in his office on the phone with Tommy Lasorda."

Lasorda gifted Fraser with cases of Ultra SlimFast products while appearing on famous television commercials in the late 1980s and early 1990s. When the two compared their weight-loss results and Lasorda admitted to not losing as much as he intended, Fraser jokingly told him the shakes were not to be had with meals, but as replacements for the meals.

"In a way, Tommy was the father my dad didn't have," said Fraser's daughter Cynthia. "Even though they were friends and not that different in age, he was a father figure or big brother to him."

Fraser took Lasorda to one of his high school reunions. When Lasorda was anywhere near South Florida, he would visit Fraser's home to have dinner and stay overnight. On one trip, Lasorda received an award, and Fraser's grandson happened to be staying at the house. When toddling into the guest room, the young boy found Lasorda asleep in the bed and enthusiastically yelled out, "Uncle Tommy!" Lasorda, despite exhaustion from travel and an awards event the night prior, eagerly greeted him and gave him the big glass trophy award he had received.

Fraser brought Lasorda to one of his grandson's Little League games to give a pregame speech. On another occasion, Lasorda took Fraser's grandsons around the Vero Beach training complex and treated them like royalty. They drove around on the golf cart together, went into the players' locker room, gathered equipment and gear, and moved to the front of the dining line.

After retiring as coach, Fraser served as an advisor for player development during Dodgers spring training. He evaluated Minor Leaguers during spring training and the instructional league and gave input about how quickly players may ascend through the system and which level best fit them. The position kept him active in baseball alongside his pal Lasorda and former assistant coach Jerry Weinstein, who served as the Dodgers director of player development at the time.

Fraser's personality and his involvement across baseball, coupled with the University of Miami's facilities and proximity to several spring training sites, created unique opportunities to invite Major League players to campus. Whether working out during the off-season, arriving ahead of spring training, or living in the area after retirement, many pros visited Mark Light Stadium. Fraser's players benefitted from accessing a who's who of baseball stars willing to share insight and experiences.

Yankees legend Joe DiMaggio visited a preseason practice soon after Fraser started at Miami. A few days later, Joltin' Joe remembered a flaw in the swing of one of the players and phoned Fraser. He provided some corrective tips, and Fraser began using them with Ernie Yaroshuk, the player whose swing DiMaggio recalled. Yaroshuk hit .448 that season and signed with the Philadelphia Phillies organization.

Ted Williams, who lived in the Florida Keys and became a fishing buddy of Fraser, visited Mark Light Stadium several times. He helped Hurricane players with hitting tips during individual batting-cage instruction and addressed the entire team after practices. Fraser talked him into being part of pregame festivities for the first regional Miami hosted.

Fraser held clinics at Mark Light Stadium, bringing in names like Williams, while he managed the Washington Senators; Bobby Richardson, the former Yankee coaching at University of South Carolina; and even Mickey Mantle.

At one session, Mantle wore a microphone to talk about hitting while demonstrating against live pitching. A problem ensued when Mantle stepped into the batter's box. The batting-practice pitcher got the yips and could not throw strikes, and Mantle became frustrated.

Fraser stepped in to save the situation and threw BP, and he and Mantle became fast friends.

"He would bring in these superstar people," said Roy Firestone, a former WVUM broadcaster who became famous for his ESPN talk shows. "I don't know how he did it, but he was able to convince his friends, or at least his celebrity friends, to help get buzz for University of Miami baseball."

Several retired players living in Florida made commercials and instructional videos at Mark Light Stadium. Williams filmed videos and photos for his instructional hitting book and DVD series. Mantle and Reggie Jackson shot commercials there. Active players worked out on campus to prepare for spring training. Location played a factor, but it was Fraser who attracted the big names to his program and facility and got them involved with his players.

"The connections were incredible," recalled Fraser's daughter Lynda. "Once he started getting some of those big names to come to campus, he brought those experiences and opportunities to his players. I don't know how he did it."

The Baltimore Orioles' spring training site in Miami led to several connections. Fraser befriended legendary manager Earl Weaver and scheduled exhibition games against the Orioles at Miami Stadium. He even convinced them to come to Mark Light Stadium for games. Orioles players spent time working out with Hurricanes and advised them about tools of the trade, leaving most players in awe.

"It was a big thrill just to play against that uniform," said Bob Sheridan, a Hurricane in 1965. "We sat on the bench admiring them— Boog Powell, Mark Belanger, Davey Johnson—and Fraser got on us and told us not to look for autographs."

When the 1990 Major League Baseball lockout disrupted the start of spring training, Cal Ripken Jr. spent nearly a month working out with the Hurricanes. He took pregame infield with the team and used its batting cages. The college players, already playing regular-season games, gave him his space but soon found out that Ripken wanted to interact more, talk baseball, and share his knowledge. Ripken acted like part of the team and did the same things as the Miami players, except he was not on the game roster. If a batting-practice round consisted of two bunts, a hit to the right side, and eight swings, that is what he did. He took ground balls and worked on double plays with the Hurricanes infielders.

"He's taking infield with us. He's taking BP with us," said Kevin DiGiacomo of Ripken's workouts with the Canes. "The other team is sitting in the dugout watching him standing there at shortstop taking our pregame with us. How intimidating is that?"

As Major Leaguers prepared for spring training, others also came and worked out with the Hurricanes. Miami players faced pitcher Dennis Martinez. Jose Canseco came and took batting practice. While attempting a 1991 comeback, Jim Palmer worked with Miami's pitching coach Lazaro "Lazer" Collazo. Fraser summoned Palmer to pitch batting practice to the team until he learned that the NCAA prohibited outsiders from doing so.

"Because of Coach Fraser, we got to meet and have access to all these guys," DiGiacomo said of the experience. "It was crazy, but it was pretty cool."

Fraser took his early teams to the Kansas City Royals complex in Sarasota for instruction and games against the organization's Minor Leaguers. He scrimmaged with the New York Yankees. Besides the Orioles, he brought in the Atlanta Braves, managed by his friend Joe Torre, who had Bob Gibson as his pitching coach. The Montreal Expos came to Mark Light for exhibition games. Bringing MLB teams to campus is unfathomable today, when the rare exhibition games played between college and big league teams are held exclusively at spring training sites.

Never fearful of any competition, Fraser used opportunities with Major League players to further instill confidence in his teams. When facing MLB teams in exhibition games, he told his players the Major Leaguers still had to swing the bat, needed to throw the ball over the plate, had to pitch, and needed to catch ground balls. Miami only won once in a combined fourteen MLB games, in 1982 against the Orioles, but the experience was unparalleled.

Fraser's players often received guest instruction from the sport's best tutors. Cookie Rojas worked with middle infielders for a number of years. Pitcher Thom Lehman had Orioles pitcher Dave McNally take him down to the bullpen and teach him how to throw a slider. One day, Fraser told Pagliarulo to ask "that guy over there" about how to make the bunt play at third base while pointing to Hall of Famer Brooks Robinson, arguably the greatest third baseman of all time.

"I couldn't get that instruction anywhere else," Pagliarulo recalled. "In one minute, Brooks Robinson told me how to make that play. Then I became one of the best at it. That had so much impact on my career, and it was created by Fraser."

Those types of lessons made monumental impacts on the college players. Pagliarulo, a Boston native, talked hitting with the Williams. The Splendid Splinter taught the importance of watching pitchers while Fraser sat back, smiled, and observed the interaction. That type of access became a benefit of playing at Miami because of Fraser and his connections. In many ways, the legends became extensions of Fraser's staff and part of his program while providing valuable resources to his players.

"It's like all those people were at Miami also," added Pagliarulo. "Those things really stand out more than anything. I was like a sponge. Those things had a big impact and stuck with me my entire career. I would have never had that experience. . . . I got that in college for crying out loud. You learn things and don't forget them when you learn from people like that."

Fraser had offers to join Major League Baseball teams but never accepted. Coaching professional baseball was not an option, though he likely could have been successful given his knack for managing players.

"What, am I going to tell some guy making $1.6 million to bunt? To hit and run?" Fraser told media in a story speculating about a professional opportunity. "My style is for college kids. You take young ballplayers, they believe in you. My style of baseball doesn't fit Major League Baseball."

Fraser found front-office opportunities intriguing and had several overtures during his coaching career. Only twice did he seriously consider leaving. One of those opportunities came in 1976. The Chicago White Sox wanted him to lead its player development department and offered nearly double his $24,000 Miami salary. Fraser turned down the offer and received a new five-year contract at Miami soon after. He called it one of his toughest decisions but felt like he belonged where he was.

Fraser tried to get his friend Burt Chope involved in buying a team and moving it to New Orleans to play in the Superdome. Chope, however, preferred to bring a team to Miami, but the commissioner's office was against the move. Fraser was set to serve as the team's general manager and his graduate assistant Tom Holliday as the bench coach. Fraser asked Holliday to answer Chope's questions about structure and costs involved in operating a franchise. Eventually, the potential deal fell through due to financial terms.

The closest Fraser came to leaving for professional baseball came a few years later, when George Steinbrenner contacted him about a position with the New York Yankees. During the 1979–80 offseason, Steinbrenner sought a recommendation from manager Dick Howser for someone from the college ranks who could oversee the Yankees' Minor League operations and scouting. Fraser, a college teammate of Howser, was the first name that came to mind. Fraser received the offer while in Holland conducting two weeks of baseball clinics.

"When Ron was approached by professional baseball, we would discuss it as a family," recalled his first wife, Liane Fraser. "He had a lot of resistance about leaving his supporters at Miami. We would come back with a counterpoint that gave him balance to make his own decision. Whatever he decided, we were all in."

Fraser wrestled with the decision. The salary reportedly doubled what he was making. Yankee Stadium was only about twenty minutes from his hometown. The job, however, required significant travel to check on the team's Minor League affiliates. At Miami he had built a perennial College World Series contender and was closing in on an elusive first national championship. Two of his daughters were in college and his youngest in high school. Plus, Steinbrenner had a reputation for not being an easy person for whom to work. Still, there was a sense in his inner circle that Fraser was going to leave.

After making calls and seeking advice, Fraser was reminded that at Miami he could do what he wanted. Working for Steinbrenner meant being on call twenty-four hours per day. Mantle and Ford called Fraser and advised him against the move because he could be fired at the drop of a hat. Jerry Reisman, who played for Fraser from 1963 to 1965 and later became a close friend, spoke with him about the decision.

"I told him here [at Miami] you are the magician," recalled Reisman. "You go to work for Steinbrenner, and you'll be the puppet. Can you handle that?"

When Fraser called Steinbrenner to decline the job, the Yankees owner said he would not take that answer from a college coach over the phone and demanded that he board a flight to meet in person. Steinbrenner's private plane was in Miami.

Fraser arrived at the airport in short sleeves, figuring he was flying to Tampa where Steinbrenner lived. Instead, he was informed he was heading to New York. Upon arrival, someone greeted him, handed him a coat, and brought him over to a car with a private driver. When the driver delivered him to the building, Fraser went to the top floor, where Steinbrenner's secretary greeted him. She showed Fraser the stadium and his private office. When he met with Steinbrenner and informed him he was staying on as Miami coach, Steinbrenner told him not to worry and that the Yankees would get him someday. The two shook hands, and Steinbrenner walked out of the room. Fraser, unsure what to do next, told the secretary he needed to get to the airport. She informed him the team would call him a cab, and Fraser ended up having to pay for his flight back home.

"He always ran his own show, and I remember him saying that he ran his own deal here [at Miami]," said Fraser's daughter Cynthia. "He wasn't used to taking directions, even from the ADs, and they didn't touch him. I think the Yankees would have been a different dynamic for him, not that he wasn't up for it, but he wasn't used to that. George [Steinbrenner] was a lot to deal with."

Bowie Kuhn, MLB's commissioner from 1969 to 1984, was a longtime friend of Fraser. At the 1987 Tribute to Ron Fraser commemorating the coach's twenty-fifth season, Kuhn was the featured speaker. Held at the Miami Airport Radisson, it had the feel of a smaller Mark Light Stadium. The nine hundred tickets sold quickly, and lucky numbers were drawn, a long-throw contest held, and outfield-fence advertisements adorned the walls in the event ballroom.

During his speech, Kuhn told the crowd that Fraser's "brilliance never shown better than the fact that he turned down George Steinbrenner's offer to be vice president and stayed right here [at Miami]."

He added that in speaking to legendary sportscaster Howard Cosell, he asked for a line about Fraser, to which Cosell responded, "In a word, incomparable."

By building relationships throughout Major League Baseball, including with Kuhn, Fraser lifted college baseball's reputation. In the 1960s, players drafted out of college were in the minority, often seen as not good enough for professional baseball because they did not sign out of high school. Players drafted from high school comprised nearly all of the *bonus babies*—players who received large guaranteed signing bonuses to get them into the parent club's farm system.

Kuhn took a recommendation that he get to know Fraser and learn about the college game. While forging the relationship, Kuhn found that the old professional attitude toward college players was wrong. Recognizing that the growth and quality of the college game could benefit professional baseball, Kuhn often praised Fraser's influence on college baseball, particularly when it came to reversing the opinions of Major League front offices about drafting college players. The more players choosing to play college baseball instead of signing professionally out of high school, the more the sport raised its quality and competition.

As a result, college baseball grew into a better product. Coaching was better. Playing seventy games a season, earning an education, and growing socially was better by comparison. More schools put money into improving their programs. An unprecedented eleven of the first twelve picks in the 1985 MLB Draft came from college, including Will Clark, B. J. Surhoff, Bobby Witt, and Barry Larkin.

"Parents don't look at signing [with the pros] the same as they used to. Now they're saying, 'They're offering [this] amount of money not to go to college,'" Fraser said in 1988.

The perception evolved to a point where comparisons were made between top-level college baseball, especially perennial College World Series contending programs such as Miami, and high Class-A Minor League Baseball. Some would argue that with additional pitching depth, the college game may compare favorably with the AA level.

Fraser led the fight for respect while college baseball grew into its own recognizable entity rather than simply serving as another farm system or player source for Major League Baseball. Coaches developed teams to reach Omaha and win national championships, much like their football and basketball counterparts. By the time Fraser's career wound down, college baseball had nearly pulled even with the high school ranks in draft pick numbers. The college game grew far more competitive, with talent spreading across the country rather than in just a few hot spots like California or Texas. Division I programs produced professional players at an unprecedented rate and in 1994 started a string of five consecutive No. 1 overall draft picks.

Beyond his influence in lifting college baseball, Fraser's promotional work drew attention from both Major and Minor League Baseball. Few in professional baseball, and even less in the college game, did any type of promotions at the ballpark. What is commonplace now was once controversial. The handful of Minor League teams that employed well-executed promotions drew criticism for creating a carnival atmosphere rather than putting on a baseball game.

Jim Paul, owner of the El Paso franchise, was a pioneer in substantial marketing at the Minor League level. At a time when nearly 80 percent of Minor League teams lost money, his efforts doubled the team's attendance in one year, and it went on to set attendance marks for five consecutive seasons. Paul invited Fraser to speak to his Promotion Seminar in the late 1970s, which provided ideas on how to market a baseball team through concessions, advertising, ticket sales, and promotions at games. Fraser was the first college coach to attend the seminar.

"Ron is certainly one of the most creative and interesting people I have ever met. . . . He certainly had the creativity," Paul told *Collegiate Baseball* in 1992.

"I learned a lot from people who were trying to do the same thing I was doing as far as selling the game and marketing it," Fraser reflected in a *Collegiate Baseball* story featuring his promotional expertise. He also incorporated his own ideas along the way to set the model for the college level.

Bill Conlin wrote in the *Sporting News*, "Remember the days when college baseball was the orphan of the athletic department? It sounds like some big league clubs could learn from the Hurricanes' promotional aggressiveness."

Kuhn did just that while commissioner. He invited Fraser to speak to

Major League owners and public-relations personnel about succeeding at the gate during 1981 Winter Meetings in nearby Hollywood, Florida.

"What makes it more impressive to me is that college baseball was not a big deal back then. It just wasn't," said former player turned close friend Al Marsicano. "For him to have the kind of influence he had not only for college but [also for] professional baseball was impressive."

Naturally, Fraser became a key advocate in selling a potential South Florida bid to land an expansion Major League Baseball franchise. As Miami and the surrounding area grew, it became an attractive option on any list of possible locations.

In 1984 Dolphins owner Joe Robbie led the charge for a South Florida Major League Baseball team to play in his new stadium. Fraser actively lobbied his immense network of baseball personnel about Miami's readiness to be a big league city. The South Florida Baseball Committee included popular Miami sports media personality Hank Goldberg and future Florida governor Jeb Bush. Fraser served as spokesman and was an honorary cochairman, alongside U.S. representative Dante Fascell. The initial goal was simply to make Major League Baseball's list.

"Very famous people in the sport called on him for advice," said Marsicano of Fraser. "He would sit back and listen and then give you an opinion and his advice. He was also able to envision what things might look like. He had wide tentacles that spread throughout the sport."

Major League Baseball's Long Range Planning Committee, led by Commissioner Peter Ueberroth, along with the American League and National League Presidents and six owners, whittled a list of thirty to thirty-five cities down to ten viable candidates. Only six would be chosen as potential expansion locations. At the time, Fraser predicted Miami as South Florida's best shot at landing an MLB team.

By 1985, the betting odds of South Florida landing an expansion team rose from 100:1 to 30:1, thanks in part to Fraser's efforts. The South Florida Baseball Committee brought Fraser aboard as a consultant before it hired marketing gurus Dick Pomerantz and Del Wilber to make their push. Local media stated that "no other baseball man here even comes close to Fraser" and called him the "ace" in South Florida's expansion hole.

When Miami made the short list for an expansion franchise in 1990, prospective owner Wayne Huizenga asked Fraser to travel to New York to meet with the expansion committee. Fraser sold the virtues of Miami's baseball fans and emphasized that its summer heat was much more manageable at night. Media attached Fraser's name to a future franchise and speculated about whether he may be in a front-office or managerial role for a new club.

"I think he could have been a high-ranking executive for MLB or a team executive as the marketing guru," said Firestone. "He always had an idea and had all sorts of stuff going on and well before teams were thinking of in terms of marketing. It was sort of a cross between Charlie Finley and Bill Veeck for college baseball."

In the summer of 1991 Major League Baseball officially granted Miami and South Florida a franchise under Huizenga's ownership. "Huizenga had the financing, but my dad sold the story," said Fraser's daughter Lynda. "He was very instrumental."

As the Marlins began officially counting down to their on-field debut, a local news poll asked who should manage the team from a list of Fraser, Yogi Berra, Bob Gibson, Tommy Lasorda, Tony Perez, Pete Rose, and Dick Williams. Fraser was an overwhelming choice, with 52 percent of the vote—a testament to his vast popularity. In comparison, Rose was runner-up at 21 percent.

When the Marlins took the field in 1993, it marked another milestone for Fraser. Not only had he built the University of Miami program into a national power, but he was also indirectly credited with helping the state land its first Major League Baseball team. The only thing holding Fraser back from direct involvement in a full-time capacity was the health issue that factored into his decision to retire as Miami coach the year prior.

Despite never holding an official position with the team's front office, Fraser's name is rightfully linked to the franchise. Both Robbie and Huizenga asked for his help throughout their expansion-team pursuits. The *Miami Herald* touted Fraser as baseball's "funnel to the city," adding that "before the majors and spring training open, there has always been Fraser first."

Huizenga liked Fraser's work so much that he not only presented him a standing job offer but also hired his public-address announcer

Jay Rokeach, mascot John Routh, and marketing and ticketing staffers. Fraser's All-American catcher, Charles Johnson, became the Marlins first-ever draft choice when taken in the first round in 1992 and was the starting catcher for the 1997 World Series champions during his successful twelve-year Major League career.

"[Fraser] was thrilled for them and really wanted to see them grow and have success in South Florida," said Lynda.

Ahead of the Marlins inaugural game in April 1993, the *Miami Herald*'s Greg Cote wrote, "For me, Fraser is the spiritual forefather of this ball club, this possible dream. I am not sure he has gotten enough credit for that."

11

Community and University Impact

"No one in the history of college baseball started with less and ended with more," said Skip Bertman of Fraser.

Fraser's legacy at the University of Miami and across South Florida lives on decades after retirement. His accomplishments extend well beyond the baseball field. The University of Miami benefitted immensely from his achievements and so did the community through his many humanitarian efforts.

Long before Miami gained the NBA's Heat, MLB's Marlins, and the NHL's Panthers, Fraser built Hurricanes baseball into the spring companion to the NFL's Dolphins in the fall. Fraser's program and Don Shula's Dolphins had comparable trajectories and attained parallel success during a golden age of Miami sports. Both legendary coaches are synonymous with greatness in the history of their respective sports. Greg Cote called Fraser and Shula "two of a kind in South Florida sports history" who "became a part of our life's timeline" and "unblemished by anything but good in doing South Florida proud."

"Ron was a huge personality in town, and everybody knew him," said friend and media icon Hank Goldberg. "He came along before people like Pat Riley and Howard Schnellenberger."

Miami baseball went from sparsely attended games in front of player's families and friends to drawing in curious baseball fans. By the late 1970s and 1980s it became a hot ticket and the place to be seen. People wanting entertainment and a night out, not necessarily all baseball fans, joined the crowds.

Fraser's never-been-done promotions drew big crowds to Hurricane games. Having one thousand fans at a game was unheard of at the time, but that was just the beginning. The initial success and promotions bred enthusiasm, and Miami baseball turned into a must-see happening. Exponential growth reached three thousand and four thousand spectators, well beyond what anyone besides Fraser could have envisioned.

"People flocked to those games and looked forward to them. The broadcasts had a huge audience. It was South Miami, and it was their sport," added Goldberg. "There was never anything like it. I mean, they had huge crowds for college baseball."

The success of Fraser's teams and promotions created an atmosphere at Mark Light Stadium that was the envy of college baseball. It was lively. It was fun. And it was always full. Nothing in the sport compared at the time.

"If you loved baseball, this was the place to be," said Paul Frishman, student broadcaster for wvum from 1982 to 1985. "The program really was, to us, on the level of a professional sports team."

What made the popularity more significant was the endless number of recreation and entertainment options in South Florida. People chose college baseball games over time at the beach less than ten miles away from the stadium.

"He had to get people away from the beaches," said Ron Polk. "There's too much to do in Miami. . . . He had to bribe them [with giveaways] to come, and there was always something going on."

And it was more than just the regular-season games that drew people to the ballpark. Friday Nights at the Light began in the 1970s as a promotion for fall exhibition games. Yes, even fall practices brought in crowds.

"I remember going out on the field the first day of fall practice, and there had to be close to two thousand people in the stands," said Jerry Weinstein, who served on the 1984 coaching staff. "I said to Ron, 'What's going on here?' And he said, 'They just came to check you out and see if you're any good.'"

Reasonably priced season tickets and G-rated entertainment appealed to families. A night at the ballpark meant the Maniac's performance, quality food, fun prizes, and exciting baseball. An endless array of promotions and giveaways without quality baseball feels like a gimmick. Fraser balanced the equation by fielding consistent winners.

Miami drew 1.27 million fans, the most in college baseball, during the 1980s. By 1990 Mark Light Stadium had to close its gates on six occasions because crowds reached maximum capacity per local ordinance. From 1981 through Fraser's final season in 1992, Miami averaged no less than 2,000 fans per game and totaled over 118,000 fans in all but one season. It led the nation in attendance five times during that span and drew five thousand spectators twenty-five times. Fraser described the draws as his most exciting moments in coaching, stating, "We went overboard and outdistanced everyone in the business."

"Fraser created this atmosphere of fun, almost like a carnival, but it was entertaining baseball, and it was bigger than life," said longtime voice of the Hurricanes Joe Zagacki. "On big nights, almost every night, the crowd would be three or four deep standing behind home plate and down the lines. They would be into it with every single pitch."

Friday and Saturday nights in South Florida meant going to Mark Light Stadium, much like high school football on Friday and college football on Saturday in the fall. It was an unofficial civic event, and Fraser loved how the fans and community rallied around to support his teams. Teens walked around the ballpark like it was the mall, and they represented their high school teams by wearing jerseys and jackets, often coming straight from their own game. "The 'in' place to be in South Florida is the University of Miami's Mark Light Stadium," wrote the *Dallas Morning-News*.

Celebrities commonly popped up in typical crowds. Those spotted at Mark Light Stadium included sports icons Bob Griese, Chi Chi Rodriguez, Martina Navratilova, and Nancy Lieberman and baseball legends Carl Yastrzemski, Jim Palmer, and Tommy Lasorda. "You just never knew who was going to be there," said Greg Vaughn, who played at Miami in 1986 before a fifteen-year Major League Baseball career that included four All-Star seasons.

At the height of Fraser's success, Miami was not the sprawling metropolis that it is today. With a 239-acre campus of approximately twelve thousand undergraduates, the university is nestled in Coral Gables, nearly seven miles from downtown Miami. Baseball crowds retained the warm and friendly feeling of a big family gathering. Fans sat close enough that they got to know the players. Some brought homemade chocolate chip cookies to the dugout or supplied bubble gum to the team. The regulars attended so frequently that if someone missed a game, the person might receive a call for a wellness check. Jay

Rokeach eloquently described Fraser as "the patriarch of our extended family" following his final regular season home game in 1992.

"There was a quaint ambiance at the ballpark that is hard to describe or even tell people unless you had the experience," said Mike Fiore. "It centered around baseball and what was being done on the field but also a sense of community where people came together. Coach Fraser built that and made it something people wanted to come and celebrate. It was unique to Miami, and I don't think it will ever be replicated anywhere else."

USA Today once called Mark Light Stadium a "county fair picnic." The carnival feel was palpable. Food was an important part of the equation for Fraser, who decided to hire a local company to take over concessions in the mid-1980s. That decision made adding unique menu offerings more feasible than awaiting approval from a nationally owned company.

Nearly any item found at a fair, from barbeque to steak sandwiches and chicken wings to pizza, was available in a tent located down the line. Hamburgers and hot dogs were charbroiled, rather than cooked on a flat griddle, and sent smoke and aroma wafting into the air and onto the field. It was uniquely part of The Light experience.

"The opposing coach once went to the umpire and said there was too much smoke on the field, and they couldn't play under those conditions," said Mitch Freedman, who started leading concessions in 1986. "Coach Fraser was thrilled about that. He really looked for any legal advantage he could."

Soft-serve ice cream, something only found at Dairy Queen or a special event at that time, appeared on the ballpark menu before the legendary Mark Light Milkshake, which remains an extremely popular item. Today's menu includes The Wizard, made of chocolate ice cream, Heath bar, and fudge.

Fraser started inviting Little Leaguers dressed in uniform to the ballpark for various promotional nights. When the kids wanted to come to games, the parents had to come along. Entire families were there, young and old, baseball fan or not. Parents could also feel safe dropping off their kids for nine innings.

Fraser often reminded his players that fans in attendance paid money to watch them play. Without them, the program would not have been possible. Fraser emphasized pace of play, and when game times crept higher, particularly past the three-hour mark, he told his players to pick up the pace or they risked losing fans. Players frequently heard the message that their games were prime entertainment for families, and Fraser expected his players to serve as role models for youth in attendance.

"He always told us if we ever turned down a kid for an autograph our days there were done," recalled Joe Nelson. "He didn't care if we signed for a thousand of them or were there signing for an hour after the game. If there are kids wanting your autograph, you're going to sign whatever they hand you."

One young admirer was Álex Rodríguez, who snuck into games by jumping the fence. He committed to play collegiately at Miami but signed professionally after being drafted No. 1 overall in 1993. In 2002 Rodríguez donated $3.9 million for stadium renovation and scholarship funding, marking the largest contribution ever made to the baseball program. Rodríguez attended games and camps during his youth and called Ron Fraser and the Hurricanes the "best show in town."

When ESPN broadcasted games, the atmosphere at The Light went up another level. Fraser and his gameday masterminds John Routh, Ken Lee, and Rick Remmert scripted various ways to present Miami baseball to the national television audiences in memorable ways. That spotlight became a big part of Fraser's magic.

"You know what ESPN *College Gameday* is for football," said Barry Leffler. "At that time, it was so rare to have the games televised that it was huge. It was definitely a big deal."

It was loud—the music, the public-address announcements, enthusiastic cheering for the game, and the promotions. The atmosphere intimidated visiting teams not used to playing in front of crowds beyond the hundreds. Abundant media coverage and radio and television broadcasts were foreign to many opponents. Music blared between innings and when Miami players came to bat. The home team fed off the support and often achieved an unexpected moment or a big comeback. Those occasions defined Mark Light magic.

"When you get to the eighth or ninth inning in a close ballgame and you know something spectacular is going to happen," said Ken Lee, baseball sports information director from 1981 to 1993. "You always had that feeling. It happened enough to where it was noticeable."

The *Miami Herald* once wrote, "It's the people. It's the fun. An atmosphere you wish you could put in your pocket and take home with you."

In the early years a group of one hundred fans known as the Hurricane Hecklers got after opponents by calling their pitchers "rag arms" and catchers "creampuffs" in good fun. It evolved into the "Walk 'Im Club"—a boisterous group of three dozen fans who sat at the top of the bleachers and continued their own chants of "walk him" followed by two claps when the opposing pitcher had a 3-0 or 3-1 count. When the opposing team brought a new pitcher in from the bullpen, fans greeted warm up pitches with an escalating unison sound of *woooooop*, while the catcher's return throw brought lowering sounds of *wooooooo*.

"Without a doubt, the atmosphere [at the Light] made for a tremendous home-field advantage," said Mike Fiore. "The crowd is a great motivator. You can feel the buzzing. You can feel the affection. When other teams played there, it tensed them up."

Fraser's program built its reputation in Coral Gables and across Miami, Dade County, and South Florida. The excitement generated by regular media coverage and stories about unique promotions, packed houses, and winning teams became woven into the community. Fraser did the unthinkable, making Miami baseball a marquee attraction in an era when South Floridians viewed college sports as a lesser option to pro sports. Fraser once said the best thing he had ever done was getting the community interested because the people were the ones supporting the program and passing it from family to family.

"He had a tremendous belief in Miami baseball and said he was going to make it great," said friend and iconic ESPN college football analyst Lee Corso, a college roommate of Fraser. "I said, 'Yeah, okay,' but he did it."

Baseball's success profoundly impacted University of Miami athletics. Fraser's team played before a packed house nearly every night, while football, mired in mediocrity, rarely produced winning seasons. Drawing crowds as small as fifteen thousand to the Orange Bowl left football teetering on survival. As baseball excelled, football was far from being any type of national factor, and the basketball program was dormant. When the university decided to drop basketball, football survived the Board of Trustees by a single vote thanks to Fraser's convincing.

"The U wouldn't have been the U without Ron Fraser," said John Routh, executive director of the UM Sports Hall of Fame. "Howard Schnellenberger gets a lot of credit and deservedly so. Coach Fraser was literally the reason Miami was able to do what they did in the 1980s because he helped keep the football program."

When named head football coach in 1979, Schnellenberger saw baseball's success and support as a model for his program. Schnellenberger, who came from the NFL, was reportedly stunned and surprised by the lack of assets invested by the university into the football program. He eventually talked the athletics department into hiring a marketing staffer dedicated to football and holding a number of promotions similar to what Fraser did. Much like baseball, football began an aggressive approach to get people into the stadium, show them a good product, and gain them as fans and repeat customers.

"I think Howard started to learn a thing or two from Fraser and how he promoted," said Firestone, a proud Miami alumnus. "He always looked at Fraser as the guy who was thinking about how he could make the program more compelling."

Fraser's work building his own advertising and marketing team inspired Schnellenberger. A first-time college head coach, Schnellenberger got to know Fraser well while seeking advice, and the two developed a bond. Fraser encouraged his new colleague to show personality and embrace the outlandish.

"Ron Fraser had more to do with us becoming a great football program than many of us will ever know," Schnellenberger said while eulogizing Fraser. "I saw him go out and do things I had never seen a coach do before. I saw him put his personal character into it and his personal reputation on the line. He gave me the courage and understanding that Miami was different than Alabama and Kentucky and all the other great places and that we had to do it differently. He laid the groundwork and showed me how to do it. I emulated him in many ways."

Schnellenberger copied a page from Fraser's promotional playbook by taking his team to Cape Kennedy to relay a football down state road A1A and along the Atlantic Ocean for 222 miles. Players ran a mile at a time and handed the ball off to a teammate. The exchange continued until reaching the Fontainebleau hotel where Miami's band and cheerleaders awaited. The football team gained national exposure while the hotel hosted an Easter Seals telethon.

It was more than just promotions that Fraser likely demonstrated for Schellenberger. Fraser's loose and fun approach with his program contrasted the strict nature of the football program from Lou Saban to Schnellenberger. When football loosened up a bit, the team started to win.

"If Ron had not been here, I think I would have tried to coach this team like Bear Bryant, and that would not have worked," Schnellenberger added in Fraser's eulogy. "Ron, I thank you very much for taking me under your wing and giving me advice on many occasions. All of us from the football side of things thank you very much for getting started what has become the most pronounced phenomenon in college football today."

Schnellenberger started Miami football's rise to prominence continued on by Jimmy Johnson and Dennis Erickson that produced four national championships in nine seasons from 1983 to 1991. Miami held the unofficial designation as college football's team of the eighties.

"I truly believe the football team started to bleed off baseball's approach—relax, have fun, go out, and play," said Doug Shields, center fielder for the 1982 national championship team. "The atmosphere carried over to football. I know that's a wild statement."

Miami's gridiron success first comes to mind because football drew much wider national media exposure than baseball. However, it was Fraser's team who first made the Hurricanes famous as a consistent winner and national power before football made it "The U." Baseball reached the College World Series in 1974 and became an Omaha regular in 1978. Fraser's teams frequently ranked among the nation's top five in the weekly polls. Meanwhile, football's 1979 regular season win over Penn State and Peach Bowl appearance a year later jumpstarted its momentum. Fraser won the university's and state's first NCAA team championship a year and a half before the football team won the Orange Bowl to claim the unofficial national championship.

By the mid-1990s the football program faced its share of controversies and NCAA sanctions. At the same time, the baseball program continued its place among the national elite. During the 1995 College World Series, the *Omaha World-Herald* described a "tale of two programs," calling Miami baseball "a class act all the way" and stating that Fraser "could have run for [Omaha] mayor and was popular enough to get the votes," a reference to his many cws trips. Given recent football history between Nebraska and Miami, local fans began rooting against the Hurricanes and took their frustration out on the baseball team after Fraser's departure.

Fraser's influence spread beyond football. It helped pave the way for other sports, including the return of men's basketball in 1985–86. He helped build momentum for reinstating the program after a fourteen-year absence. The successful baseball and football programs helped create a push to bring the sport back. "I really think he's responsible for a lot of the successes the athletic department had back in the day," said Rokeach.

When Miami joined the Big East Conference in 1990, only the baseball program did not. Football was the impetus for joining the conference, but baseball remained independent solely for financial reasons. Fraser's program grossed $1 million and outdrew men's basketball. The Big East was a one-bid baseball league, and none of its most successful programs—Rutgers, Boston College, Virginia Tech, and University of Pittsburgh—factored nationally at the time. The Hurricanes typically played 75 percent or more of their games at home, and the thought of giving up home games to travel and play lesser-stature teams in cold weather was irrational competitively and financially. It was the first and only instance of a baseball program bypassing Division I conference realignment when the rest of the school's programs moved.

"I cannot think of a guy who was more instrumental in turning Miami's athletic program," said Firestone of Fraser. "There would be no Miami program if it weren't for Coach Fraser. He was that great, that influential, and that successful."

Fraser had business connections and knew what coaches needed to succeed. He developed and ran a model program independent from the rest of the athletic department. Fraser's accomplishments and influence should have made him a viable candidate for Miami's athletic director position. The role opened multiple times during his coaching career, but he was continuously passed over.

In 1978 Miami hired its football coach Saban, who lasted less than a year in the AD role. Following that hire, Fraser received a consolation prize adding an assistant AD title and tennis, golf, swimming, and soccer oversight. In April 1983 Fraser was again touted as a leading candidate and stated that he would listen but had no plans to apply. Again, the university went elsewhere to fill the role.

"I think he would have welcomed it because he recognized what the coaches go through and deal with," said Fraser's daughter Lynda Armitage. "I think he wanted to be a different kind of AD, an athletics-based AD, instead of a financial guy."

Fraser likely would have been a successful athletics director and a trailblazer. His protégé, Skip Bertman, excelled in the role at LSU from 2001 to 2008 and paved the way for another baseball coach to become AD when South Carolina hired Ray Tanner in 2012.

"Ron would have been a great AD," said Dave Scott, who was an assistant coach under Fraser before moving to an assistant athletic director role overseeing football. "Who knows what he would have done to the Orange Bowl [home to the Hurricanes football team]? He was one of those guys with the vision that the stadium would have still existed today."

Miami became a national brand name under Fraser. Despite not playing many road games, Fraser's program became an attraction everywhere it went. He took his teams all over the country and developed a national following, comparable to what the Yankees had done. Whether playing at state rivals, against Texas or Maine, or in Tulsa against Oral Roberts University, the Hurricanes packed stadiums. Through its national media coverage and on-field success, Miami baseball became one of college sports' most recognizable brands. The Old English *M* and colorful orange and green uniforms left an impression on viewers nationwide.

"We could go anywhere and have big crowds," recalled Joe Nelson. "Maybe they didn't draw well when they played someone else, but when the Hurricanes came to town, they were going to get their biggest crowds of the season."

Fraser's vast network of boosters followed the team to other states. Many showed up at away games just to be part of the baseball program. The pinnacle was going to Omaha for the College World Series.

When they played in the College World Series, Miami became one of the local fan favorites. During the team's initial trips in the 1970s,

Fraser brought hats and T-shirts to give away to kids all across town. Fans cheered his team's exciting and aggressive play.

"You had all these kids running around wearing Miami hats," recalled John Routh. "No other team gave them anything, but we gave them hats, so they became Miami fans. That's what really built up the reputation in Omaha—just simply taking care of people around you. Little life lessons you learned from Fraser."

"Omaha loved us. They loved Fraser," recalled Rick Raether, the ace relief pitcher on the 1985 national championship team. "They loved the mystique of the South Florida team, and it felt like good Midwest hospitality. That meant a lot to us, and we really enjoyed being around them."

Fraser's influence extended across the university and community. He was a successful, recognizable, and likeable figure. Everyone wanted him on their team.

After his 1992 retirement, Fraser accepted a role as national spokesperson and honorary chairman for the university's ambitious three-year fundraising campaign aimed at strengthening the College of Arts and Sciences and the Richter Library. Named the Cornerstone Campaign, it ended early after raising over $50 million. Fraser, who assisted full-time in building a national alumni program, was excited about the results and about an opportunity to give back to the university.

Fraser fought for WVUM and its students when the university began cutting funding for many student programs in the early 1980s. The radio station faced losing a large amount of its budget. After broadcasting every home and road game for nearly a decade, the cuts meant WVUM would no longer travel and could only broadcast home games.

Fraser requested a meeting with university president Tad Foote and brought along Barry Leffler, WVUM's sports director. Rather than focusing discussion on importance of game broadcasts, Fraser emphasized the loss of funding and its effect on the students. He argued for the value of learning about their careers and gaining valuable experience and responsibility while practicing their craft in different conditions. His successful lobbying restored the majority of funding back to WVUM.

"He was always student-centric, whether it was his players, support staff, or radio broadcasters," recalled Leffler. "I know in the background he had a vested interest in having the games broadcast back home, but that wasn't his main argument. He was sincere for the reasons he stated on our behalf."

Fraser loved the community and believed that leaders should take leadership roles to help take care of the people who lived there. He believed in giving back and felt involvement was a very important part of life. Fraser helped raise an estimated $75 million across his many charitable efforts. Most of the beneficiaries were people he never met.

The wide range of Fraser's involvement is impressive. He chaired committees for Easter Seals and Make-a-Wish Foundation and served on the board for the Leukemia Society of America. He worked with the United Way, March of Dimes, the Miami City Ballet and various causes for abused children, children's genetic diseases, muscular dystrophy, and diabetes. He was director of the First City Bank of Dade County, located across the highway from Mark Light Stadium. He was grand marshal for the 1992 Orange Bowl Parade, the university's 1992 Homecoming Parade, and the 1997 Weston Little League Parade. He held hundreds of baseball clinics for the underprivileged and gave countless speeches to civic and charitable organizations across South Florida.

One of the organizations closest to Fraser was the Alpha-1 Foundation for alpha-1 antitrypsin deficiency (A1AD). His second wife, Karen, had the hereditary condition, often mistaken for asthma, chronic bronchitis, or allergies, that slowly destroys the lungs and typically does not allow sufferers to live beyond their mid-fifties.

In 1997 Fraser helped organize a Grand Slam Celebration fundraiser that coincided with the Yankees-Marlins series and featured Jim Leyland, Joe Torre, and several players. It marked the first in a series of luncheons that raised over a half million dollars combined. Fraser recruited influential voices to speak on behalf of the Alpha-1 Foundation. Tommy Lasorda walked the halls of Congress to encourage and secure federal funding in support of alpha-1 research. The work Fraser began, to generate awareness, increase research funding, improve therapies, and extend lives, impacted thousands.

Fraser spoke to nearly every Kiwanis and Optimist Club and anywhere else he could give a presentation. *USA Today* wrote of Fraser's 1985 speech at a Miami Chamber of Commerce event: "You can't get

850 people together in South Florida in September for anything but football or Bruce Springsteen."

Baseball tied into some of Fraser's community work. He began a program designed to prevent elementary school children from falling prey to gangs in the middle school years. He invited handicapped residents from Fellowship House to games, describing the outings as big events for them.

Fraser instilled the importance of community service in his players. It was not enough to don a uniform and play on the field. He believed the team owed something to the community. Each off day, Hurricanes players worked as volunteers at hospitals, schools, centers and clubs, little leagues, and other charitable organizations. Players chose where and when to help with an expectation to serve a designated number of hours. It was a significant part of the baseball program and a life lesson carried on years later.

"Coach Fraser's impact on the community and what he expected his players to do transcended the team," recalled Hernandez. "I think that's why a lot of former players remain actively involved and do a lot of things in the community. It goes back to Coach Fraser's character and who he was as a man and as a person in the community."

After playing and coaching for Fraser, Warren Bogle became a middle school teacher in Miami. Fraser invited him to bring his students over to the university for a field trip centered around the athletic programs. Some of Bogle's students came from the lower-income area of South Miami and ended up going to college. Some competed as student-athletes or gained jobs at the University of Miami. The doors opened for many of the students when Bogle introduced them to Fraser during field trips, and they expressed their interest in getting involved.

A statue of Fraser stands outside the front entrance to the ballpark he created. A crowd of hundreds, including university dignitaries and his entire family, including wife Karen, former wife Liane, three daughters, and five grandchildren attended the 2015 unveiling ceremony. Head Coach Jim Morris spoke at the event, and members of the 1985 national championship team gathered to pose for photos with the statue.

"We're so grateful just to know that Ron is going to be back at Mark Light Stadium," his widow Karen said at the unveiling, "knowing that's he's going to be there forever in the place he loved."

Fraser's statue became just the fourth on campus, joining the university's first president, Bowman F. Ashe; former Board of Trustees vice president and booster Neil Schiff; and Sebastian the Ibis. The sculptor, Zenos Frudakis, previously completed tributes to Joe DiMaggio, Arnold Palmer, and Jack Nicklaus. The plaque adorning the statue reads, in part:

This magnificent statue stands in grateful recognition of the life he lived at the ballpark he built, for the university he loved. For as long as the game is played, Ron Fraser will be lovingly remembered as The Wizard of College Baseball.

Forever standing in tribute to Fraser's contributions to the university, its athletics, and the community, the statue portrays him in a coat and tie rather than a baseball uniform, just like he went to work (except when in uniform during games). The back of his jacket is pulled up slightly, the same way he had it tailored. He holds a bat over his shoulder, a nod that baseball, while his main job, was not what defined him.

"Every time I walk by that statue, I feel like he's inside," said Zagacki. "It radiates Ron Fraser. The University of Miami is known for its football championships and its glitz and glamour, but he's the guy that paved the way for that."

The seven-foot-tall statue greets fans attending games today. Fraser's legacy is present at Mark Light Stadium decades after his incredible career. His retired number is placed prominently on the outfield fence.

"Every time we walk into the stadium, we bump fists with Coach Fraser's statue and say, 'Hey, coach,'" said Nelson about his teammates. "We take pictures with him and honestly feel like he's still there. His presence is always there."

The statue, ballpark, and tradition all evoke thoughts of Fraser. Mentioning his name elicits several memories and stories, especially for those closest to him as players, staff, or acquaintances.

"A lot of people remember him as if he retired yesterday," said Cynthia Fraser. "People will say how they loved my father or how he influenced them, and a lot of them never knew him personally. It was a testament to who he was."

In the decades following Fraser's retirement, the Hurricanes won two more national championships and consistently remained among college baseball's most identifiable programs. Even with all the success in the years that have passed, Miami baseball remains synonymous with his name. Fraser's daughters and family are grateful to the coaches who followed, for keeping his legacy in the forefront amid their coaching achievements.

"Coach Fraser is still revered. Nobody will ever touch him." said DiMare. "There's the saying that nobody is bigger than the game or sport, but Coach Fraser might have been one of those guys bigger than everything else. That's how he was to people."

"When you put on the Miami uniform, the front might as well say 'Fraser' because he built this thing," said former Hurricane player, Matt Tyner.

12

Player Mentor

Fraser coached more than one thousand players during his thirty years at Miami. More than 150 of them played professional baseball, including seventeen Major Leaguers. He was just as proud of the 850-plus former players who became contributing citizens in other occupations. Fraser always told them, "Whatever you do, be great at it," and that advice lasted well beyond their college days.

Fraser had the utmost respect from his players, in part because of his ability to relate to them. At the beginning of his career when he was only a few years older than his team, he had an older-brother presence. As Fraser completed his first and second decades, he became more of a father figure. Whether his players needed that presence in their lives or just someone to lean on while away from home, Fraser was there for them. It was about far more than baseball. It was about life, family, and developing young men to contribute to society in their occupations and communities.

Tommy Lasorda said of Fraser, "After leaving him, players knew what it was like to get into the big world and be able to face it."

"He was a combination of our coach, our teacher, and our father figure. It's hard to put all that he did into one sentence," Jim Maler said of Fraser's impact.

Fraser instilled an emphasis on details, a lesson that helped his players on the field and later in life. He spoke about putting in hard work, never being satisfied, and not taking things for granted. The underlying message was success did not come from talent alone.

"When you look at Coach Fraser's teams, they weren't the biggest, weren't always the fastest, didn't always throw the hardest, but when you played against them, the little things mattered," said Luis "Wicho" Hernández. "There was a ton of focus on the little details that make a big difference. It's how I live every day of my life—it's the little things."

Fraser's ACES theme was the basis for success. The acronym stood for attitude, commitment, enthusiasm, and service. If you have attitude, you'll have the right approach. If you're committed, you'll be a winner. If you have enthusiasm, you'll be respected. And if you serve others, you will have a glow of success. Whether speaking about the four ACES to his team or in corporate settings, he interspersed stories and humorous anecdotes relating to each area.

"I tell my players they are the best, [so] make it happen. If your attitude is not right, make it right. You want to be a happy successful person," Fraser said in his speeches. "Commitment is important in your life. Enthusiasm is a key to success. Service is most important—to your family, to your religion, your community, your country—most of all, service to other people who maybe are not as fortunate as you are. There is no greater feeling than to help people who need help.

"In a nutshell, you control what you want to be. If you want to be No.1, you can be No. 1. If you want to be successful, you can be successful. You are the master of your life. The master lives in you. You make it happen. You can do anything you want to be successful."

Fraser stressed the importance of education. He reminded his team that only a small percentage of players go on to Major League careers. Fraser's top priority for his players was earning their degree so they had something to fall back on. He reminded them that their education was one hundred times more important than leaving to sign professionally. Fraser told them that a lot of things can happen to keep them from making it to the big leagues and they needed an insurance policy in case it did not happen. That insurance policy was an education, and the University of Miami offered an outstanding education.

"He'd say, 'Do something other than play baseball. Go into business. Do something that interests you,'" recalled Kevin DiGiacomo. "He expanded our view and our horizon. He didn't want you to feel like you weren't successful if you didn't make it in professional baseball."

It was essential that his student-athletes handle the demanding practice and game schedules for a nationally ranked team while balancing rigorous classwork at a renowned academic institution. They were not there to play baseball, but to get a degree.

"I feel like it's important for me to tell them a little about life," Fraser once said. "I try to put everything in perspective and say, 'Even if you don't make it in baseball, there is a life afterward.'"

After suffering a sweep at Florida State, Fraser held an early-morning practice the next day at Mark Light Stadium. His players were dragging and not wanting to be there. The sound of busy U.S. 1 traffic was audible on an otherwise quiet morning. Fraser stopped practice and gave a motivational speech that went something like the following:

"You think you guys have it tough? You have to get up at 6:00 a.m. and come down here. You've got to go to class and get your grades. Hear those cars? Those people got up early this morning, made their lunch, are sitting in traffic with their coffee and lunch bag in the front seat, and are going to work all day trying to make a living. They've got it tough. You'll be doing that the next forty years of your lives. You guys don't have it tough. You have a great opportunity. You're here at the greatest program in the country, and you're having fun playing a kid's game. Enjoy it."

It was a lesson about not taking their current lives for granted and understanding that their obligations would get tougher in the future. "We're looking around thinking, *What is he talking about?*" recalled Jeff Alkire. "As we got older and out of baseball and had families and a business, we realized he's right. The reality is there is going to come a day when life is tough. You've got to work and provide for your family. Those types of lessons and stories were good. They were always at the right time too."

With his expansive network of contacts across the business world, Fraser connected his players with high-ranking executives who could help them land jobs in the future. He was always talking to someone or introducing people to get them together. That is how Fraser operated.

Hugo Rams, who played shortstop for Fraser from 1974 to 1977 and majored in premed, applied to the University of Miami's medical school as a senior. While discussing recommendation letters for acceptance, Fraser told Rams he would get him one he needed. Without telling Rams anything further, Fraser went to the office of university president Dr. Henry Stanford, whom he had won over as a baseball fan, and said he needed a recommendation letter for one his players.

Stanford said he could not make a recommendation because his position as president may influence decisions. Fraser insisted and said, "You write it for him, or I'm not going to leave." The conversation continued for a few minutes before Fraser stood up on Stanford's desk and informed him that he would not get down until he got a yes. Stanford acquiesced and wrote the letter. When Fraser stepped down from atop the desk, Stanford showed him where he had scratched it. With quick wit, Fraser responded, "No, Mr. President, I added character to the desk."

"That's how much he cared about his players," said close friend and cardiologist Dr. George Vergara. "By then, he was so popular he knew he couldn't get fired. That story tells you what he was like."

Fraser did whatever it took to help his players in their pursuits. Rams completed medical school, finished his training, practiced gastroenterology, and built a renowned thirty-five-year reputation in the field. Fraser became one of Dr. Rams's patients. A photo of the two talking prior to an at bat hangs in Dr. Rams' office today with an inscription from Fraser reading, "I'm so proud that you were part of UM baseball."

Fraser taught his players lessons about choices and changes. He drew an analogy of walking down the street and seeing a piece of paper sitting on the street in a beautiful Miami neighborhood. He told them they had a choice—either pick that piece of paper up and keep the street beautiful, even though they did not drop it (while often adding, "I know you wouldn't do that [i.e., drop it] because you're a Hurricane") or leave it. So many people walk by that piece of paper. You don't have to pick it up. Only those that want to make a change do.

When players visited Fraser's office, the conversation often revolved around business news and the stock markets rather than baseball. Fraser advised them to learn about business because they would be involved in it the rest of their lives.

"He was into stocks, and I wanted to be a stock broker when I was out of college and done playing baseball," said Alkire. "I thought, *This is so cool. Who sits with their head coach, especially a coach like Ron Fraser, and talks stocks?*' He was a big Home Depot fan, and that was the first stock I bought."

Fraser dressed in a sport coat and tie when in the office. He required that his players dress respectfully. When traveling, that meant a sport coat and tie. If the player did not have one, Fraser found him one. He taught players how to tip at restaurants and for services. When they shook someone's hand, he told them to look the person in the eye, hold the hand, and feel it.

Through personal conversations with his players and by asking what was going on in their lives, Fraser developed a tremendous rapport. His door was always open, and he spent countless hours talking with his players and telling them stories. "I don't even have a secretary to block their way to my door," Fraser once said of his availability.

"He was a very big personality but could relate to different situations," said Will Vespe, a pitcher from 1986 to 1989. "He made you feel comfortable and confident and taught so much on a personal level. His influence on us as young men was just incredible."

Fraser stressed the importance of family. His program was a family, something demonstrated through his actions, not merely by words. He frequently invited players and their girlfriends to join his own family for Thanksgiving if they could not afford traveling back home. Fraser wanted to make Miami home for all players, regardless of where they came from. He was always there to support his players anytime they needed it.

"He really instilled in me how important family is, and I've lived by that," added Vespe. "He was right—at the end of the day, when things go wrong or tragedies occur, it's your family that is going to be there."

In the late 1960s John Danchik's mother fell ill and was hospitalized after a kidney transplant. He didn't have the money to get back to Pennsylvania to see her. After hearing of the situation and her need for blood transfusions, Fraser organized a university-wide blood-donation drive. Enough blood was raised for Danchik's mother plus the entire kidney ward of the Cleveland Clinic to last a full year.

Ron Scott had divorced parents in California who were unable to ever attend his games. After the team lined up for introduction at the 1974 College World Series Championship game, Fraser walked by Scott and asked if he noticed anything different behind Miami's dugout. Scott looked over and saw his mom there. Fraser had her flown first class from San Francisco to Omaha to see her son play. "What he did for my mom and [me] was special and something I'll never forget," recalled Scott.

Fraser fit the description of a player's coach. When addressing an issue, he did so individually, not in front of the team. There was no airing of dirty laundry nor any yelling or screaming at an individual. If faced with a difficult player, Fraser tried to draw him a little closer and be part of a bigger solution. He knew the right time for advice or compassion and when to push players and focus on them.

"He was incredibly respected by all the players," said Skip Bertman. "He always knew what to say to every player and what not to say."

Fraser believed in giving the benefit of the doubt and providing second chances. Situations were handled with calm and careful thought about the scope and the effect on the individual involved.

A player once tried to steal a ten-gallon ice cream drum from a university cafeteria. The student union, not happy about the situation, called Fraser and asked that he discipline the player for his actions.

"That very night, the kid hits a triple and slides into third where Ron is coaching," recalled Bertman. "Ron's laughing. A few pitches later, he scores on a fly ball [and] comes into the dugout, and I asked him what they were laughing about. He told me, 'Coach asked what flavor ice cream I was trying to steal.'"

When Danny Smith was caught plagiarizing during his freshman year, the coaches talked about a plan to send him to junior college and have him return later. Fraser sat mostly quiet during a meeting with his coaches and Smith before saying, "Let's give him one more chance." Relieved, Smith knew it was his last chance. He made the most of it during the 1982 national championship season when he earned selection as College World Series Most Outstanding Player.

"If he didn't give me that extra chance, none of that happens," Smith, a police officer and high school baseball coach, recalled of the lesson he learned and now relays to others. "If I have a guy who screws up, I tell them that story, they come back, and most of them go on to do good things. I tell them I was given that chance and believe in giving everyone else that chance."

Fraser had an ability to put himself in his players' shoes and understand their personal situations and decisions. When rumors circulated that freshman All-American pitcher Alex Fernandez was considering a transfer to junior college in order to enter the draft one year earlier, Fraser called him in for a meeting. Fernandez was nervous and admitted the rumors were true. Fraser stopped him there.

"I'll never forget what he told me," said Fernandez. "He said, 'I want what is best for you. It may not be best for me and our program, but it's best for you. So, whatever you think is best for you, I will support you.' Some of his success relied on me as one of his players. He gave that up for me and my family. It put me at ease."

If someone wanted to talk, Fraser made time for him and never passed him off to someone else. He made everyone feel special, and one-on-one meetings were both professional and heartwarming. It was teaching, not preaching.

"He knew how to treat each player and what they needed. That is special," recalled Kenny Henderson, a highly touted freshman pitcher on Fraser's final team in 1992. "Not every coach can do that, and you have to be able to learn what each guy needs. He was an expert at it, and it was kind of neat to watch."

Fraser had a remarkable knack for motivating his players. It was never through threats or tirades but through conversations and stories. The result instilled confidence, and his players did not want to let him down.

"Coach was an incredible human being, not only as a baseball coach but [also] as a mentor," said Rams. "He was almost like a second dad to most of us. The way he motivated us was incredible. He brought out the best in every individual player."

Before the opening game of an important series, Fraser pulled aside Matt Tyner, whom he put in the lineup despite hitting eighty points lower than the player he replaced that night. The starter had a migraine, and Fraser needed Tyner to fill in. He asked Tyner if he had ever heard the story of Wally Pipp. When Tyner said he had not, Fraser explained that Pipp was once the New York Yankees starting first baseman, but no one had ever heard of him. As the story goes, Pipp told his manager he could not play a game because of a headache. The manager wanted to try out a young player anyway and put him in the lineup. It was Lou Gehrig, who had three hits, scored a run, and never sat on the bench again, going on to start a record 2,130 consecutive games. As he ended the story, Fraser asked Tyner what number he wore. "Four," Tyner answered. Then Fraser told him that was Gehrig's number and to go have a "Gehrig night." Tyner responded with two doubles and a home run and never came out of the lineup again.

"I felt like one of Fraser's dudes that night," recalled Tyner. "I had to play like I couldn't let him down. It changed my life forever. Coach probably thought, *I'll tell Tyner the Wally Pipp story because he's No. 4 and Gehrig was No. 4.* He had that innate ability."

Fraser's aura was intimidating for young recruits. He had an impressive résumé filled with national championships, College World Series appearances, and lofty national rankings. Fraser was a bigger-than-life star in many ways. When he entered a room, the attention turned to him. He endeared himself to parents who wanted their son under his guidance during college.

"I was so nervous when I got to his office that I just melted seeing him sitting behind the desk," Smith recalled of his recruiting visit. "I accepted the scholarship right there. Then he asked me what number I wanted. When I told him No. 1, without knowing he wore No.1, he said, 'You better find someplace else to play.' I panicked, thinking he took my scholarship away. He said, 'I wear No. 1. Nobody wears that number but me.' I said, 'Okay, no problem' and picked another number."

Fraser empowered his players to provide input and feedback. Once it involved a request to introduce new hats to the team uniform. An array of colorful uniforms combinations existed, but all were worn with the same hat—the iconic green with orange bill and white Old English *M* on the front. That was the program brand. In the early 1990s when his players wanted white hats with an orange bill and the *M* in orange to wear for Sunday games, he allowed it. However, in the game the hats debuted, Miami played poorly. Fraser told his team midgame to take the white hats off, use them as beach hats, and get their regular hats on. They were never worn again, and the standard green and orange hats were worn exclusively until he retired.

A coach of Fraser's reputation could have easily put on airs and acted as an authoritarian above his team. Instead, he embraced and even became involved in some of his players silly antics. Fraser made everything fun until it was not supposed to be. He had a great sense about separating those moments.

"It was always a riot, all the time," said Bertman. "Without him, it would be just baseball."

When one of his pitchers began wearing an earring, and the team became upset over it, Fraser, who was late in his career, decided to make a point with his own fashion accessory. While playing tennis with good friend George Vergara, he wore a fake diamond earring. Vergara asked him why and recalled Fraser's response.

"He said, 'If he sees me wearing an earring, he's going to get so disgusted that he'll take it off. I'm not going to say a word and just go out there with the earring, and the players will get upset because their role model is wearing an earring,'" said Vergara. "I asked him the next day how it went, and he told me the guy took off his earring and he doubted he would ever put it on again. And he never did."

"He was such a great player's coach," recalled Gino DiMare. "He demanded respect, but he also was a lot of fun to be around. We had so much fun."

The 1989 players made a deal with Fraser that if they won the Gainesville Regional and advanced to the College World Series, the coach would shave lines in the side of his head, like many on his team, as a style of the time. They won, and Fraser let them shave lines in his hair.

"Not something you would think a guy like Coach Fraser, who's always in a coat and tie and looking like he's on Wall Street, would do," recalled DiMare, a freshman that season. "He stepped out of his comfort zone for his players. That our coach would do something like that fueled us, inspired us, and motivated us."

That same season, several players used April Fools' Day as an occasion to play a prank on Fraser. During pregame batting practice, pitcher Joe Grahe was in the outfield making acrobatic catches, which Fraser did not like seeing. Grahe staged being hit by a line drive and teammates doused him with ketchup. As the commotion ensued, the players yelled for the trainer, who was also in on the gag. Fraser, usually watching from the dugout or entertaining guests above the dugout, came running out to the outfield to check on the situation. When he got there, they yelled 'April Fools' and erupted in laughter. The next year, they staged a similar prank under the guise of a collision between two outfielders with both being badly injured and one breaking his leg. They tricked Fraser both times, and while not happy about it, he let it go quickly and was a good sport in acknowledging the well-executed prank.

Fraser had an annual prank of his own. Each fall, he would have a state trooper come in and arrest a freshman on a bogus charge while his teammates watched. Fraser found it amusing and great for locker-room camaraderie.

The bond between Fraser and many players remained strong years after their college careers. In some instances, they developed close friendships. Years, even decades, after their time at the university, Fraser's players called him for advice or simply to talk. They updated their coach about events in their personal lives—engagements, having kids, job changes, moving to different cities. Fraser was willing to help them at any point in their life, no matter what the situation.

Six years after graduation and following a three-year run on Broadway as Ringo Starr in Beatlemania, Phil LoMedico sought a return to baseball. Always one for a good story, Fraser leveraged LoMedico's background when contacting teams and alerting scouts. He threw LoMedico batting practice at Mark Light Stadium with a Reds bird-dog scout present. When a hard line drive hit the scoreboard, Fraser remarked, "I'm trying to help you out, but you're trying to break my scoreboard."

Fraser invited LoMedico to continue his return by playing for the 1980 USA Baseball team, but other matters prevented him from participating. Instead, LoMedico went on to make a name for himself in the baseball business by patenting the ProHitter, a hitting aid worn on the thumb of many players across all levels. He conceived the idea while creating a pad to protect a bad hand bruise during his Miami career.

When the Indians drafted Orlando González following his 1974 National Player of the Year season, Fraser took him under his wing. He assisted Gonzalez with his contract and flew to Cleveland to help him get acclimated and make introductions to key personnel and contacts.

Regardless of where life took them or how long it had been since they played, countless former players made every effort to return to campus for alumni games and other events. Seeing Coach was a top priority of their visit.

"When they had their first-ever baseball alumni-game weekend, Fraser was more paternal and happy than I ever saw him," recalled Dan Canevari, who served as an assistant coach under Fraser and later Bertman at LSU. "It was like a giant family reunion, and all his sons came back to see him."

"What made him so happy—and he would tell me when I'd take him to a ballgame—is seeing his players bring their children to the games," recalled Fraser's daughter, Liz Kraut. "That meant so much to him—getting to meet the kids and seeing his players do well and be good parents and people."

Even in the years since Fraser's passing, team-reunion turnouts remain remarkably strong. Former teammates still hold a tight bond forged in their coach's ability to bring teams together. When the 1985 national championship team returned to campus for its thirty-fifth reunion, thirty players attended from all over the country. They lived Fraser's mantra of remembering where they came from because it's someplace that will never leave them. "Four years to play and forty years to remember," Fraser told them in college.

At Fraser's 2006 induction into the College Baseball Hall of Fame, a large contingent of his former players descended on Lubbock, Texas, in support of his honor. "I remember him coming up, putting his arm on me, saying how glad he was I came and that it was good to see me and hear about how I was doing," Kevin DiGiacomo recalled about speaking with Fraser at the Hall of Fame induction. "I certainly wasn't a star there, and for him to do that spoke a lot about his character. It meant a lot to me."

Fraser especially adored the players from his early teams who shared the blood, sweat, and tears of building the program's foundation from nothing. Danchik, who became a close friend after playing for Fraser, recalled an unforgettable heartfelt reflection the coach later shared about his early years at Miami: "I've done a lot of things in my life and have a lot to be thankful for, but the greatest memories and times were when it was the toughest, and that was the early years in the 1960s," Fraser told Danchik. "That's when I realized how much I love this game. When I get down, that's what I think of most—you guys in the 1960s. Don't get me wrong, I loved all my players, everybody who came through here, but you guys were the first. You were there when we really struggled."

Fraser's adoration extended beyond his former players and included batgirls, staff, and anyone surrounding the program. "Eight of us batgirls saw him at homecoming, and I know he was having memory issues, but he still was surprised to see us. He even got teary eyed," recalled Linda DiMare, batgirl from 1970 to 1974. "It was very moving. He really valued and appreciated us. Those years as batgirls were very formative. He kind of raised us and gave us the character qualities we were searching for."

Fraser followed and encouraged his Major Leaguers, often checking in and letting them know he was watching. When Major League Baseball expanded to South Florida, it provided Fraser an opportunity to see his former players as big leaguers when they came to play the Marlins. Jim Abbott from Team USA, former Cane Greg Vaughn, and other Miami alums appreciated the opportunity to visit with their former coach during the trip.

"He would tell me that I was having a good year, but he had a team of kids there who wanted my job. He said never be complacent or satisfied, always be ready to go, and never be outworked," said Greg Vaughn, who played fifteen seasons in the Majors and called Fraser "Uncle Ron." "The Lord put me in a good place to be around people who were part of my village, and I know he played a very important part in mine."

Many of Fraser's players look back at their decision to attend the University of Miami and play for the Wizard of College Baseball as a life-changing experience.

When Miami native Wicho Hernández was deciding to attend Florida State or Miami, Fraser paid a recruiting visit and advised him that he would have a great career at either school and everyone would love him. The difference, Fraser told him, was if Miami was going to be home as an adult, playing for the Hurricanes would open doors in a big way professionally and in business.

"That was Coach Fraser and the genius of saying, 'It's not just baseball, it's about setting yourself up for the rest of your life,'" said Hernández. "When I look back, I realize that conversation in my parents' home as a seventeen-year-old high school junior, literally changed my life."

"Even today when you go somewhere and someone finds out you played for Coach Fraser and the Hurricanes, they look at you a little differently," said Joe Nelson. "It certainly opens up a lot of conversations. It carries a lot of weight in job interviews. They know about the Hurricanes and how special that was."

The experience in playing for Fraser created a life's worth of memories and lessons. Players carry many of the values he instilled on them today.

The speeches Fraser delivered may not have resonated in college but are held closely years later as a professional. "I do everything I can to realize I'm not just satisfied being the best in South Florida," said Dr. Marc Mestre, a former Miami player. "You strive to be the best in the country. A lot of that carries over from Miami baseball under Coach Fraser—a program where trying to be the best was instilled in me."

13

Personal Life

Ronald George Fraser, was born June 25, 1933, in Nutley, New Jersey. His father was a boxing prize fighter who once fought a preliminary bout at Madison Square Garden. He did not make much money, fighting primarily in Brooklyn's Police Athletic League. His mother had only a sixth-grade education and married Ron's father at sixteen.

The family had very little money and was on government welfare. Ron used pieces of linoleum as insulation in his shoes during the cold winter months. He wore socks over his hands for warmth. A steady diet of corn-starch pudding, consisting of only corn starch and water, made him very thin growing up. Ron boxed as a youth, though never considered good enough by his father. His mother, who exuded optimism, put a positive spin on everything in their life.

When Ron was eight years old, his father died. With older brothers out of the house, Ron, just nine, took care of his mother with loving adoration. Following his father's death, his mom had a difficult time and left the family for a while.

His mother sent Ron to live with friends and other people in the neighborhood rather than letting the authorities take him to a foster home. She put some clothes in a brown paper bag and told Ron he was going to summer camp and to have a lot of fun. Red Cross personnel picked Ron up and dropped him at the bus station. He arrived at a camp for underprivileged children, where their heads were shaved for lice, and morale was low.

"Once you lived that way, you never want to go back," Fraser once told *Collegiate Baseball* newspaper. "You never want to be hungry again, never want to be lonely again."

Ron returned to home environments and bounced around from older brother to older brother. He moved out on his own when he graduated from high school at age seventeen. His family had a strong work ethic and believed in getting a job and moving up the ladder rather than attending college. In Nutley the only occupations available were factory worker, firefighter, or police officer.

Ron and his first wife, Liane, met when they were both fifteen, and her parents stepped in to fill some of the parental void missing in his life. Her father let it be known that Ron would need to go to college if he wanted to marry his daughter.

Fraser worked construction during the summers and was a three-sport (baseball, basketball, and football) athlete in high school, earning the title of Most Athletic during his senior year. He was set to attend Murray State University to play baseball. When he arrived, school officials informed him he needed to play football because there were no baseball scholarships.

Fraser dreamed about playing professional baseball. He hitchhiked to Florida and attempted to join the Washington Senators, but he was underage and had no one to sign on his behalf. He had a 1952 tryout with the Brooklyn Dodgers as part of the team's Rookie Stars of Tomorrow program to fill its rookie squad. The Dodgers provided instruction from team scouts, coaches, and players, including Tommy Lasorda, and played a series of games in the metro New York and adjacent states. Fraser was not signed.

When it came time for Fraser to head to Kentucky for college, Liane and her parents took him to the train station to send him on his own. After his freshman year at Murray State, he returned home and back to his mother. When Ron told her he was home for a couple of months before he had to go back, she was surprised, initially assuming he was done with college.

A friend at Murray State transferred to Florida State and convinced Ron to join him because baseball scholarships were available. He enrolled at FSU as did Liane after transferring from the University of Maryland, and joined the baseball team. Living in the school's athletic dorm and without money, Fraser worked in the kitchen at some of the sorority houses on campus. On the side, he made bologna sandwiches to make extra money, slicing the bologna so thin it appeared transparent. He set the sandwiches out with a payment box after hours and attached a sign reading, "Only God Knows If You Steal" to reaffirm the honor code.

He then landed a job at the Theta Chi house and joined the fraternity. Among Fraser's roommates were Dick Howser, a teammate on the baseball team and eventual World Series–winning Major League manager; Lee Corso, later made famous as a college football coach and ESPN analyst; and "Buddy" Reynolds from the football team. "Buddy" was just a nickname to his friends. His real name was Burt Reynolds, who went on to star in television and movies.

Despite developing arm trouble, Fraser posted a 5-1 record with a 4.57 ERA as a senior. He used to say that when he pitched, he would put dirt over the pitching rubber and move three to five feet closer to home plate because the lights at FSU were so bad.

He and Liane married in 1956. Liane had already graduated and was working at the university while Ron completed his degree in Physical Education and spent one year as a graduate assistant baseball coach. Fraser was the first in his family to attend college. His mother, whom Fraser's daughters fondly describe as the "sweetest woman," traveled to Tallahassee for the graduation ceremony and beamed with pride.

In 1960 Fraser was invited to coach the Dutch National team for six months. He stayed for three years before returning to the United States to seek a baseball position. He called his former coach at FSU, Danny Litweiler, who advised him against pursuing an opening with the Mets. Fraser decided to pursue a college coaching position. Auburn had an opening, but it was quickly filled. Miami was the other vacancy. Some serendipity and a recommendation from Litweiler landed Fraser in Coral Gables. The rest was history.

Fraser's daughters, and later grandchildren, called him Popie, the Dutch word for father. He was a loving dad to his three daughters, Cynthia, Lynda, and Elizabeth (Liz). They were as close as those in any father-daughter relationship, even later in life, talking daily, going to movies, and going out to dinners. "He loved his girls, and they were always at the field," recalled Mike Fiore.

Fraser's daughters grew up at the ballpark. They loved it and never resented the coaching lifestyle. As youngsters, and to give their mom a break, they hung out while Popie was coaching. They made sandcastles with bullpen dirt and played in the piles of red Georgia clay used on the field at Mark Light Stadium, the playground of their youth. Fraser was fully on board with having them there during practice while Liane was working and pursuing her master's degree and PhD at the University of Miami.

Like royalty, the girls had their run of the ballpark and acted respectfully. When his girls were not at the ballpark, Fraser emphasized that they could call the dugout phone, much like a regular office, at any time if they needed to reach him. At times, even during games, there might be a phone call asking permission to go to a friend's house or informing him about something at home. They never considered the game situation and only thought of it as being Popie at work.

"He adored his girls," said Doug Shields. "When the girls came around, he was not a coach, he was a doting dad. You saw it in his eyes and watched him talk to them and laugh and smirk. It was pretty cool."

Fraser was very sympathetic to his girls when they got bumps and bruises as kids. "I wiped out on my bike and had road rash all over," said Liz. "I remember putting hydrogen peroxide over all the scrapes and it hurt him to ever see us, his babies, in pain."

Fraser never brought baseball home with him. When the girls went to school and were asked how their dad was doing after a tough game or series, they thought nothing of it because it was never discussed. He maintained a calm demeanor regardless of the situation at home much like he did with his players in the dugout. "He would walk into the house after the worst possible loss or having been swept during the weekend and be the same person he always was," said Liz.

"When he got home, he was husband and father," recalled Liane Fraser. "We laughed, we joked, and we had good times. We never talked about games. We did not bring them up. When he came home, he enjoyed the kids."

He dealt with his boys and their problems all day and came home to his girls, which was a completely different world. The family always ate together and stayed at the table talking after meals, especially during weekend breakfasts. Fraser took tremendous interest in what his girls were doing and was quick to give opinions. He frequently left notes and reminders for them.

Fraser's one unsuccessful coaching stint came during a season assisting Liz's Big Red Machine youth softball team in the local Khoury League. The team went 0-13, but Fraser had fun. "We had a great life. We really did. It was a great childhood. We just had fun," said Liz.

As his daughters reached high school and college age, it felt like one extended family with the players of similar age. Fraser had a strict rule of no dating players. Instead, the bond was one of brothers and sisters, with the players looking out for the girls. The players reported back to Fraser about his daughters' social plans or places they were seen even before they did. As a result, Fraser almost always knew what was happening but never let on. "He was never going to ask a question unless he knew the answer," said Liz.

Much like his players, Fraser never instilled a fear of consequences with his girls, instead loving them and trusting them to do the right thing. "I didn't want to do anything that would disappoint my father, or mother," said Cynthia. "We weren't scared of them; we just never wanted to disappoint them."

"He gave you this feeling and trust, and you didn't want to go against it or lose any respect you were given," said Lynda. "I think the players felt that way too."

When boyfriend issues arose, Fraser was almost always spot-on with his advice, even if it was difficult to hear. He hated seeing his daughters with a broken heart. He'd say, "Flush him" and swipe his hand across his chest as a signal to erase it.

"I truly have to say I had the best father," said Lynda.

"We were spoiled—not in riches, but in love," said Liz. "He was the most loving person to all of us."

When the College World Series conflicted with Cynthia's college graduation, Fraser was heartbroken that he had to miss it, apologizing to her even until the day he died. She played tennis at Wesleyan College in Macon, Georgia, and Fraser missed his own regular-season games to attend a father-daughter weekend and participate in the father-daughter doubles tournament, which they won.

"It's all he could talk about for years," recalled Cynthia. "He always said, 'Do you remember when we beat your [tennis standout] friend?' I'm thinking, *You won the College World Series*, but he hung his hat on that. It was a big deal."

When Cynthia transferred to Stetson, Fraser pulled some strings to help while he was coaching. During the pregame umpire meeting against Stetson, Fraser asked Pete Dunn, coaching his first game against Miami, for a big favor.

"I look at him thinking, *Are you kidding me? You need help from me? What in the world can you need from me?*" recalled Dunn, who was admittedly in awe of the legendary coach.

Fraser asked Dunn to pass Cynthia's name along to admissions at the very selective school. She was admitted and even became a batgirl for Dunn's team. Fraser gave Dunn effusive thanks each time they met, though Dunn emphasized that her admission came on her own merit.

Liz attended Florida Southern and introduced herself to baseball assistant head coach Mike Gaski. She asked to start a batgirl program like her father had at Miami. It led to similar promotions, including car giveaways and money scrambles. Even the San Diego Chicken made an appearance. The program saw attendance and revenue increases as well.

"Liz, in the footsteps of her father's initiative, started a batgirl program that was way beyond picking up bats," said Gaski. "She was a genius equal to her father in many, many ways."

Lynda went to Wingate University in North Carolina, which then had an NAIA baseball program coached by Bill Nash. "It's not a mistake that we all went to smaller schools with successful baseball programs where he was very good friends with the coaches. He wanted to protect us." said Lynda.

The family nucleus was very important to Fraser. When he had grandchildren, it became even more important. Lynda named her son, Fraser, after her dad, who was both thrilled and choked up. As Fraser's daughters married and had families of their own, they all moved to the same neighborhood in Weston, Florida, making frequent family gatherings possible for the rest of his life.

Fraser and Liane divorced in 1985, yet they remained very close friends for the remainder of his life. He wed Karen in 1988. Both were fully involved in the family, and vacations often consisted of Fraser, his current wife, his former wife, his daughters, and their spouses and children. When Liane was undergoing chemotherapy, Karen and

Ron would take her to the hospital. Ron was dropped off to sit with her. "That was extraordinary to me," said daughter Lynda.

"Both our mom and Karen came to our houses for every event—birthdays, christenings, whatever it was. We all got together, and it was never a problem," said Cynthia. "People are still amazed. We were very lucky."

"He had such a wonderful family," said Skip Bertman. "Ron was so good that his new wife, his former wife, and his children all ended up working together."

Following his retirement, Fraser moved into a new home, joining Dolphins Dan Marino and John Offerdahl and Angelo Dundee, famous boxing trainer for Muhammad Ali, in a newly developed residential area. Fraser could see the sixth hole of Weston Hills Country Club from his home. He never thought he would pick up golf but took lessons and became addicted. He was happy to break a score of 100 and called learning to play golf one of the hardest things he had ever done.

One favorite pleasure in Fraser's life was going to Siesta Key, Florida, before it became a popular destination. He took his family for two to three weeks on the beach each offseason. Fraser loved to fish, and he took his daughters along, even teaching them to scale, gut, and prepare the catch for breakfast.

Fishing was a beloved hobby. One of Fraser's ultimate fishing thrills was catching an eighty-one-inch, fifty-five-pound sailfish off Cape Florida in 1990. He also fished in the Florida Keys, which sat about a forty-minute drive from his home in Palmetto Bay (part of Miami at the time), to get away from coaching. Sometimes, he took his family on a Saturday evening after a game to visit friends, then get up early and fish before heading back for Sunday's game. It was his way of relaxing.

Sometimes his fame prevented him from seclusion. Close friend and physician Dr. George Vergara recalled trout fishing in the back country in the Everglades. When they encountered someone calling for help to start their boat, Fraser was greeted with "Oh, Coach Fraser, it's nice to see you."

Fraser once fished with Assistant Coach Bill McClain on Orange Lake in Central Florida. They rented a boat and went out without a fishing license, a requirement rarely enforced, except on that particular day when a game warden stopped them. Fraser, ever the salesman, persuaded the warden out of issuing a citation. "By the time he finished talking with the warden, he almost had the guy ready to buy a season ticket to our baseball games," recalled McClain.

Fraser's favorite place in the world was his house overlooking Grand-father Mountain in the Blue Ridge Mountains of northwest North Carolina. He spent almost twenty years fishing and golfing in the serene location. The house sat on a golf course filled with wooden bridges over creeks. Fraser drove his golf cart up to the clubhouse daily and visited with several members from Miami. When he wasn't playing a round of golf, he would go out in the evening and putt, sometimes using the excuse of showing the holes to visitors to get out on the greens.

Fraser's sports-related hobbies were tennis, golf, and fishing. Ironically, he did not have an avid interest in watching games on television at home.

"I remember being at a party, and a man introduced his wife to Ron and added that he was the baseball coach at the University of Miami," said Fraser's first wife, Liane. "She said she wasn't much of a sports fan, and Ron responded, 'Neither am I.' People didn't believe that we didn't watch sports. Not that we didn't enjoy it occasionally, but it was not entertainment for him."

Instead, Fraser enjoyed foreign movies and Westerns, with *Silverado*, *High Noon*, and John Wayne classics among his favorites. He watched cop shows on television and war movies like *Tora! Tora! Tora!* When traveling, he and Liane sought out great art museums.

Fraser enjoyed food, wine, and clothes. He was a foodie before the term was coined. Fraser enjoyed Italian cuisine, steak, barbeque ribs, and baked beans, but also the finer meals. He was a wine connoisseur. "He'd swirl the wine or let it breathe. He was somewhat of a sommelier," said Bertman.

Fraser once underestimated a dinner bill on a trip to a favorite restaurant in Tampa when requesting a "good bottle of wine" for his party of four. The bill came to $480 when meal per diems were about $20. He paid the bill but admitted that he needed to dip into the next day's meal money to do so. McClain, who was at dinner, recalled Fraser's speech to the team the following day.

"He told them, 'I let you go yesterday pretty easy. We played two bad games. I'm just not going to tolerate it. We don't win a doubleheader here, you're not getting any meal money at all,'" said McClain. "Our guys were so upset they didn't know what was going on. They knew they played badly the day before, but never before did it cost them meal money."

Miami won both games of the doubleheader. McClain laughed and asked Fraser how he was able to do that, to which he responded, "They don't call me the Wizard of College Baseball for nothing."

"After that, we were real careful about what we were eating and drinking when we went to dinner," said McClain.

Fraser was a chocoholic, and chocolate ice cream topped with hot fudge was a favorite. With doctor orders to reduce chocolate and sugar consumption and wife Karen keeping an eye on his diet, Fraser developed a signal system to Mitch Freedman, who oversaw the concessions from a tent adjacent to the home dugout at Mark Light Stadium.

"He would come out of the dugout, go through signs, and give a hand gesture as though he's ladling soup," recalled Freedman. "That meant sneak a little hot fudge on it."

As a diabetic, Fraser had to watch his diet, and Karen helped keep tabs on his health. When at work, he would ask his office assistant Colleen Anderson, a Sugarcane and close friend of his daughter Liz, to take care of errands, including picking up lunch. He asked her to go to the Wendy's across the street, handed over a twenty-dollar bill, and told her to keep the change. The order had additional requests—if the meal included a burger, she had to request a chicken sandwich wrapper. For the soft drink, the diet button on the plastic lid needed to be pushed in. That way, if Karen checked the garbage and asked Fraser what he had for lunch and he said a chicken sandwich and Diet Coke, the evidence corroborated his story.

Fraser dressed impeccably. Except during games, he was always in a coat and tie, typically a blue blazer with gray slacks. He always wore a silk handkerchief poking out of the breast pocket of his suit jacket—a pocket square before the fashion accessory became widely popular. He wore trendy crewnecks, like mock turtlenecks, under his jacket. Fitting of his tropical location, he often wore loafers without socks.

His daily appearance looked more befitting of a business executive than of a baseball coach. Fraser's radio show aired commercial spots for Baron's clothing store, and in exchange, Fraser requested a suit rather than cash compensation. When in Tallahassee, Fraser frequented Nic's Toggery, his favorite store for custom suits, and managers even closed the doors for his personal shopping. He always had "a guy" for some type of fashion or other alteration. "He had the nicest suits you can imagine," said Ron Polk.

Fraser even helped his daughters with their fashion decisions, both as teenagers and adults. "He picked out our prom dresses," said Lynda. "He was in charge of all things fashion."

When it was time for their weddings, it was Fraser who went with them to the bridal salon for dress shopping.

Fraser offered his input on trends. He did not like women's Capri pants or jeans with holes.

"I'd wear clam diggers or capris, and he'd go, 'You know we can afford the whole pair [of pants].' I'd say, 'I know, but this is the style,'" recalled Liz. "He hated jeans with holes and would say to me, 'Can I give you some money to do something with the jeans? I know a guy who can sew those up.'"

Filled with kindness and compassion, Fraser treated everyone like a friend. Often, he called people "coach" or "big guy" as terms of endearment. He had a special knack for connecting with anyone at any time in any setting. Fraser had a tangible presence about him that drew people in. "He was absolutely one of a kind," said Cynthia, "one of the most giving, loving, generous, and authentic men."

A sportswriter once noted, "I don't think anybody ever had a bad word to say about Ron. His players are fond of him. I'm sure somebody out there probably didn't like him, but you never really heard any criticism about him."

The Frasers and Bertmans were close; the relationship began before Skip became an assistant coach. His wife, Sandy, and Fraser's first wife, Liane, both taught at the same school, which was how Fraser first met Bertman, who was coaching at Miami Beach High School. After Bertman joined Fraser's staff, the wives and daughters alternated gatherings at each other's homes to listen to road games on the radio.

The friends closest to Fraser were genuine and willing to help him execute his vision for Miami's baseball program. "People cared about him so much that he could ask anybody for anything, and they would gladly give," said Vergara. "That was his secret."

Burt Chope was one friend who became a significant program benefactor. Chope lived in an enormous, secured, waterfront home in the most elite place in Coral Gables. The Fraser family became frequent guests, even vacationing together on Chope's incredible bus, the same one he let the team use. Fraser took Chope's son, who had a physical disability and loved Miami baseball, to be batboy at the 1971 Pan Am Games.

Possessing an exceptional business mind, Fraser often saw other's moves before they happened. His charisma and stories drew people to him in any setting. Fraser was the definition of a magnetic personality. "He made friends with everyone. It didn't seem hard for him to become friends, regardless of their status in life or status they claimed," said Jerry Reisman.

When Joel Green had his knees operated on at the University of Miami hospital, Fraser paid him a surprise visit. "I got this message that my priest was coming to see me," recalled Green, who had just come out of surgery. "I'm like, 'My priest?' In comes Coach Fraser. He said he was my priest so he could get in and see me after hours."

Fraser had deep appreciation for servicemen, firemen, and police. If he was at a restaurant and saw anyone from the armed forces, police, or fire and rescue, he anonymously and immediately picked up their tabs. It was a done deal and not negotiable. He always thanked them for their service.

Dinners at restaurants often were interrupted by someone wanting to meet Fraser, thank him, ask him about the team, or check their kid's batting stance. He was always willing and never said no. They became common interactions during family outings.

Fraser had a big heart. His second wife, Karen, recalled in an interview how Fraser would notice someone who seemed lonely or down and could use some kindness. He approached the stranger, complimented them and struck up a positive conversation to raise their spirits.

With his young daughters in tow after home games, he regularly stopped at a convenience store next to Mark Light Stadium to get a soda and a bag of pretzels before driving thirty minutes home. Four or five guys may have been sitting on the curb drinking out of a paper bag, seemingly down on their luck. Fraser always walked over and talked to each of them. Meanwhile, his daughters were tired and hungry and anxious to get home. "When they'd say, 'Hey, coach,' I remember thinking that we're definitely here for another hour," Cynthia recalled about the conversations. "He had such an affinity for people going through hard times because of his background."

During games, people frequently came to the dugout to greet Fraser, talk to him, or bring him something. He always took time to interact and never brushed off anyone, even while the game was ongoing. "Coach was phenomenal at looking people in the eye, letting them talk about themselves, and showing interest in them," said Stan Jakubowski.

Following his hiring, the university's *Miami Hurricane* newspaper mentioned a resemblance between Fraser and legendary comedian Bob Hope. He also exhibited some of the same sense of humor, often with short, one-line zingers. "He reminded me of Bob Hope when he would say a joke and look at you out of the corner of his eye, like, *Did you get that?*" said Doug Shields.

"You could be ten minutes away from it before you realize what just happened," said Lynda. "He had a brilliant sense of humor."

Fraser's gamesmanship and competitiveness mixed with his humor and playfulness. Vergara described him as a big, funny, life-loving kid who loved to play. The two frequently played noon tennis matches against each other during the hot summers. Many of the matches were back-and-forth and sometimes drawn out. More than anything, Fraser hated to lose. He didn't like trailing a match either. He did anything to gain an edge.

"He walked over to his bag, pulled something out, and stuck it under his armpit, and we resumed playing," said Vergara of one match. "Something fell out of his shirt onto the court. He picked it up, showed me, and said, 'Oh, it's my pacemaker.' He borrowed a pacemaker because he knew if I saw that, it would change my thought process. Sure enough, he beat me."

The scouting report on Fraser's golf game was that he could crank it pretty far but wasn't too good around the greens. He had a penchant for taking mulligans and not counting them.

"He was a bandit on the golf course," said friend Hank Goldberg. "He would negotiate strokes with you. He would do anything to win—a very competitive guy."

Green recalled bringing a friend who was quite good at golf to play a round with Fraser. "He told my friend he was having a problem with his knee and couldn't bend over to tee up the ball or get it out of the hole and asked if he could help him," Green said. "My friend said he would be glad to help. Then Fraser turns and winks at me. For eighteen holes, my friend is teeing up and getting the ball out of the hole and there was nothing wrong with Fraser's knee. He played him."

Fraser could talk to anyone but did not stay up on pop culture. On a 1984 road trip to Oral Roberts in Tulsa, Fraser stayed on the concierge floor at the team hotel. He told Assistant Coach Jerry Weinstein he ran into a guy named Lionel Ritchie one morning at breakfast. During the conversation with Ritchie, Fraser, who was unassuming and not familiar with the top musicians of the time, asked if he played the [jazz] vibes. Ritchie told him, "No, no, that's Lionel Hampton [the famous jazz musician]." Fraser asked Weinstein whether he should have asked Ritchie for an autograph for his daughters.

When introduced to *Miami Vice* television star Don Johnson, Fraser told him he looked small for a tight end.

Johnson said, "I'm not the Don Johnson who plays for the Miami Dolphins, I'm on a show called *Miami Vice*."

Fraser covered his tracks and said, "Yeah, I've heard of that."

Stories played a large role in Fraser's memorable and inspiring speeches. His success, popularity, and personality made him highly sought for speaking engagements to community groups or corporate employees. Cash payments for his appearances helped supplement his salary.

Fraser incorporated elements of his ACES philosophy into his speeches but otherwise went unscripted and spoke about whatever came to mind. Many times, he relayed one of the many incredible stories from his coaching experiences.

"I'd ask him as he went up to give his speech what he was planning to say, and he'd say, 'I don't know,'" recalled Cynthia. "There were five hundred people in the room, or we'd be at the baseball coaches convention, and he would just extemporaneously tell stories off the top of his head."

Fraser spoke to Space Shuttle technicians at Cape Kennedy the week before a launch. Leaders at the corporate headquarters of Burger King and Ryder were among the business executives requesting Fraser to speak. They asked for thirty minutes and he gave them much more, which was never scripted.

"[Thirty minutes] was just his opening," said Lynda. "[Duration] didn't matter because everybody hung on his every word. People were enamored by his stories."

Former player Thom Lehman lined Fraser up for a speaking engagement at the University Club, and allocated thirty to forty-five minutes for the speech.

"About an hour and fifteen minutes into his speech, he looked over at me, and I motioned for him to cut it off," said Lehman. "He had some great stories, and I could have sat there for hours listening to him tell them."

Fraser's storytelling ability and insight helped lead him to television work following his coaching retirement. He joined the CBS team of Greg Gumbel and Jim Kaat as roving reporter for the 1993 and 1994 College World Series. Fraser paired with play-by-play man Jay Randolph for a few seasons on Miami's SportsChannel broadcasts. He was a natural.

"He could have been college baseball's Lee Corso, quite frankly," said Cynthia, comparing her father's baseball broadcasting potential to his former college roommate turned famed ESPN college football analyst.

Fraser kept his long battle with Alzheimer's quiet. The signs were not present until the end.

Bob Sheridan and some of his teammates from the mid-1960s went to Fraser's house to visit him. They told stories, and he remembered everything, even when he put Sheridan in to get hit by a pitch. When he needed care, former players and Sugarcanes would take shifts, tending bedside and sharing stories to him. Talking about names and memories and looking at old yearbooks and memorabilia was therapeutic.

Fraser died at his home in 2013 surrounded by family. Two of his longtime friends and fellow baseball legends, Stan Musial and Earl Weaver, passed away one day prior.

Approximately one thousand family, friends, and fans gathered for Fraser's celebration of life ceremony two months later and before a Hurricanes baseball game. Mike Fiore, Rick Remmert, Jim Morris, Tony Segreto, and Howard Schnellenberger eulogized Fraser. A series of video tributes from Lasorda, Jim Abbott, and many close to Fraser and the Miami program were shown.

Fittingly, lucky numbers were called for various prize giveaways and commemorative T-shirts sold with proceeds funding his statue. It was the epitome of Ron Fraser.

Appendix

Ron Fraser by the numbers

0	Losing seasons in thirty years
.742	Career winning percentage (best all-time in NCAA at retirement)
1	His uniform number (retired by Miami)
2	National championships (1982 and 1985)
3	NCAA Coach of the Year Awards
11	Halls of Fame
12	**College World Series** appearances / 50-win seasons
26	**College World Series** victories
1,271	Career wins (ranked 2nd all-time in NCAA at retirement)
2006	College Baseball Hall of Fame inductee (inaugural class)

Ron Fraser year-by-year

YEAR	W	L	T	PCT	POSTSEASON
1963	18	9	0	.667	
1964	20	9	1	.683	
1965	23	12	1	.653	
1966	19	18	1	.513	
1967	23	15	1	.648	
1968	27	11	1	.705	
1969	31	11	0	.738	
1970	28	15	1	.648	
1971	35	11	0	.761	NCAA District
1972	32	17	0	.653	
1973	42	17	0	.712	NCAA District

Ron Fraser year-by-year (*cont.*)

YEAR	W	L	T	PCT	POSTSEASON
1974	51	11	0	.823	**College World Series** runner-up
1975	45	14	0	.763	NCAA Regional
1976	41	15	0	.732	NCAA Regional
1977	44	13	0	.772	NCAA Regional
1978	50	12	0	.806	**College World Series**
1979	55	11	0	.823	**College World Series**
1980	59	12	0	.831	**College World Series**
1981	61	10	0	.859	**College World Series**
1982	55	17	0	.760	**College World Series** champion
1983	61	21	0	.744	NCAA Regional
1984	48	28	0	.632	**College World Series**
1985	64	16	0	.800	**College World Series** champion
1986	50	17	0	.746	**College World Series**
1987	35	24	1	.592	NCAA Regional
1988	52	14	1	.784	**College World Series**
1989	49	18	0	.731	**College World Series**
1990	52	13	0	.800	NCAA Regional
1991	46	17	0	.730	NCAA Regional
1992	55	10	0	.846	**College World Series**
total	1,271	438	9	**.742**	

Ron Fraser awards

HONORS

1960–62	Three times Best Coach Award winner as Netherlands coach
1973	World Amateur Coach of the Year
1974	NCAA, *Sporting News*, and District Coach of the Year Rawlings/Adirondack Big Stick NCAA Coach of the Year University of Miami Iron Arrow Honor Society
1979	NCAA District Coach of the Year
1980	NCAA District Coach of the Year

1981	*Sporting News*, All-American Baseball News, and District Coach of the Year *Collegiate Baseball* Magazine Superstar Award
1982	NCAA, Florida, and District Coach of the Year
1984	NCAA, Southeast, Florida, and District Coach of the Year
1985	NCAA and District Coach of the Year
1987	International Baseball Federation Coach of the Year
1988	Lefty Gomez Award *Miami Herald* Spirit of Excellence Award Coral Gables Outstanding Citizen Award

HALLS OF FAME

1981	Florida State University Hall of Fame
1983	University of Miami Sports Hall of Fame
1985	Netherlands Hall of Fame American Baseball Coaches Association Hall of Fame Florida Sports Hall of Fame
1989	Greater Miami Hall of Fame
1990	Nutley High School Hall of Fame
2006	College Baseball Hall of Fame (inaugural class)
2014	National Association of Collegiate Directors of Athletics Hall of Fame
2015	Omaha College Baseball Hall of Fame

Ron Fraser timeline

1933	Born June 25 in Nutley NJ
1952	Graduated Nutley High School / Most Outstanding Athlete
1953–54	Murray State University baseball and football
1956–58	U.S. Army, pitcher and assistant coach
1959	Florida State University, pitcher (5-1 record as senior)
1960	Florida State University, freshman coach BS, Physical Education
1960–62	Netherlands, director of baseball Coach of Royal Dutch national baseball team 1960, 1962 European champions
1963	Named University of Miami head coach March 21, First Victory (3–1 over Army)

Ron Fraser timeline (*cont.*)

1969–70	Team USA, world amateur coach
1971	Team USA, Pan American Games coach (silver medalist) George Light makes donation to build "million-dollar complex"
1973	Team USA, world amateur coach (champion) Netherlands, coach (European champion)
1974	Miami makes its first **College World Series** appearance (national runner-up)
1977	Hosted $5,000-a-plate dinner on infield of Mark Light Stadium
1981	ESPN televises first college baseball games (Miami vs. USC, February 6–8)
1982	Miami wins its first NCAA Championship, the first for any Florida-based university
1983	Inducted into University of Miami Sports Hall of Fame Miami Maniac introduced as mascot
1985	Miami wins its second NCAA Championship in four seasons
1987	Team USA, Pan American Games coach (silver medalist) University of Miami dedicates Ron Fraser Building (offices) at Mark Light Stadium
1988	Earns Coral Gables Outstanding Citizen Award
1990	Named NCAA Coach of the Decade (534–177–2, .750 from 1980–89)
1992	Announced retirement Miami finishes season one win from **College World Series** championship game Team USA, Olympic baseball coach (finished fourth)
2006	Inducted into College Baseball Hall of Fame (inaugural class)
2013	Died January 20 at his home in Weston FL
2015	Ron Fraser statue unveiled outside front entrance of Alex Rodriguez Park at Mark Light Field

Note on Sources

Publications consulted for research include University of Miami baseball media guides and Ibis yearbooks, along with the books *Hurricane Strikes, The Road to Omaha*, and *The College World Series*. Articles consulted were in the *Miami Herald, Miami News, Miami Hurricane, USA Today, Omaha World-Herald, Sporting News, Sports Illustrated, Collegiate Baseball, Cane-Sport*, and the *Washington Post*.

People interviewed from 2020 to 2023 for this book include the following: Jim Abbott, Jeff Alkire, Lynda (Fraser) Armitage, Bob Bartlett, Mark Batten, Tom Baxter, Peggy (Donohue) Berk, Red Berry, Skip Bertman, Warren Bogle, Holmes Braddock, Jim Callis, Dan Canevari, Eddie Carieri, Terry Cardwell, Tracy Cardwell, Gary Chrisman, Nicki (Dacquisto) Cluney, Marty Connors, Rob Cooper, Lee Corso, Mike Coutts, John Danchik, Justin Dedeaux, Kevin DiGiacomo, Gino DiMare, Linda DiMare, Pete Dunn, Alex Fernandez, Mike Fiore, Roy Firestone, Cynthia Fraser, Liane Fraser, Mitch Freedman, Paul Frishman, Mike Gaski, Hank Goldberg, Orlando González, Joel Green, Rick Greene, Ty Harrington, Kenny Henderson, Luis "Wicho" Hernández, Tom Holliday, Paul Hundhammer, Stan Jakubowski, Richard "Itch" Jones, Rick Jones, Dave Keilitz, Steve Klitzner, Danny Knobler, Liz (Fraser) Kraut, Phil Lane, Ken Lee, Barry Leffler, Thom Lehman, Phil LoMedico, Preston Mack, Ron Maestri, Chris Magno, Paul Mainieri, Jim Maler, Al Marsicano, Mike Martin, Jim Martz, Bill McClain, Marc Mestre, Jim Morris, Pat Murphy, Joe Nelson, Randy Olen, Mike Pagliarulo, Kyle Peterson, Jim Pizzolatto, Ron Polk, Wally Pontiff, Dennis Poppe, Linda Porter-Cox, Larry Pyle, Rick Raether, Hugo Rams, Jerry Reisman, Jay Rokeach, John Routh, Earl Rubley, Vinny Scavo, Larry Schmittou, Dave Scott, Ron Scott, Tony Segreto, Bob Sheridan, Doug Shields, Barry Shollenberger, Allan Simpson, Danny Smith, Ish Smith, Dave Snow, Sam Sorce, Turtle Thomas, Steve Traylor, Matt Tyner, Charles Urbanus Jr., Greg Vaughn, George Vergara, Will Vespe, Jerry Weinstein, Jim West, Bill Wrona, and Joe Zagacki.

Bibliography

Martz, Jim. *Hurricane Strikes: University of Miami Baseball*. Huntsville AL: Strode Publishers, 1983.

Madden, W. C., and Patrick J. Stewart. *The College World Series: A Baseball History, 1947–2003*. Jefferson NC: McFarland, 2004.

McGee, Ryan, *The Road to Omaha: Hits, Hopes, and History at the College World Series*. New York: Thomas Dunne Books, 2009.